MW01153937

DESCENT AND RETURN:

AN INCEST SURVIVOR'S HEALING JOURNEY THROUGH ART THERAPY

The Inner Journey and Art Work of
Jacqueline Leigh

Text by
Louise Lumen, A.T.R.

www.ChironPublicatons.com

Interior and cover design by Danijela Mijailovic
Printed primarily in the United States of America.

ISBN 978-1-63051-381-8 paperback
ISBN 978-1-63051-382-5 hardcover
ISBN 978-1-63051-383-2 electronic

Cover image and photography of client's artwork by Louise Lumen.

Photo color adjustments and cropping, and author portrait by Phil Grout and Lance Garber.

Library of Congress Cataloging-in-Publication Data Pending

Fig. 1 "TOTEM POLE"

At the base of this collage is a photo of a wooden sculpture of an animal's head, but half of it is a black, human face, smiling ominously and surrounded by the red of passion and rage. Astride this human-animal is a doll whose face looks old - a child grown old too soon. Without hands, the doll-child is powerless. Dominating the image is a Samurai warrior. His mouth is wide open in derisive laughter. Standing behind the child, he should serve the function of protector; instead, he has his hands around the child's neck as if to strangle her or keep her from speaking. He is well-protected by the armor her silence provides.

He guards The Secret, rather than The Child.

A totem pole is the record of a family's history and ancestry.

Fig. 1 "TOTEM POLE: RECORD OF A FAMILY'S HISTORY AND ANCESTRY"

"THE FOOL'S JOURNEY"

Fool has cast off from safe harbor
  to embark on a voyage
  of healing.
Fool's eyes are open wide:
  this odyssey
  is a conscious choice.
It is Fool who has chosen to blow the wind
  that fills the sails,
  and has set the boat on its course.
Storms will be encountered
  and mythic monsters will rise
  from the unplumbed depths.
Fool will speak truth to the king,
  whether heard
  or not heard.
Tears will be shed.

It is the Wise Fool *
  who has the courage to set sail
  in search of the sacred Center of the Self.

     Louise Lumen

*The Fool is a term from many traditions signifying one who makes the journey into wholeness.

DEDICATION

To Jacqueline Leigh
with respect and affection,
in acknowledgment of her courage in making this healing journey
and her generosity in sharing it to aid the healing in others.

Fig. 2   "THE FOOL'S JOURNEY"

ACKNOWLEDGMENTS

This book has been a work in progress for twenty-seven years. Countless friends, colleagues, and family members have supported the work throughout many revisions, endless computer problems, and searches for a publisher. They have held the vision that one day it would be a book that could be a healing influence for many persons, and over the years they have continued to inquire as to its progress. I cannot thank them all, but special gratitude goes to:

Jacqueline Leigh, artist and client for generously sharing her healing journey. It was truly an honor to know and work with her.

Kathy Bernstein, healer, numerologist, and dear friend who knew this story from the beginning, and who continues to be my wise companion on the inner journey.

Sally Riley, my long distance computer-tutor who from the beginning was always available, knowledgeable, and patient in guiding me over the phone through my endless problems with the ever changing and evolving computer programs, which were never in sync with my nature.

Helena Claire Pittman, artist and author, my writing "coach" who generously and skillfully worked with me to refine the language, never letting anything unclear or incorrect in the content slip by.

Dr. John Peck, Jungian analyst with whom I was privileged to do dream work for several years. In appreciation for his endorsement and for all the times he would relate relevant myths and legends to help me stay with the writing process whenever I was about to give up.

Without these constant supports this book would never have seen the light of day.

Dr. Donald Kalsched, Jungian analyst for his generous endorsement of this book.

Rev. Harlie Bemis, Jungian colleague, who gave me my first lessons in the use of this magic box as I worked many months to type up the first draft of Part I, and who exhumed it from the depths of oblivion when I put in the last change and then hit delete instead of save!

Rev. Frank Poole who provided excellent supervision throughout the three years of this work.

Sondra Geller, Jungian analyst and Art Therapist who escorted me on the first leg of my own inner journey, where I experienced the potency and magic of Art Therapy.

Dr. Katherine Williams, director of The George Washington University graduate program in Art Therapy and all members of the faculty, who prepared me to enter this wonderful field.

Nancy Joly, healer, who over many years helped me to acknowledge the integral wholeness of both the Light and Shadow aspects of my Self.

For endorsements by two dear colleagues at Albertus Magnus College, New Haven, CT:

Dr. Ragaa Mazen, Clinical Psychologist who created the three-year Masters of Art in Art Therapy program. Each year she invited me to present this work to her graduate students and always anticipated its publication.

Abbe Miller, art psychotherapist and director of the MAAT program, her creative spirit and energy continue to enhance the training of students by emphasizing the centrality of art in this process.

Rene Bouchard, Jungian art therapy colleague and friend who first broached the idea of publishing this material in a book he had planned. He would have celebrated its completion.

Elmira Ingersoll and Mary Muhlhausen, my unconditionally loving spiritual mothers, who introduced me to most of the people and ideas that are important in my life, and always believed in and supported this endeavor. I had hoped they could have seen it completed.

Renee Bauer-Wolf, therapist, poet, and artist: the third member of our amazing foursome.

Felicity Weghorn, extraordinarily wise, creative, and spiritual friend to whom I first entrusted this manuscript, but who could not see its completion. "We have always been sisters."

Dorothy and John Fix, spiritual and creative fellow sojourners of a lifetime.

The early members of the Groton, CT Library Writers' Group, **Jude Rittenhouse, Melanie Greenhouse, Platt Arnold, Herta Payson, Elaine Bentley Baughn,** and **Dr. Maura Dollymore** who welcomed this artist into their poetic midst and always encouraged my efforts.

And so many other friends, colleagues, teachers, and spirit guides.

My parents, **James and Frances Rudloff**, who gave me such a safe and loving home and were the model of always being kind and helpful to others in need. They would have rejoiced in this.

My sisters, **Ann Clark and Una Telscher**, and all the members of my extended family who have always been interested and supportive of this work. In particular, my nephew, **Rudy Telscher, Esq.,** who was my legal advocate through the publishing process.

And to all the dear friends who so generously supported this publication financially, especially **Liz Jackson, Jean Wilson, and Halinah Busack,** I offer my fondest love and gratitude.

Finally, my enormous appreciation to the staff of **Chiron Publications: Dr. Steve Buser, publisher, Dr. Leonard Cruz, Editor-in-Chief, Jennifer Fitzgerald, General Manager, Ron Madden, Copy Editor,** and **Danijela Mijailovic, Graphic Designer**. They saw the value of this work and with skill and kindness brought it, at last, to fruition.

TABLE OF CONTENTS

NOTE TO THE READERS:

All the artwork in this book was done by Jacqueline in the three years we worked together. Taken from detailed notes I wrote after each session, this record has been read and approved by Jackie. Although this is one woman's healing journey stated in feminine terms, it applies with equal compassion to persons of either gender who have suffered the violence and indignities of abuse, sexual or otherwise, because the pattern of emotional response is similar. In the captions beneath each collage the words "Child" and "Woman" are used as a kind of universal "Everyman" designation.

It is our hope that this book may serve the needs of a wide diversity of people affected in one way or another by childhood sexual abuse: those who have been victimized, their families and friends who may need help to understand the lasting negative effects of the experience, student or professional art therapists or other types of counselors, religious ministers, or teachers who will be asked to work with sexually abused persons. Consequently, some readers will be familiar with the issue of abuse or with Jungian psychology, and for others this may be new material. Therefore, some may be helped by the explanations in the footnotes, and for others that material may not be needed.

CONFIDENTIALITY

Whenever case material is shared with others for educational purposes, it is always done anonymously and only with the client's permission. In art therapy, the client's name on the artwork must also be masked. In this case, in sharing her journey for the benefit of others, Jacqueline has chosen to do so under her own name because she wishes it to be known that claiming the hard work of healing is part of her experience of feeling empowered.

LIST OF ILLUSTRATIONS

FRONTISPIECE

DEDICATION

INTRODUCTION

PART I

INTERIM

PART II

AFTERWORD

I have a feeling
that my boat has struck,
down there in the depths,
against a great thing.
And nothing happens.
Nothing.....Silence.....Waves.
Nothing happens?
Or has everything happened
and we are standing now,
quietly,
in the new life?

Juan Ramon Jimenez

Spanish poet, 1956 Nobel Prize for Literature, 1881-1958

Jacqueline Leigh, client / artist:

When I was thirty-eight years old, I began having spontaneous flashbacks in which memories of having had an incestuous relationship with my father, throughout my childhood, erupted into my consciousness. These unbearably painful, but undeniable, memories destroyed everything I had ever believed in: who I thought I was, was gone; every idea about my family, the world, life, and God, was gone. I didn't know what to think about anything anymore and felt I couldn't trust anyone. I thought I would never again feel good about myself. I became suicidal and for three and a half years remained in what I always referred to as "The Abyss" of depression. Finally, I decided that I needed to get help through therapy in order to deal with those memories, rather than continue to keep The Secret, silently and alone, within myself.

After several attempts at verbal therapy, I was referred to art therapy. This turned out to be a very compatible way for me to work and I continued this process with Louise Lumen for about three years (two fifteen-month segments separated by six-months). During that time I worked through the rage I felt toward both my parents, as well as my own shame, guilt, grief, and lack of self-esteem. I also worked on finding my own deep spiritual center once again, and empowerment as a woman. The art therapy process was deeply meaningful and effective in helping me to regain an authentic sense of self-worth. When this shift was complete, I decided that I would like to share my healing journey.

My purpose in doing this is to offer it as encouragement to anyone who is a survivor of sexual abuse: know that if you do your own healing work in therapy, you really *can* feel good about yourself again.

See yourself as you plainly are.
You've got a hidden wound,
and this is no time for posing.
When inward tenderness
finds that secret hurt,
the pain itself will crack the rock
and, ah! let the soul emerge.

> Julaluddin Rumi
> 13ᵗʰ century Persian mystic poet

Louise Lumen, art therapist/scribe

I have had the honor of escorting Jacqueline on her *Descent* into the dark, painful Underworld of psyche; remaining as she experienced the death of her former self-image; her healing; and then, at last, witnessing her *Return* to the Upperworld of everyday life in a far more integrated state. During the three years we worked together, I kept detailed notes, recording the progress of her inner journey. When the work was completed she asked me to photograph her art and gave me permission to share this healing process with others by writing about it.

Moving through the pain of resolving old wounds in therapy was Jackie's part of the work; witnessing, guiding, and supporting her process was my task and now I chronicle her story.

I have undertaken this endeavor for several reasons. Most important is that Jackie would like to share this body of work in order to help others. In addition, since the beginning of her art therapy I have been moved by the depth of her commitment and integrity as she struggled to resolve her traumatic feelings and issues. As a Jungian art therapist, I was captivated by the dreamlike quality of these composite collage images. It was clear to me this contemporary woman was experiencing an ancient archetypal pattern: the *Descent* into, and *Return* from the fearsome realm of the unconscious for the purpose of healing. In addition, as an artist, I was enchanted by the beauty, strength, and elegance of these magazine collages.

In telling this story it is our hope to foster healing in others who suffer the unresolved effects of childhood abuse.

THE ARCHETYPE OF DESCENT AND RETURN - CONTEXT FOR THIS JOURNEY

Life - Death - Rebirth. This is the cycle of life as we experience it in the changing of seasons, the respiration and cellular life of our bodies, and the living and dying of all life forms. The psychological counterpart of the physical life-death cycle has been recorded throughout history. Known as an archetypal pattern, it is universally symbolized in religious rituals, all forms of creative expression, legends, myths, and dreams.

Ordinarily our waking ego is all we know of ourselves, and we hold strongly to our self-image: who we think we are, what we believe in and value, our skills and preferences. As children we may have been taught that a "good person" does not get angry. However, since this emotion is a natural reaction in situations such as abuse, many problems are caused when that feeling is repressed rather than being expressed and resolved. The concealed rage becomes part of the unconscious aspect of the personality, causing a psychological-emotional-spiritual crisis. In denying the issue, we become ensnared in the death aspect of the life cycle, resulting in depression and an inability to find joy or meaning in life. There is a lack of physical and sexual energy, and a spiritual emptiness known throughout history as the Abyss.

The cause of this miasma is an experience so profoundly painful or shaming, it has been split off from conscious awareness. A severe or protracted trauma may precipitate the collapse of the ego's defenses, and in that supremely vulnerable state, we become aware of what we have refused to own as part of who we are. The extreme form of that repression is amnesia.

In order to bring into congruence the known and unknown aspects of the psyche, our waking self at times must descend into its own mysterious depths and allow the superficial self-image to "die," in order to experience a healing transformation. This individuation and maturation process requires an encounter with what C.G. Jung termed the "Shadow."[1] In it he refers to what is "unknown" rather than simply "dark" because the Shadow can encompass both positive and negative qualities within us. When we can own aspects of ourselves of which we were previously unaware, such as our creativity and humor, or others that do not fit into our idealized sense of self, such as rage, shame, guilt, fear, grief, and mortality, we experience a "rebirth" of a more vital and integrated core. Healing requires a willingness to examine the issues and relationships involved with the help of one who has also made the inner journey.

This book, illustrated by a series of magazine collages and several drawings done in art therapy, is an example of allowing a psychological "death" in order to experience the "rebirth." This client entered into that frightening dimension of the deep psyche and became aware of universal images, described as "transpersonal" because they refer to that which all humanity has in common.

Looking at a large crucifix one day it occurred to me that here was the quintessential archetypal pattern of a Descent (of God to earth), a sacrificial death, followed by the Return in the Resurrection. This pattern or drama is deeply embedded in the Western and Near Eastern psyche, with Christ's fate and role having been prefigured in the suffering gods of several older cultures. This experience in a contemporary therapeutic

---

[1] C.G. Jung. *The Archetypes and the Collective Unconscious*, Collected Works, vol. 9.I Trans. R.F.C. Hull. Bollingen Series XX, (Princeton University Press, New Jersey, First printing 1980, tenth printing 1990).

context, the archetype of the crucifix—of Descent and Return—has well-known antecedents in spiritual, psychological, shamanic, alchemical, and mythological literature worldwide.

An intense experience in therapy may be related to what the 16th century Christian mystic St. John of the Cross referred to as *The Dark Night of the Soul*.[2] St. John speaks of two kinds of darkness or "purgation." The first is of the senses and is experienced by many, for example, during periods of fasting. The second relates to spirit and is an even more terrible and refined inner cleansing. In both cases, St. John tells us this leads to an arid "melancholy," replacing the comfort previously attained in spiritual practice. *This was true for Jacqueline. She told me she had been part of several spiritual study groups over the years, which were very meaningful to her. However, as she said in her opening statement, all the core beliefs she ever had about herself, her family, and God were obliterated by the onset of the flashbacks. That experience dropped her into the death phase of the life-death-rebirth cycle and, she said, the loss of her sense of a spiritual core that could guide her life was the most painful result of the memories as they erupted into consciousness.*

From a psychological perspective, psychiatrist Dr. John Weir Perry discusses the effect of repressing trauma in his book, *The Far Side of Madness*.[3] He notes a significant difference between the acute and chronic schizophrenic conditions. Perry delineates the reasons for, and ten stages of, a short-term psychological breakdown. These phases correspond in certain ways to the transpersonal experiences of the mystics, such as St. John of the Cross described. They include among others: "cosmic conflict, death, return to beginnings, threat of the opposite sex, a new birth, and the Center." Dr. Perry developed a program to lovingly support individuals, enabling them to move through this dark and terrifying mental state and return to their everyday lives revitalized. His process requires that the symptoms not be repressed or dulled in any way, but rather, be experienced fully to enable the underlying meaning to become conscious and effect a healing.

In giving an example of one woman's acute breakdown, Dr. Perry states that the dynamics of it "center upon the image of the self, of the way the individual experiences herself. When it is too limited, isolated, one-sided, or debased, this 'self-image' becomes due for a reorganization, and various compensatory mechanisms come into play. If these are not successful because of the ego's resistance to them...a more drastic and turbulent process...gets under way to enforce the needed changes."

Dr. Perry goes on to explain that persons in this condition will find their usual interests and involvements shift away from everyday activities and plunge down into the realm of primordial images of the unconscious mind. Jung speaks of these as the "archetypes of the collective unconscious." Perry prefers the term "affect-images" because they are not only symbols, but are also accompanied by an emotional charge. These mythological images are an *essential part* of what he calls the "renewal process." *Jacqueline's dream-like collages are a prime example of archetypal affect-images, and have now become a visual record of her inner journey.*

Perry says:

> It is part of the nature of archetypal imagery or process to be, in its fundamental ground-plan, universal...[and] this whole archetypal process becomes the vehicle in the individual psyche for a

---

[2] St John of the Cross. *The Dark Night of the Soul*. translated, edited, and with an introduction by E. Allison Peers, 3rd Revised Edition, (Image Books, a Division of Doubleday & Co., Inc., Garden City, New York, 1959)
[3] Perry, John Weir, MD. *The Far Side of Madness*. (Spring Publications, Inc., Dallas, TX, 1974)

fundamental reorganization of the self.... I would stress that these "transpersonal" archetypal affect-images here act as the vehicles for the resolution and setting straight of these very personal emotional life issues...[after which] the individual comes back out of his or her withdrawal into a new way of experiencing people and things, with new concerns and with new investment in relationships.... The renewal process...may be considered nature's way of setting things right.... Even though this compensatory process may become a massive turmoil, the turbulence is a step on the way toward the living of a more fulfilled emotional life.

In *Shaman, The Wounded Healer,*[4] author Joan Halifax sites Dr. Perry's description of the intense inner experiences of persons in an acute schizophrenic breakdown, and she states there is an almost identical series of stages shamanic initiates go through on their descent into the Underworld. (The Underworld refers to an altered state of consciousness—in psychology: the unconscious.) When a novice shaman first makes that psychic journey, it is an initiation in which he or she will have intensely painful and frightening dreams and visions of being decapitated and dismembered, having their organs removed and cleansed, special herbs placed in their bones for renewal, etc., as well as meeting spirit guides.

Through this process the novice is cleansed and taught spiritual and practical lessons in the work of healing. The experiences and learning of the shaman are not for that individual alone, but must be shared with the clan. Later he or she will be able make that descent to "retrieve the soul" of others in the tribe who are in need of physical, emotional, mental, or spiritual healing. This "soul retrieval" has a correlation to the therapeutic process of reintegrating "split-off" dimensions of the psyche. *I find a correspondence here, too, in Jacqueline's spontaneous wish to share her healing journey in order to encourage other abuse survivors to do their own therapy and so resolve whatever trauma they continue to bear.*

In his book, *Rites and Symbols of Initiation,*[5] Mircea Eliade also elucidates the universal patterns involved in shamanic initiations, including the primary motifs of decapitation, dismemberment, or of being reduced to skeletons. He recounts descriptions by shamans who experienced these terrifying inner visions when in ecstatic trance states. The stories come from widely diverse native cultures on every continent. Eliade: "Now, as we know, for archaic and traditional cultures a symbolic return to chaos is equivalent to preparing a new creation. It follows that we may interpret the psychic chaos of the future shaman as a sign that the profane man is being 'dissolved' and a new personality being prepared for birth." This has a parallel in Dr. Perry's approach of supporting a person to move consciously through their fearsome hallucinations toward the goal of renewed psychic integration, rather than simply repressing the symptoms.

Throughout Jackie's work the image of decapitation was a repeated motif, starting with her first collage Fig. 7: "Memory: the Beginning of the Child's Journey" and ending with a final decapitation: that of Freud in Fig. 52: "Spirituality, Psychology, and Woman." In Fig. 10: "The Bacchus Slaughter" there is a beheading and dismemberment of the young girl, in addition to the decapitation of Bacchus. Jackie's relation to this motif evolved as her rage decreased in the course of therapy. At times she cut off the head of a figure in a collage, at other times she did it and then repaired it, or alternatively, thought about doing it and then changed her mind. In several instances, she cut the head off a figure in a photo while deeply embroiled in her raging emotions, but then did not retain conscious memory of having done it and was startled when

[4] Halifax, Joan. *Shaman, The Wounded Healer,* (Thames & Hudson, Ltd., London, 1982)
[5] Eliade, Mircea. *Rites and Symbols of Initiation: The Mysteries of Birth and Rebirth by Mircea Eliade,* (Spring Publications, Inc., Putnam, CT, 1994, revised ed. 2012.)

it was pointed out during the art therapy sessions. These were spontaneous, meaningful actions, powerfully expressing her feelings at the time. On a psychological level decapitation is a severing of the head—which we generally see as holding consciousness and memory—from the body where physical sensations and emotions reside (although we now know there is also cellular memory throughout the body). Such symbolic decapitations and dismemberments made with art materials, were for Jackie, the single most powerful and effective expression of her rage.

Inner healing, as distinct from a physical cure, is a spiritual process. One must always undergo the experience of transformation from an everyday, prosaic level of consciousness to an awareness of the higher realms of being that are revivifying, before one can guide and assist another person involved in a deep level of healing. Our work in depth psychology is a contemporary Western variant of this universal process practiced by Shamans and spiritual Alchemists throughout the world.

Alchemy throughout many cultures arcing back across time to ancient Egypt has been an attempt to transform a base material into something refined and purified: "gold." The word, from the Arabic, means to transmute or change the internal structure of something. Generally, there were two branches of this tree: the physical effort to transform a base metal into ordinary gold; and the spiritual/philosophical alchemy that viewed the process as the experience of such a transformation within the human being—the elevation of our foundational animal nature into the "gold" of an enlightened consciousness.

In his explorations of the processes of alchemy,[6] C.G. Jung found corroboration of his personal experience of the "night sea journey," which he recounted in his "Red Book."[7] Jung saw in the alchemical stages a psychological parallel to the steps in the analytic/therapeutic process, in which the *prima materia* of the troubled human psyche moves through successive stages of dissolution and consolidation. The *nigredo* stage was the experience of one's own dark, mysterious, and frightening depths, in which the illusions of who we think we are unravel, letting one move toward final unification, a *coniunctio* or joining of all opposites. Jung described this process of finding one's Self or Centre, "Individuation." *Spiritual alchemy is another major example of the archetype of the Descent into one's depths and the Return to life in a more integrated state, such as Jacqueline experienced.*

This book is about Jacqueline's work of renewal in Art Therapy. Her "dark night of the soul" is the kind of acute psychological upheaval Dr. Perry and others describe, and it has an ancient prototype.

Mythologically, the symbolic death and rebirth cycle is discussed by Jungian analyst Sylvia Brinton Perera in her book, *Descent to the Goddess: A Way of Initiation for Women.*[8] Her touchstone is the oldest known account of this kind of experience—the ancient Sumerian myth, "The Descent of Inanna." It was written on clay tablets in cuneiform hieroglyphics nearly 5,000 years ago. Myths function both as a container that provides some supportive boundaries to our journeys and as a mirror that reflects to us some specific patterns of the life process. In this way they add a dimension of universality that grounds the individual's journey in a larger context.

---

[6] Jung, C.G. *Psychology and Alchemy*, 2nd ed. revised. Trans. R.R.C Hull, Routledge, London, 1952.

[7] Jung, C.G., *The Red Book*, ed. Sonu Shamdasani, trans. Kyburz, Peck, Shamdasani, Philemon Series, W.W. Norton & Company, New York, London, 2009.

[8] Sylvia Brinton Perera. *Descent to the Goddess - A Way of Initiation for Women.* (Inner City Books, Toronto, CA, 1981)

Perera elucidates the ways in which the various aspects of that myth symbolize the internal psychological experience of a "death" and "rebirth." She says, "Inanna's path and its stages...present a paradigm for the life-enhancing descent into the abyss of the dark goddess and out again...She descends, submits, and dies. This openness to being acted upon is the essence of the experience of the human soul faced with the transpersonal. It is not based upon passivity, but upon an active willingness to receive." *Jackie's explicit commitment to persevere through the fear, rage, guilt, grief, and shame that resulted from her experience of incest, was that kind of "active willingness to receive."*

Perera goes on to say this dark journey forces us to go below the conscious, rational levels of cognition, and descend to the affect-laden, magic dimension and archaic depths that are embodied, ecstatic, and transformative. These depths are pre-verbal, often pre-image, capable of taking us over and shaking us to the core. In these depths we are given a sense of the one cosmic power; there we are moved, and taught through the intensity of our affects that there is a living balance process." Perera continues: "On those levels the conscious ego is overwhelmed by passion and numinous images. And, though shaken, even destroyed as we knew ourselves, we are re-coalesced in a new pattern and spewed back into ordinary life. That journey is the goal of the initiation mysteries...even as it is the goal of therapeutic regression (for both men and women)."

As human beings we all have within ourselves both unrecognized positive qualities and also negative experiences which we have banished from our ordinary state of awareness. It is clear from spiritual, psychological, shamanic, alchemical, and mythological writings that the inner Descent, or exploration of the painful aspects of the Shadow is a profoundly difficult process of growth and transformation. We also see that if earlier, less intense stages of the renewal process are unsuccessfully navigated or prematurely shut down, an acute schizophrenic breakdown may result. That is an intensely confusing and painful experience of the reorganization and balancing process of the self, requiring psychological help for healing.
(The only more serious experience is when extreme and protracted trauma causes a person's ego to shatter into the state of what previously was known in the Diagnostic and Statistical Manual of Mental Disorders (DSM)[9] as "Multiple Personality Disorder," now designated as "Dissociative Identity Disorder."
If successful in moving through this reintegration process, however, the individual—whether spiritual seeker, shamanic initiate, student of spiritual alchemy, or client in the therapeutic process—will emerge on the other side of the psychological death, reborn. That person will experience a renewed and revitalized sense of Self that is far more integrated, resulting in a greater capacity for living life more fully, meaningfully, and enjoyably.

"The story of Inanna's descent" Perera tells us "is the revelation of an initiation ritual, and it is directly relevant to feminine experience today." This record of Jacqueline's inner healing journey through art therapy is an example of such a process.

---

[9] American Psychiatric Association: *Diagnostic and Statistical Manual of Mental Disorders*, Fifth Edition. Arlington, VA, American Psychiatric Association, 2013. Dissociative Identity Disorder 300.13 (F44.81), p. 292-298.

Brief Summary of the Myth of Inanna

The myth of Inanna was written in cuneiform hieroglyphics on clay tablets in the fifth millennium B.C., which is referred to as the time of the matriarchy when feminine religious symbols predominated.

Inanna, goddess of the Upperworld of light and life descends into the Underworld to comfort her sister, Ereshkigal, goddess of that realm, who is grieving the death of her husband. Her sister is enraged and says Inanna may enter only if she is treated according to the laws and rites of anyone entering her kingdom. Inanna agrees and is stripped of her royal raiment and bowed low, the customary position of Sumerian burials. She then is killed by her raging sister. She remains entombed for three days until her female assistant Ninshubur persuades Enki, the god of wisdom and waters, to send two mourners to help. They commiserate with the pain and grief of her sister and by that action are able to gain release of the goddess' corpse and affect her rebirth upon return to the Upperworld of Life.

From a Jungian perspective, each of the characters in the story represents an aspect of the human psyche. The story tells us we're not only the positive aspects we'd like to be, like the goddess of the Upperworld. We also have a dark dimension that reigns in the Underworld of our psyche and that we must integrate in order to be whole. But the process requires we be stripped of our illusions of being only good and acknowledge the raging and grieving aspects of our being that we have repressed. The story shows us how Inanna has disowned her own dark side and projected her grief and rage onto her sister, hidden deep in the Underworld (Inanna's unconscious)

This process of transformation often feels like a "death" of who we thought we were. The story teaches us about both the risks and the value of making a descent into the unknown and sometimes terrifying inner depths. We also learn that the essential element in healing our deepest wounds is compassion—both receiving it from others and also having compassion for our own suffering, just as the little mourners had for Inanna's sister. And finally, we need a companion like Inanna's friend, who will make certain we do not get lost in the dark and will guide us back into life.

DESCENT AND RETURN:

AN INCEST SURVIVOR'S HEALING JOURNEY THROUGH ART THERAPY

INTRODUCTION

"Fool has cast off from safe harbor to embark on a voyage of healing."

Fig. 3   "THE SHAMAN'S DRUM: INVITATION TO THE ABYSS"

A shaman from the East stands at the edge of The Abyss. His face is distorted with pain, and the dark scar over his heart bears witness to the wounds he has incurred and healed. He beats the rhythm of a heartbeat on his hand-drum, beckoning those who would follow. The shaman has entered the cathedral of the deep wood, has stepped beyond the great "X" formed by the trees - a caution to the faint of heart. Now trees have grown up like an iron grille that has closed behind him, and the path has brought him to The Edge. Below lies the entrance to the Underworld, marked by the skull of an animal, long dead.

You are invited to witness the journey.

Fig. 3   "THE SHAMAN'S DRUM: INVITATION TO THE ABYSS"

INTRODUCTION

When someone has been severely victimized and the trauma begins to demand attention, that abuse becomes the catalyst for embarking on a healing journey. The precipitant may have many forms; in this case it was incest. However, regardless of the specific problem that initiates it, the Descent and Return has basic universal characteristics, as defined by St. John, Perry and Halifax. As Jackie's therapy proceeded, it was clear she was experiencing many of the classic stages of this archetypal pattern. Her artwork, dreams, and discussion were revealing the kind of acute psychological breakdown and subsequent healing that Dr. Perry described, and in some ways her process paralleled a shaman's descent into the mythic realm. The images that emerged from the depths of her unconscious, described with nonverbal eloquence all she was going through. Her work in therapy also corresponded to the stages of the first symbolic record of a psychological descent, the myth of the Sumerian goddess, Inanna, written so long ago.

As we experience this example of the psychological Descent and Return, Jacqueline's art will guide us. Her work illustrates the dangers and rewards of plumbing the depths of the psyche to heal old incapacitating wounds and find one's authentic Self.

Whenever someone senses a need for healing, that individual has either experienced a violation, or feels guilty for having hurt someone else. This story involves the former. A wound may be inflicted on one level, for example, the physical, but in truth its negative influence continues to penetrate ever deeper, ultimately affecting emotional, psychological, and spiritual aspects of one's being. Conversely, in initiating the healing process, an intervention can be made on any level and all the others will be affected positively.

This record of Jackie's healing begins with the most painful feelings she experienced in response to sexual violation and gradually moves through a full spectrum of emotions, which survivors of abuse typically report, and are described below. Throughout the process, these emotions and the beliefs she formed about herself and her abusive parents were addressed, until finally she experienced a genuine sense of self-worth and the renewal of her spiritual Center.

Rage
Jackie arrived at her first art therapy session mired in deep depression, self-loathing, and despair. She was angry, confused, guilt-ridden, and bent on confrontation and vengeance. The wound she described was paternal incest from the time she was a very young child until she was fourteen years old. She also described having amnesia for twenty-five years regarding the trauma, until dark memories of it erupted into her consciousness, turning her life upside down. This happened three years prior to our first meeting.

The Secret.
Jackie's incest experience was the Secret she held alone and in silence since childhood—like a presence that dare not be named. Typical of sexual abuse survivors, Jackie was told by her father not to tell anyone what he was doing to her. As the story began to unfold in the art therapy sessions, her childhood fear surfaced again because she was just now beginning to challenge the power his threats had over her. It is also typical for victims of sexual abuse to be threatened that they or others whom they love, including family members, friends, and even beloved pets, will be hurt or killed if the victims disclose what has been done to them. Through this tactic, the abuser protects him - or herself from recrimination for their violation of the innocent child.

Shame.

For as long as she could remember, Jackie felt shame—that there was something very wrong with her. Even as she began her therapy, she felt dirty and guilty about what was done to her, although as a child she didn't have any way to understand it.

Guilt.

As an adult, Jackie still continued to experience confusion and deep guilt about having felt any pleasure in that early sexual experience. She needed to be assured that it is normal for the body to respond to touch with pleasure even in that situation, and that sometimes the incestuous touch feels good and may be the only affection or approval a child ever gets. Jackie said this was true for her, but it was confusing because she knew there was something very wrong with this behavior. Had his actions been appropriate for a father, he would not have threatened her with the most severe consequences if their secret intimacy were ever revealed.

Terror.

Jackie told me that her father was intensely domineering and controlling and that terror simply permeated their house at all times. This level of fear is common when a child experiences violation and/or penetration by an adult who is big and strong. Physically hurt, sometimes violently, a child can't understand why the other parent or any trusted adult doesn't come to the rescue. In the course of my work with women who were sexually abused as children, individuals describe states of terror in which they were barely able to breathe.

Dissociation.

> *Dissociation - the extraordinary psychic phenomenon in which the conscious mind spontaneously separates from the body when what is happening is too painful, shameful, terrifying or guilt-provoking to be owned as part of one's personal experience.*

Jackie recalled that when she was five years old she often had the sense of floating out of her body, down the stairs, and out of the house. There was no physical sensation. It seems inexplicable, yet when sexually abused children dissociate from their physical pain and emotional confusion, they sometimes experience themselves floating about the room: in the corner with their teddy bear and dolls, flying up near the ceiling, into the safety of the closet, or even out a window. Away. Anywhere. This spontaneous process enables the child to survive psychologically by severing all conscious connection with the abuser and the pain, shame, and confusion they feel.

Amnesia.

> *Amnesia - The absence of conscious memory or awareness of certain experiences or entire periods of one's life. A spontaneous shut-down, not consciously chosen.*

In some situations, depending on the type, magnitude, and duration of the abuse, as well as the temperament of the child, dissociation will be so extreme as to result in amnesia or a fragmenting of the ego.[10] On a deep, non-verbal level of emotion, an abused child will feel this cannot be happening. In

---

[10] *The most severe level of dissociation and fragmentation is Dissociative Identity Disorder, formerly known as Multiple Personality Disorder. In that case the trauma is so intense and prolonged that an individual's sense of self actually splits into two or more distinct personalities. Each aspect holds part of the memory and each has distinct traits, preferences, etc. Fortunately, this was not Jackie's experience. There is controversy within the psychiatric profession about the validity of this diagnosis.*

order to maintain psychological integrity, all memory of the experience will be unconsciously repressed. When this happened to Jackie, she no longer had conscious memory of the sexual abuse, although it continued to affect her life in powerful ways. She later commented on how amazingly complete the lack of memory is in the condition of amnesia. She said "It was the saving grace" for her ego's sense of self (even though it was destructive to the unity of her whole Self.)

At some point, the incest will stop; in Jackie's case it was due to the onset of puberty. However, the connection between conscious and unconscious levels of awareness is never truly severed. Decades of studies of human consciousness have shown unquestionably that everything we have ever been or experienced—all ages, stages of development, thoughts, and emotions, are recorded on the deeper levels of our consciousness. All our life experiences are available to be recalled in specific detail. This retrieval can be experienced through deep relaxation and hypnosis, energy-healing work, breathwork, medical probes of the brain, the life review of persons who have had a near-death experience, or the sudden, intense awareness of long-forgotten traumatic experiences known as flashbacks.

Flashbacks.
> *Flashback: The abrupt and unexpected remembrance and re-living of severely traumatic experiences that happened at an earlier time in one's life and were repressed into apparent oblivion.*

Now the psyche yields under the long-sustained pressure to keep the Secret. Like a volcano in which internal heat and pressure are so extreme as to turn solid rock into molten lava that spews in all directions in order to relieve the underground pressure, so too, the long-repressed, raging, roiling, emotions erupt into conscious awareness once again in a way that is confusing and terrifying, but never again to be denied. Jackie said the worst time of all was when the memories of her incest experience first surfaced because they destroyed everything she had ever thought was true of her life.

The psychic traumas of war and sexual abuse are the two most common causes of amnesia and the subsequent abrupt and unexpected flood of memories. In these flashbacks one does not simply remember, with some emotional distance, what happened. Rather, the person mentally re-experiences the events as if they were happening again physically. We know from observing dream states that the mind does not discriminate between internal and external reality. For example, the body moves, perspires, changes breathing patterns, may be sexually aroused, and so on, in response to dreams that are experienced as real while we are asleep. Just so, in a flashback, an experience from one's past is mentally relived in a way that is just as terrifying and traumatic as it was in the original physical experience.

What follows now is the account of Jacqueline's archetypal Descent into her psyche's Underworld and her Return to the light of a renewed and revitalized life through her work in art therapy, dreamwork, active imagination, and energy healing.

We begin in **"The Abyss."**

DESCENT AND RETURN:

AN INCEST SURVIVOR'S HEALING JOURNEY THROUGH ART THERAPY

PART I

"Fool will speak truth to the king, whether heard or not heard.

Tears will be shed."

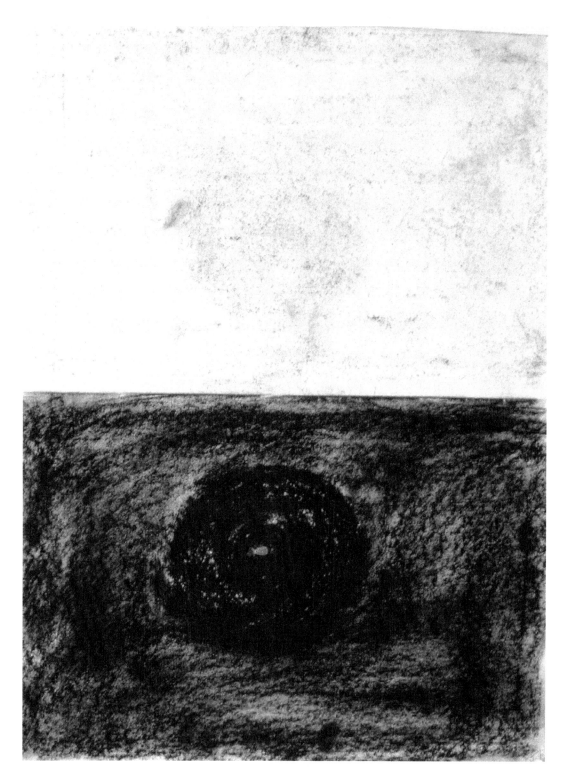

Fig. 4 "THE ABYSS"

The red of Child's rage is constricted by the heavy black that swirls all around it, as if confined in the ominous and deceptive calm of the eye of a hurricane. Woman senses that this rage is dangerous and believes it must be contained by the dark Abyss of her depression.

Fig. 4 "THE ABYSS" 2/27/89

Black fills half of an 18"x24" piece of drawing paper. A darker swirl of black is in the center and at its core are three spots of color: red, yellow, and blue.

February 27, 1989   First session

It's winter and I'm sitting comfortably in the warm family room of a country church's parish house. The space is pleasant, two couches are at right angles to each other, with two wing-back chairs opposite and a wooden coffee table in the center. Several lamps provide soft lighting, and a bank of windows gives a good view of the trees on the other side of the parking lot. There are plenty of well-tended plants by the windows, a wreath on the paneled wall, and a banner that reads "Go in Peace." Well-stocked bookcases line the walls of a separate part of the L-shaped room, and a round table with chairs and brighter lighting provides an adequate place for doing art work.

Jacqueline arrives for her first art therapy session, and I stand to greet her. She is a large woman, significantly overweight, with short dark hair, wearing a mumu, and small gold earrings. I sense a strength in her and also a well-defended anger. We each sit in the angle of the two couches so that we can see each other comfortably. She says to call her Jackie, and I go simply by Louise.

Without many preliminaries she quickly defines her issue. Jackie has written a letter to her parents describing a spontaneous eruption of flashbacks—devastatingly clear memories of many years of paternal incest that had long been lost in amnesia. She plans to confront them with her letter in a few days. Jackie talks about the intense depression she has experienced since the memories surfaced three and a half years ago and refers to that state as "The Abyss." Jackie has always enjoyed drawing and is able to enter into the art therapy process without any encouragement or explanations. I ask if she can show me what The Abyss feels like, using art materials.

Jackie begins by folding the 18" x 24" white paper in half and proceeds to draw on only one side. She works with intensity and produces a very black piece of paper—"not black enough," she says. Nested in the middle are a few tiny spots of the three primary colors, red, yellow, and blue. Jackie says the red in the very center of the black represents *her*. She says black is "isolation, but mostly it's safe."
Note: *To distinguish for the reader between what was said aloud in the sessions and my unspoken thoughts about what was happening, I have put my internal processing in italics.*

This reduction in the size of the paper immediately suggests to me the emotional constriction she feels; and identifying the red in the center as herself indicates to me the rage that is held at the core of her depression. I recognize that for her, isolation is a safe buffer and less painful than experiencing the magnitude of her anger.[11]

> *Since all colors can be mixed from the primary ones of red, yellow, and blue, and colors are associated with various emotions, I see Jackie's use of these three as an unconscious suggestion of the potential for a full spectrum of feelings that resides in her core—beneath the massive black of her depression. It is a small, but hopeful indication.*

---

[11] *Often the meaning of these drawings and collages became clear as we discussed them together. Whenever an insight about an image was Jackie's, I refer to her or quote her directly. Otherwise what is said here is my understanding.*

As an art therapist, I am always careful not to assume that any given color signifies one particular emotion in all situations. There are two basic levels of meaning: personal and universal. Some widespread correlations are repeatedly seen, for example, red for rage or black for depression. However, red for one person might also symbolize other things such as: love and passion, and for someone else, blood—which might represent either the vitality of life or violence. For this reason, I feel it is essential, first of all, to glean from clients what their associations are to the colors they use. This often yields helpful clues as to what emotions are being held in their unconscious. In addition, the art therapist may also be aware of some broader symbolism, and will determine on an individual basis whether or not it is appropriate to discuss this other level of significance at that time.

It is interesting to note that this first image is half-black and half-white, suggesting the balance of opposites signified by the ancient Yin-Yang symbol of China. In this case, having black on the bottom may be seen to represent the darkness of pain and fear that Jackie has experienced for so many years. In contrast, it was my sense that the light on top signified her "higher Self" that contains her wisdom and compassion, which this process will attempt to bring forth.

Fig. 5   "RED IS FOR RAGE"

Here lies the symbol of the crime. The long, sharp dagger, itself slashed by red and black, represents both the violating phallus of the male and the female's instrument of retribution. Thus destructive violence and rage on both sides are symbolized and expressed.

Fig. 5 "RED IS FOR RAGE"   2/27/89

A dagger with a brown hilt and steel-gray blade is nearly obliterated by red and black slash marks.

February 27th (continued)

Jackie is aware of the intensity of her feelings and wants to be able to speak with her parents without losing control. She has been working on her anger and recently felt a shift that she feels will make that possible. I ask her to show me what the now-diminished emotion would look like.

Drawing a dagger, Jackie states "this is what I've fantasized killing him with." She makes red slashes all over the page, shifts to black, then back to red. Now experiencing intense rage, she continues "I feel like I could go on without ever stopping." *This simple act of drawing has immediately gotten her in touch with the intensity of her emotions, and it is obvious that her fury has not yet been resolved.*

I speak of the "wounded child" within—the aspect of her being that was violated when she was young. As an adult, Jackie wants to talk with her parents with reasoned control; however, that "child" is still very hurt and outraged about the abuse she experienced, and her drawing clearly illustrates how volatile those emotions still are. I suggest it would be better to be in touch with her anger rather than deny or repress it—she can use the art materials to express her feelings safely with me. Then, since she will surely feel vulnerable as she talks with her parents, her rage will be less likely to erupt during the confrontation.

I assume that, like everyone, Jackie has good qualities. I acknowledge her sincerity as well as the wounded, raging aspects, and let her know that all her feelings are acceptable here. Jackie says she is aware of her inner strength and she knew that part of herself even as a child, in the midst of continued violation.

*   *   *

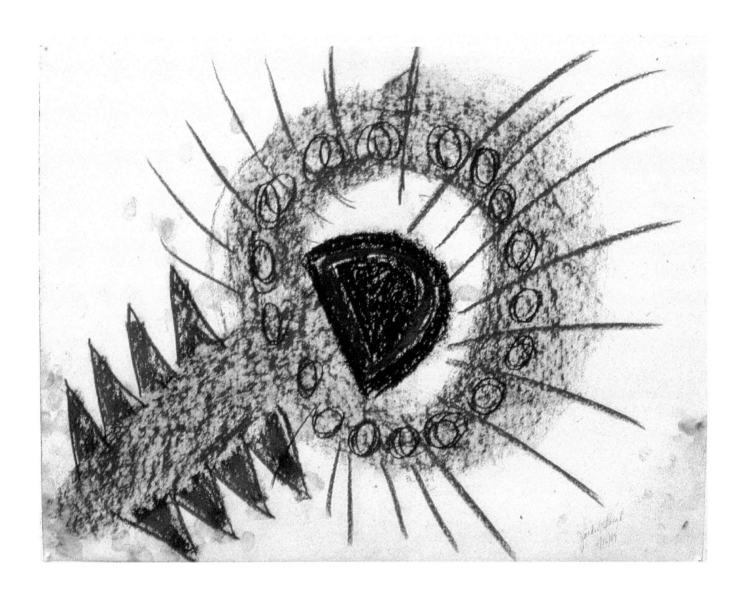

Fig. 6   "'D' IS FOR DADDY"

A rageful red "D" is encased in the black head of a dangerous penile form that is thrusting itself into the blue feminine circle. In this way Woman has symbolized the painful violation of her inner child, victimized throughout childhood by the incestuous acts of the father.

Fig. 6 "'D' IS FOR DADDY" 3/16/89

A wide blue line with pointed red shapes like shark's teeth on either side penetrates a large blue circle. Within it the blue line becomes solid black with a band of red paralleling the edge. The blue circle has small red circles within it and dark blue lines radiating out from it. Fingerprints are on the side.

March 16th

As we begin our second session, Jackie informs me that during the past week she told her grown son and daughter about the incest. Her sister and brother and life-long best friend already know. Now she feels she has revealed her secret as much as is necessary; there is no need to tell anyone else. She says that no longer having to hold the shameful secret alone is a great relief.

She begins to draw, and this abstraction (Fig. 6) evolves without any preconceived notion of what it will be. She describes the straight blue line as "a path with jagged red teeth on either side" and says that the lines projecting out of it and the small red circles within the wide blue circle are "protection," *like barbed wire*. The teeth along the path are "protection, too, like a bear trap." Finally, she says she is *in* the red "D" shape in the black.

Although I generally do not interpret clients' drawings for them, this time I cannot resist offering a possible reading that seems obvious, in light of the fact that Jackie has already told me the issue we are dealing with is incest. Ordinarily, I would first elicit from clients their own memories, associations, and feelings about their images, as well as any emotions that may have arisen while they were drawing.

Jackie has brought in several journals and shows me many line drawings she made in the past to help express her rage.[12] I suggest the straight blue line is a phallus penetrating the feminine circle. The "teeth" are just like the red "dragon's teeth" which she said represented her father in many of the journal drawings she has shown me today. The red within the black forms a perfect "D" at the tip of the penile form: "D" as in Daddy. Finally, the radiating lines suggest much pain to me. Jackie is startled by the notion that the red inside the black is in the shape of the letter "D" and what it seems to signify. Having just said she felt she was inside that red shape, she becomes tearful. Jackie acknowledges she had a slight feeling at first that the blue line entering the circle was a phallic symbol, but had dismissed the idea, not wanting to see it.

I feel that now the stage is set for the work we have to do. The problem has been clearly defined along with some of the emotions that accompany it. Also, I see an example of Jackie creating an image that is perfectly relevant to her experience, but not fully allowing the knowledge of it to be conscious.

The images from Jackie's journals are significant, but we don't have time to review them all in this session and so she offers to let me take them home. Jackie had gotten tearful earlier in this session, saying how

---

[12] *It is important to note that the use of any creative medium in therapy, for example, art, music, dance, poetry, or psychodrama, is a powerfully effective means to vent intense feelings symbolically so that they will not injure oneself or anyone else. Such expressive media can help that person quickly get beyond the surface level of their verbal defenses and tap into a full spectrum of authentic emotions from rage to joy. In "art psychotherapy," such as we are doing here, clients gain access to their deeply wounded feelings through the use of art materials; conscious insight is then achieved by using words to describe the images and feelings that arose during the art making. At the other end of the spectrum is "art as therapy" in which involvement in the creative process is experienced as healing, without any need for verbal processing to achieve insight into the source of the problem.*

awful it is not to be able to trust anyone. I comment that she has just entrusted her very precious journals to me for the next two weeks until we meet again. She comes back and gives me a hug.

We will proceed very gently.

*   *   *

March 23rd

Today Jackie tells me that a few days ago she had an especially clear memory of her father forcing her to have oral sex with him. I ask if she would like to draw in order to release the emotions that are coming up. She agrees, but then is reluctant to begin. Suddenly she's enraged and tells me she's fantasizing castration—cutting off her father's genitals.

Many years after the oral sex incident, and still two years before the memories emerged, she began seeing a male therapist, having become undeniably aware of the rage buried so long in her unconscious. The experience of violent, spontaneous fantasies in which she would see herself torturing men in gruesome ways such as castration and dismemberment, led her to try to identify the source of this rage—whatever it might be.

Jackie shows me some more of her journals from that time with many drawings she made in an effort to understand the reason for her fury. She would sit with pencil and notebook, inviting the issues and feelings to surface in drawings. The result: men and women confronting each other, often with a surreal quality—men having weapons for hands, or only one eye.

After the flashbacks began, Jackie imagined killing her father with a dagger and then remembered that as a child she had often had that same fantasy. (*Fig. 5*) She remembers once having sex with her husband when she had been unwilling, but complied. Under tremendous emotional stress, she began to imagine herself stabbing him. At that time, memories of the incest had not yet surfaced and she was startled that her reaction to her husband was so fierce. However, since the flashbacks, Jackie can see how her husband's behavior paralleled her father's and now understands the intensity of her reaction to him. She also realizes why she gained such excessive weight: as a way to protect herself from any further sexual advances.

Silently, I reflect on how powerfully the years of incest had destroyed her capacity to speak up for herself, perhaps for fear of physical reprisals, or because of that terrible paradox of a child regarding survival—abandonment even by a tormenting adult. Instead of expressing her needs strongly, she repressed them and they manifested in that violent fantasy.

Memories of sexual ordeals with both her father and her then-husband trigger Jackie's long-held rage once again. She does an angry drawing (*not shown*) and then draws a cage around it for fear her fury might explode. *Doing this drawing provides a safe way for Jackie to express her feelings and brings her some emotional relief.*

Jackie has only one positive memory of her father. He once made a see-saw for her and her siblings and constructed it in such a way as to insure a soft rather than hard landing. She feels such an expression of caring for his children was ironic.

*   *   *

April 6ᵗʰ

Jackie comes into our fourth session brimming with tears she is trying to contain. She has been feeling suicidal for several days over a financial situation that has presented itself with her father. She is angry, but has slipped back into the role of victim and feels as though she is a "bad girl." She has withdrawn from her friends and has begun to isolate herself again. She is afraid to really cry and touch all the pain she feels inside.

I offer art materials. She accepts, but then hesitates. Jackie tells me she occasionally uses visualizations on her own, so I suggest we try a simple type of energy work involving inner images.[13] Although she is cautious about moving more deeply into her pain, she is open to this. Jackie is able to close her eyes and visualize how the stagnant energy of her repressed pain looks in her body. It is a "large, red, angry, stuck place" in her gut; she is also aware of a "golden yellow and turquoise area" in her forehead. I suggest that she allow the lighter colors to disperse the dark ones, in the same way detergent dissolves heavy grease, if she feels that's appropriate. At first Jackie is tearful and a little hesitant, but she moves into the process and within a surprisingly short time, is feeling calm and relieved.

This simple, but powerful, internal visualization process has been effective in several ways. First of all, Jackie was able to relax and release her intense feelings of being victimized. This is of vital importance because she now knows from personal experience that she has within herself the power to alter her mood without depending on any outside influences. Second, the process has deepened the growing bond of trust between us. At the end of the session Jackie asks for a hug and leaves laughing, an enormous shift from the distraught state she was in when she arrived.[14]

*   *   *

April 13ᵗʰ

I suggest a book for Jackie to read: *I Come as a Brother, A Remembrance of Illusions*.[15] I tell her that in a time of personal crisis some years ago, a friend introduced me to this book. Through it I was reminded that the surface level of my being, the ego, needed to acknowledge and safely express the tormented emotions I experienced at that time, and also that there was more to me than my pain. Buried beneath the suffering was my soul-Self, which was strong, light, and full of wisdom. I tell Jackie that finding that deeper dimension within herself is essential to her healing, and this book may help in the process. I also emphasize that its perspective is broadly spiritual, but has no particular religious affiliation.

---

[13] *"Energy Work" is a term that covers many different approaches to healing. It is distinguished from "talk-therapy" and also from the "expressive therapies," which use various creative processes, such as art. In general, energy work refers to ways of working that either 1) utilize the breath, 2) clear blockages to the flow of life energy as it moves through pathways in the body known as "meridians," 3) work with chakras and the electro-magnetic field around the body, known as the "aura," or 4) use sound, visualization, or touch.*

[14] *As a therapist, I love working with inner visualizations because it is so empowering for the one who is seeking help. The client learns processes that can be undertaken alone or with others that effectively shift an emotional state with no unpleasant side effects.*

[15] *Bartholomew. I Come as a Brother, A Remembrance of Illusions. Taos, NM; High Mesa Press, 1986. This book is purported to be channeled from an angelic spirit, whom the unnamed scribe refers to as "Bartholomew." Whatever the book's source, as a trained psychotherapist I found the book to be inspiring and full of psychologically sound insights that I felt could be helpful and encouraging to Jackie.*

I also tell her I have learned through my own dark journey toward healing that it is impossible to resolve a problem at the level on which it exists. In order to achieve the most profound healing, an individual needs to drop beneath the logical, verbal mind where we typically can stay defended against our pain. In the process of feeling our emotions directly and having them witnessed with compassion, we are able to move through them into the deepest aspect of Self where we experience our own inner light. The book, *I Come as a Brother*, emphasizes that we have intrinsic worth, despite messages to the contrary we may have received due to abuse, neglect, or abandonment. My hope is that Jackie will begin to understand she is a person of great value and worth, despite the trauma of incest.

Jackie says she may look it up, but is reluctant to consider anything she feels could be a "sweetness and light" whitewash of her rage, or which might minimize the depth of her pain.

*   *   *

April 27ᵗʰ

In the week since our last meeting Jackie read part of the book I suggested. She liked some of it, but feels other parts seem to deny the harsh reality of the world. In this session, she creates an image (*not shown*) that expresses the dichotomy she feels, describing it as "a mixed message." According to Jackie, the main thing she has learned from her incest experience is that nothing is as it appears to be. She is understandably filled with rage at this point, and it is obvious from what she says that at this time she has no wish to release her tormenting emotions.[16]

*   *   *

May 4ᵗʰ

Jackie begins by telling me that on her way here she wondered if she really had anything to do in therapy today, but then started to cry in the car. She jokes that she feels like Pavlov's dog: just the thought of coming for her therapy triggers deep painful feelings, even when her conscious mind is unaware of the

---

[16] *As I listen to Jackie's reluctance to engage with anything that might mitigate her anger, I recognize this attitude as one that is characteristic of many abuse survivors. My experience has shown me that holding onto one's rage is often believed to be the only way to feel strong and safe, while to let go of it would seem to discount the enormity of the effect the abuse has had one one's life.*

However, paradoxically, instead of being a protection, the unwillingness to release that rage has the effect of maintaining the position of victim: helpless, and hopelessly tied to the past, unable to move into the present with a feeling of genuine self-worth. The wound of sexual abuse will fester in the psyche until it is witnessed compassionately by someone who acknowledges the reality of it.

When survivors become aware of the larger dimension of Self deep within that is strong and whole, the dark and terrifying elements of psyche can be addressed from a place of strength. Those frightening aspects are part of what C.G. Jung termed the "Shadow." On the other hand, tapping into the wise, inner Self enables us to hold our small suffering ego with tenderness; and then gradually, as the healing work matures, extend that gentle empathy to others.

The Shadow also contains positive potential which we have simply not yet recognized or developed, such as humor, creativity, or other skills. The wide ranging psychological explorations of Jung and his orientation to the deeper realm of spirit have always appealed to me as a container for my own inner journey, as well as for my work with other souls in need of healing.

specifics that need to be addressed. *This spark of humor about her emotional reaction is a healthy sign because it indicates that even as she is allowing her pain to surface, she can also have some objectivity about it that keeps her from being overwhelmed.*

Moving into the session, the issue of trust arises again. Jackie asks how she can ever fully trust another person after her long years of incest. As we talk, she asks me not to look at her. She says she feels naked when her tears and vulnerability show. I comment: when she was naked and exposed as a child, her feelings were deeply violated, and so now, as she lets herself experience those old wounds, of course she feels naked again.

As we continue, I keep my eyes closed, honoring her request. After a while, intuitively feeling a need for some connection, I hold out my hand and ask if fingertip contact would be alright with her. She agrees to that and very lightly touches the tips of her fingers to mine. I ask her to draw what the contact feels like. Jackie draws two lines that mirror the angle of our hands and are in contact at one end, just as our fingers were. She then interrupts the connection of those two lines by drawing a larger vertical bar between them. Referring to the central line separating the other two, I suggest that in her fear of trusting others, she has drawn the line in relationships, just short of real contact. I copy Jackie's diagram and draw a circle around it. It becomes a peace symbol. She responds that for her there is peace within the barrier. *Jackie is at the threshold of a deep well of anger and grief she has avoided feeling for so long by staying in the numbness of depression and isolation. I sense her ambivalence as she now begins to consciously experience those emotions and allow me to witness them.*

I assure Jackie I honor her need for safety—there is every reason for her to feel cautious about continuing to open to this work. In addition, if she needs that separating distance in order to feel safe in relationships, she may want to maintain it. An alternative would be to continue the therapy process, knowing she can always move at her own pace and she can stop the work at any time.

I tell Jackie whenever one brings old feelings and behavior patterns into consciousness it creates the freedom to respond differently. When a survivor no longer remains a victim of the past, that person won't unconsciously act out deeply held pain in ways that are destructive. My years of work as an art therapist have shown me that completing the healing process of releasing ancient rage and resolving trauma is liberating and brings inner peace. But as Ellen Bass and Laura Davis state in the title of their book on healing from sexual abuse, it takes "courage to heal."[17]

*   *   *

May 11ᵗʰ

Jackie tells me that simply talking, and even doing drawings to vent her rage, have not been fully effective to lift her out of the depression and hopeless feeling of being trapped in the dark Abyss that she described in her first session (*see Fig. 4*).

---

[17] Bass, Ellen and Davis, Laura. *The Courage to Heal.* Collins, New York, 4ᵗʰ ed., 2008.

Now in our eighth session, as Jackie wonders aloud how it would ever be possible to get beyond the nightmare of it all, I offer her a form of energy work called "Vibrational Healing."[18] I describe the process and my training, and assure her that I know it to be safe from my own experience. Jackie says she would like to try it in our next session.

*   *   *

May 17th

It is our ninth session and Jackie is ready to experience Vibrational Healing. Since I do not have a massage table in this office, I put some couch cushions on the floor. When Jackie is settled comfortably, I sit beside her. As a way to help her relax, I begin with a process known as "Co-meditation,"[19] in which one person synchronizes their breathing rhythm with the breathing of another. This results in a profound feeling of union and is often used to calm the fears of a dying person.

After a short while, I move into the Vibrational Healing process with my voice. In about fifteen minutes Jackie bursts into tears, opens her eyes and looks at me. She is surprised to see I am still sitting beside her with my hands in my lap. As I was intoning different sounds and mentally directing healing energy to her abdomen, she had the distinct feeling of being touched there. This has brought up the pain of her father's incestuous touch. When she sees I am not making any physical contact with her, Jackie relaxes and becomes deeply quiet for the remainder of the session. I am satisfied that she now feels safe with this way of working with the body's subtle energy.

*   *   *

---

[18] *"Vibrational Healing" is a process developed by Flo Calhoun, a nurse and practitioner of energy healing, whom I encountered prior to this work with Jackie. (She has not written a book on this particular process, but her work can be found on Facebook.) In this process the therapist voices a particular type of toning, and mentally directs those sounds into the client's major joints and energy centers known as chakras. Done without any physical contact, the vibration of the sound creates a resonance in the body, which has the effect of bringing up intense emotions that have been repressed, enabling the client to release them. Using sound vibrations in this way is only one approach to working with the body's energy systems. This healing genre is far more subtle and complex than this initial work with Jackie would indicate, and takes many forms.*

Modern work in the field of energy healing has ancient antecedents, especially the art of acupuncture which dates back approximately 5,000 years, as originally recorded in China and later in India and Japan. In China the body's subtle energy is known as "chi" and in Japan as "ki." The word "chakra" means wheel and refers to the spinning vortices of energy that are located in specific parts of the body, the major ones generally being aligned with the endocrine glands. Memories of our experiences are stored not only in the brain, but also throughout the body and are referred to as "cellular memory." It's common knowledge among people who do energy work that the primary area where intense emotions are held is the lower abdomen where the second of seven major chakras is located. Acupuncture and many types of energy healing work with these centers to restore balance and a flow of life energy.

In addition to acupuncture, some other contemporary processes are: shiatsu, bio-energetics, polarity, energy balancing, chiropractic, and therapeutic massage. I have studied or experienced nearly all of these. The life force can be impinged upon by either physical or emotional constrictions. In any of these systems the premise is that the body will heal itself when the blocks to the flow of energy are removed and a healthy balance is restored to the various polarities within us. There are also healing processes that have a specific spiritual focus. Integrated Kabbalistic Healing developed by Jason Shulman in his school, A Society of Souls, has been particularly helpful to me personally.

[19] Boerstler, Richard and Kornfield, Hulen. *Life to Death, Harmonizing the Transition.* Healing Arts Press; Rochester, VT, 1995.

May 25th

Jackie relates a dream she doesn't understand: but as we explore it, she understands the dream to symbolize her mother's denial of her inability or unwillingness to protect Jackie from her father. She asks to do the Co-meditation / breathing process again today. In doing it, she becomes tearful as she relives the dream of her mother and recognizes its ramifications for her childhood.

As we near the end of the session, I ask Jackie how she felt about last week's work with Vibrational Healing. She says it was a good introduction to this very different way of working because she felt the reality of the energy and her trust in me deepened. Jackie also tells me that the inner quiet she experienced was so profound that on the way home she didn't even turn on the car radio, as she usually does, so as not to lose the feeling.

*   *   *

June 1st

As we begin our session today, Jackie again requests the Vibrational Healing. I ask her to state an intention for the session, so I can join her and not, unwittingly, have a separate agenda. Her intention for today is "to release any blocks I may have, in order to find answers within myself about how to resolve my incest-rage." We move into this process and, because we are in a suitably private space, I tell her she is free to make any sound that arises within her.

As I start the toning and direct the healing vibration into her heart, Jackie spontaneously begins to release her rage in sound—repeatedly screaming at full volume and with tremendous intensity. What is surfacing from the dark, painful depths of her psyche into the light of consciousness is, first of all, a keen awareness of how very psychologically unstable her mother was. Second, Jackie recognizes how manipulative her mother's passive-aggressive controlling tactics had been. The screaming has provided her with a great release from the burden of emotional pain she has carried for so long. It has also demonstrated to her that, as her therapist, I will allow a full expression of all her feelings, as long as it is done in a safe way. After the energy work, we still have plenty of time to verbally process what has come up in her memories and feelings, and the session comes to a quiet close.

*   *   *

June 8th

Today Jackie returns feeling extremely upset. Ever since our last session she has been experiencing a deep rage toward her mother, and says that for years she has wanted to kill both her parents. That emotion was expressed non-verbally last week as she gave full voice to her rage, but she hadn't recognized that the screaming was the trigger that brought up those feelings so intensely this week.

Jackie relates a dream in which she saw a green, transparent glass or rock protruding from the ground, with maggots surrounding its base. She knew this had to do with her mother and that it represented just the "tip of the iceberg." *This comment suggests that Jackie knows there is much more regarding her mother that she will need to address as we continue the work.* Jackie also experienced a spontaneous image while she was awake: her mother's head was on the dining room table of her childhood home and it had octopus-like tentacles reaching out and wrapping around everyone. Last week's work has released a torrent of rage toward her mother. I suggest drawing to process those feelings before moving to new issues. Jackie agrees and draws both of those images. *(Not shown)* While drawing she tells me that after screaming out her rage last week she felt as though she had lost twenty pounds, and again says that since then her feeling of connection with me has deepened.[20]

*   *   *

June 15th

In the week following the last meeting, I received a letter from Jackie telling me about a number of painful memories that she hadn't previously mentioned, relating to how her mother treated her over the years. She wrote: "We seem to have opened a Pandora's box, everything is a tangled mess, and I feel scared." Today she tells me that since I now know the depth and complexity of her need, she feels very vulnerable with me.

Despite the feelings expressed in her letter, today Jackie also says she is now "totally committed to staying with the healing work until it is completed. I don't want to miss a single session." After we talk Jackie requests another toning session. For a second time, she screams out her rage and says what a relief it is to experience that emotional release.[21]

*   *   *

June 29th

Jackie tells me she has been angry with me for something she thought I said last week. She couldn't express her feelings directly at that time, but is able to do so today. Something I said or perhaps a tone in my voice conveyed to Jackie that I thought she wasn't committed to this work. This may have been some unconscious projection or countertransference on my part, or simply a misunderstanding. In any case, once again I assure her I am fully committed to staying with her throughout this process, and am certain she can do the work and get free of her depression and the rage it covers. *I take it as a healthy sign of growing self-confidence that Jackie can express her anger at me this week.*

*   *   *

July 6th

Jackie's full engagement in the art aspect of her therapy is evidenced by the fact that she brings in four paintings done this week at home *(not shown)*. She says the most important thing she experienced while

---

[20] *The discharge of rage from her body's energy field has created the distinctly different sensation of weight loss on the physical level, in the same way she had earlier felt the vibration of my toning as physical touch. Clearly, a change on one level of our being does affect all others.*

[21] *In-depth psychotherapy requires the active involvement of the client, as well as a therapist who has examined in therapy their own deep fears and issues. In this process the therapist grows in both knowledge of, and compassion for, what their clients are experiencing. The therapist is then fully present for the person whose journey they are witnessing and guiding. This kind of presence fosters the development of genuine trust in the client who will then feel safe enough to engage in the difficult process of examining painful experiences and beliefs that negatively affect their life.*

My experience of working on the psychiatric unit of several hospitals over the years has shown me that it is seriously dangerous for a person to try to function in the capacity of therapist or any type of counselor if they have not done their own in-depth work in therapy or some other form of healing. It is essential for the one who serves as guide, to explore the Shadow aspects of their own being in order to be aware of the danger of projecting their unresolved personal feelings and beliefs onto their clients. It is a truism that as therapists we cannot help another person go into painful places that we have been too afraid to explore within ourselves.

working on the first two was an awareness of how much she was enjoying scraping away layers of paint. A good metaphor, I suggest, for her healing process, and better than adding layers to cover up what is under the surface. She hadn't thought of it like that, but it is precisely what she has been experiencing.[22]

July 13th

As a pre-teen Jackie loved the color lavender and had chosen it for her room. This week I received a letter she wrote one night when she was distraught. She experienced a memory-image in which a lavender pillow was coming down over her face. She had the distinct and terrifying sensation that her mother was trying to smother her. Now she realizes the reason why for years that color has triggered a feeling of "absolute and total terror," so different from how she originally felt about lavender. Jackie talks about several other highly charged memories of her mother's abuse. When they came up she felt as if she were going crazy and began to doubt her own intense experiences. Yet she says the emotions were the same as when the memories of the incest erupted in flashbacks, except then she hadn't felt crazy.

Recently Jackie had not been remembering her dreams as much as she had previously; however, since these memories of her mother surfaced, she is recalling them again. *Apparently as that crucial memory was nearing the surface of consciousness, there had been a spontaneous repression of dream material, but the recovered memory has released that block.* In this session, Jackie needs reassurance that she is not losing her mind. I tell her it takes courage to allow this intensely painful childhood material to become conscious in order to be healed.

*   *   *

July 20th

Jackie asks to do another session of Vibrational Healing. Her intention is "to release all the old trauma from all of my cells." The process lasts about forty minutes and, unlike the last two energy sessions, it is deeply quietening, just as the first one was two months ago. All week Jackie has been amazed by the change she is experiencing. She says "I feel wonderful and have begun to really like myself on a deep level." She senses these feelings of self-worth are mostly a result of the energy-release of rage; and especially the memory of her mother trying to suffocate her. She is starting to feel empowered, no longer guarding the secret, a silent victim of her past.

In a note to me, Jackie comments "this constant feeling of liking myself is so strange and great." She says poignantly, "this positive sense of myself has been so long in coming...so, so, long."

Jackie's recent memories have been pivotal and represent a significant benchmark in our work. In the energy work it was not simply screaming that caused the change. The therapist's compassionate witness of the client's suffering helps to transform the rage and is essential in healing work. In addition, the broad spiritual perspective of the book, I Come as a Brother *and the deep energy attunement of Co-Meditation have also contributed significantly.[23]*

---

[22] *This is a good example of how working with art materials in therapy provides a symbolic process of which the client may not even be aware, that is often non-verbal and non-rational, yet meaningful and satisfying on an emotional level.*

[23] *In my experience all deep healing is spiritual in nature, though my work has no particular religious affiliation. There is a sacred quality to this work and I have found it humbling to be present and hold the life energy in a way that will aid another suffering soul. It is, in fact, healing and energizing for both individuals involved.*

Fig. 7   "MEMORY – THE BEGINNING OF THE CHILD'S JOURNEY"

A young girl stands alone amidst the chaos of the "war zone." Her rage is seen in the blood-red aura that surrounds her, and crumbling castles attest to her broken dreams. Child looks at a darkened window that reminds her of the all-seeing eye of her abusive and fanatically controlling father.

Fig. 7 "MEMORY – THE BEGINNING OF THE CHILD'S JOURNEY" 7/22/89

A young girl stands on an area of blue water, looking at a window behind her, while below is a pile of blankets. On the left, old castles are in ruins. She is surrounded by red, and a single word "Memory" is also in a band of red. Just above this word and to the left is a picture showing the excavation of a statue of an Egyptian pharaoh lying horizontally. Only the head is visible.

July 22ⁿᵈ

Today Jackie arrives with this small collage. For nearly five months she has been drawing in the art therapy sessions, as well as doing energy healing and dream work. This is the first time she has made a magazine collage, and it appears to contain a number of significant elements. We explore this complex picture, just as we have distilled the meaning of her dreams and drawings.[24] *This is an interesting development since I have never suggested collage, nor have I mentioned doing artwork at home alone.*

The young girl who is the focus of this work, is surrounded by red and Jackie describes her as "the child who is a victim, standing in her own small, safe area in the war zone." She stands on a variety of undefined textures, meant to convey the feeling of chaos. *These layers suggest to me the various strata of feelings and issues that she has already begun to encounter during this inner excavation work. The pile of blankets below the child looks to me like a row of dead bodies, which seems appropriate for an incest bed because that experience is so destructive to the child's essential spirit.*

To the child's right *(our left as we face the picture)* are castles that Jackie describes as "the ruins of childhood." The young girl looks at a window to her left *(to our right as we face the picture)* that Jackie says represents the "all-seeing eye" of her domineering father. There is another significant element, nearly hidden in the chaos: the sculpted head of an Egyptian pharaoh. *Appropriate because the pharaoh was the god and father figure for all the people.* The face with its headdress is just above and to the left of the word "Memory" that is in a band of red that Jackie deliberately used to represent her rage.

We explore the significance of the pictures Jackie has spontaneously chosen for this image. As I look at them and hear the comments she is making about what they symbolize for her, I see that in the medium of collage she has found a powerful new vehicle with which to express her feelings and process her memories.

July 27ᵗʰ

In today's session Jackie again talks about her mother. As we sit opposite each other, I ask, "If I were your mother, could you reach out and touch my hand?" Her immediate response is a feeling of panic because any closeness with her mother feels like a threat. She says the phrase "reach out and touch..." was her first association to a phone in a recent dream. In it, her mother left a message on Jackie's answering machine

---

[24] *The experience of exploring images and symbols for their inherent psychological meaning is essentially the same whether they are created with art materials, in dreams, or in the active imagination process while awake. I think of dreams as internal art therapy because the psyche is creating images whether awake or asleep, and when they are translated into words, the metaphor of the image becomes clear.*

saying she knew about the incest. Jackie now wonders if her mother did know about the sexual abuse while it was going on, and she begins to cry deeply from the pain this possibility causes her. Once again she expresses her caring for me. *In the therapeutic transference, I sense she has begun to perceive me as the good mother she never had.*

*   *   *

August 3rd

After about five months of work I mention to Jackie that, at some point in the process, forgiveness can be a healing experience *for the person who has been deeply wounded.* This statement brings up her second expression of anger at me. Jackie thinks to forgive means she would have to approve what had been such a terrible violation—a misconception I have found to be common in abuse survivors. I realize we are defining "forgiveness" differently and read a definition from the dictionary, which provides her with a meaning closer to my intent. That is, "to cease to feel resentment against, on account of wrong committed; to give up claim to requital from, or retribution upon (an offender)."[25]

Because I have introduced the notion of forgiveness, Jackie is angry at me as well as at her parents. Using a technique similar to the interactive process of Gestalt Therapy,[26] I suggest we might act this out in a safe way in order for her to discharge that emotion. Jackie agrees, so I pick up a couch cushion and invite her to swat me with it, which she does. I use a second cushion to swat her back. I actively engage in this mock battle in order to encourage her to fully drop into her feelings. It takes only a minute or two before Jackie collapses into deep weeping. This physical activity has not been hurtful, and has had the effect of releasing her tension.

Expressing her anger at me has triggered a release of long pent-up rage at her parents—a catharsis. This has had a positive effect on an emotional level, but intellectually it is another matter. As the session draws to an end, Jackie tells me she is still very disturbed by the concept of forgiveness, as she understands it.

*   *   *

August 4th A *letter from Jackie*

Jackie is embroiled in a mighty struggle with the notion of forgiveness. In a letter she writes that since the eruption of flashbacks, she has wanted to get revenge on her father, but surprisingly, doesn't feel that way toward her mother; and even feels some ambivalence now about her father. Suddenly, she is "ANGRY, ANGRY, ANGRY, ANGRY" and feels like crying. Subsequently, she indicates she had paused to "go within" to check on how her "inner children" were feeling.

Previously, Jackie mentioned to me that for years, she has been aware of two "inner children" who are personifications of herself at approximately two and thirteen years old, and that she usually visualizes them beneath a great tree.[27]
Resuming the letter, she tells me she looked in on them and found the toddler extremely agitated and the teen feeling very unsafe. In her imagination she comforted them and gave absolute assurances that she will keep them safe from any further hurt by her parents.

---

[25] *Webster's Third New International Dictionary of the English Language,* unabridged. Merriam-Webster Inc., Publishers, Springfield, MA, 1961.
[26] Perls, Frederick S., Hefferline, Ralph E., Goodman, Paul. *Gestalt Therapy: Excitement and Growth in the Human Personality.* Dell Publishing Co., New York, 1965.
[27] Joan Chodorow. *Encountering Jung: Jung on Active Imagination.* Princeton University Press; Princeton, New Jersey, 1997.

Having recognized the specific emotions that were welling up, Jackie was able to return to considering the ramifications of forgiveness. She has decided that to forgive her parents does not mean she has to embrace them, nor even be near them, and "I don't think it means I have to love them." Jackie says she wants to talk with me more about this, and about my understanding of forgiveness. Her letter continues: "I decided that I'm not going to focus on forgiving, but I do want to explore it; and I decided that I am willing to go wherever my process takes me - period. I am going the distance, whatever that is—for <u>me</u>—I'm doing it for me."

Jackie has entered into an "active imagination" process with which she is familiar. After breaking with Freud, Jung developed his own school, "Analytical Psychology." He wrote extensively about the process of Active Imagination that became his primary way to work with clients. He pointed out that when one stays focused on an inner image with eyes closed, in a short while the image will move and take on a life of its own that is not controlled by rational thought. The characters begin to speak, or the scene may change, spontaneously. The person doing the Active Imagination then engages in dialogue with those inner figures. Jackie had learned this process in a previous therapy. She often finds it helpful to use alone at home.

In doing the visualization this week, Jackie consciously recognized that on an inchoate, emotional level she fears that if she were to release her rage and "forgive" her parents, she would feel like a child and be vulnerable to their whims again. In this experience, she has felt the depth of fear that "forgiveness" of her parents implies to her, and the intense anger she feels about it. Jackie's ability to engage in this internal process on her own is a measure of the ego-strength that enables her to tolerate the pain she feels, as she does this healing work.

*   *   *

August 17th

Jackie asks to hear more about my understanding of forgiveness. I assure her that to forgive others for a violation, never means their malicious behavior is acceptable. Years of working with sexual abuse survivors has shown me that staying in a state of rage, demanding retribution, an apology, or explanation that probably will never be forthcoming causes depression—a paralysis of emotions. Research in the field of psycho-neuro-immunology indicates that emotional depression, in turn, causes a suppression of the body's immune system, and so holding onto rage can cause disturbances on all levels of one's being. Consequently, when someone has been abused, they may in their own time, feel a need to express a full range of emotions with supportive guidance, which offers freedom from the heavy negativity of rage.

I understand forgiveness to mean that through the tender and difficult process of expressing all the emotions that result from abuse, one is able to let go of expectations of the other person, even though the wound will not be forgotten. Jackie says she might be able to consider forgiveness from that perspective. At this point, besides being angry at me about this issue, she again expresses the deep trust and caring she feels for me.[28]

---

[28] *I understand Jackie's affection to be on two levels. Consciously, it is directed to me personally, as an expression of the love one often naturally feels for the therapist who is escort and guide on the journey into the dark unknown within. Beyond that, it is apparent that Jackie is experiencing me as the "good mother" she never had. In her transference I am now the recipient of both the love and the anger that rightfully belong to her mother. Clearly, the therapeutic bond between us has been powerfully forged by the fiery expression of her deep rage in the energy work. As often happens in abuse cases, Jackie's rage was directed with equal intensity at both parents—not only did her mother not protect her, she was also actively abusive.*

Jackie begins to use art materials and draws a large blue circle and begins to color it in. Then suddenly she starts to draw very aggressively and allows the color to spill over the boundary, saying she is choosing to "go outside the lines" in her life now.

Previously, Jackie has always worn a lot of face makeup, which tended to give her a mask-like appearance. Today I note that, for the first time, she has come to the session without wearing any. I wonder if this is also an example of "going outside the lines."
Is she pealing away an old mask? My sense is she's owning her own beauty, not needing to hide anymore.

*   *

August 24th

Today Jackie relates four or five breakthrough insights—her healing has taken on a momentum of its own. Over the months, she has spoken of two internal male figures that she perceives in the same manner as her "inner children." The negative one is her father image, which she calls "Alfred," and the positive one "Charles." The latter has been a phenomenon of more recent years. She has rarely mentioned him to me, although she has often mentioned Alfred.

Jackie has begun to feel good about herself, and says she wants to kill Alfred and bring to an end the old internalized, self-flagellating voice she developed as a result of her father's constant criticizing. However, knowing how harmful it can be to try to kill off an aspect of one's psyche, even "just" on the imaginal level, I suggest she go within and see if she can become aware of an appropriate function for Alfred.

Jackie agrees to try this. With eyes closed in the state of active imagination she sees herself standing with Charles and confronting Alfred who is "like a giant." Silently Jackie tells Alfred they have to find a new function for him and Charles says he will now accompany Jackie on the next part of her journey. Jackie reports there seems to be a lot of non-verbal communication among the three of them, and then, to her astonishment, Alfred begins to shrink until he is only about a foot and a half high. I suggest that Alfred might now have a helpful role in her psyche, such as a wise judge who can discriminate between real and false dangers and warn her "inner children," rather than always beating her down. Jackie likes the idea and leaves the session feeling very good about this new development.

This is a fascinating demonstration of Jung's articulation that inner images can move with a life of their own.

*   *   *

August 31st

Following last week's visualization of Alfred and Charles, Jackie returned to her job and found she was totally unable to concentrate or remember what work she had just completed. She says it felt as though her brain had simply been disconnected. That sensation lasted into the weekend, but by Monday she was able to function in her usual way at work. She says it was a strange experience and a bit scary, but now she's feeling fine. *When Jackie's creative imagination spontaneously reduced the size of the negative male image, it signified the psychic reality that she was actually freeing herself from the influence of her father's incessant criticism. In recent months, the energy work has facilitated several important breakthroughs, and now the process of Active*

Imagination has brought Jackie through another major transition. She is changing in deep and significant ways—I feel like I'm watching a flower open in time-lapse photography.

Jackie says she hasn't had any hope in the last three years of ever feeling anything other than pain and rage about the incest, but again tells me she is now actually feeling positive about herself. She is amazed that in the past week her mother, father, and brother have all called her which they rarely do.

*   *   *

September 7ᵗʰ

Jackie is excited today as she tells me two important dreams. In the first one, she was making love with a man very pleasurably; because of that, another man threatened to kill her, but she was not afraid. Jackie says this is the first time she can ever remember having a dream of making love with a man pleasurably. *It occurs to me that the man with whom she was making love may be a personification of the good male, Charles, and the man who was threatening to kill her perhaps represents Alfred—that internalized negative voice that previously had always shamed her about any sexual experience with men. If that is the case, her dream makes clear that she is no longer afraid, and is free to make her own choices now.*

In the second dream, Jackie was standing in the surf watching a great whale breach the surface and was accompanied by a man with whom she was comfortable. She comments that until now, the image of a whale has always been terrifying for her, but she doesn't know why. *In Jungian psychology, the whale is considered a phallic symbol, and in breaching the surface it symbolizes the contents of the unconscious coming into awareness. Jackie says she had no knowledge of that.*

Jackie talks a lot about Alfred symbolizing her abusive father; yet she also expresses the insight that this negative male is part of her psyche as well, and recognizes she, too, is capable of hurting others. She is beginning to realize how often her responses to everyday interactions bring up deep memories of past rejections that cause disproportionate feelings of anger and sadness. Jackie tells me she is also increasingly aware of how her anger has been projected onto both of her children and other men. She has decided to attend more carefully to those relationships, especially with her son and brother.

Fig. 8   "THE MOTHER-WOUND: FALSE APPEARANCES"

The "good" mother holds her precious child in a beautiful sacred space. However, Child is bleeding profusely from her heart and the blood leads us to the underlying truth. Tombstones and rubble symbolize the inner reality: confusion and pain and psychic destruction have transpired beneath the surface appearances of a loving home life of order and beauty.

Fig. 8 "THE MOTHER WOUND: FALSE APPEARANCES" 9/10/89

The setting for this collage is the nave of a High Renaissance cathedral, which is the epitome of rational order in classical architectural design. Placed in the center of it is a painting of the Madonna and Child by the sixteenth century painter, Raphael. Red paint signifies blood that flows down from the child's heart to a pile of tombstones and rubble beneath them.

September 14ᵗʰ

I am amazed to see Jackie has arrived with four collages today. This first one expresses the deep pain she feels about her relationship with her mother. In order to specifically, but non-verbally, identify the victim and victimizer, she has superimposed photographs of herself and her mother, from the time of her childhood, onto the Madonna and Child. *In each of these collages I have masked her parents' faces for confidentiality.* Red paint for blood binds the wounded child to the tombstones and rubble below, representing the realm of death and destruction: Jackie's personal Underworld of psychic pain.[29]

Jackie tells me the unresolved, painful history of her relationship with her mother is, in a peculiar way, even more hurtful than the incest with her father. She cannot imagine what it must be like to have a healthy, loving father, saying "that's a long-dead issue." What Jackie misses far more is not having had a mother to protect and care for her, and again says how much she cares for me. In this collage Jackie has expressed powerfully and poignantly her profound longing for a mother's love.

*   *   *

---

[29] *What Jackie consciously remembered before the flashbacks, was a healthy family life. In this image the contrast between the rational order of a beautiful and sacred Renaissance structure above, and the rubble and tombstones below, illustrates the discrepancy between the outer appearances and inner reality of Jackie's early life. However, the inner chaos and destruction of her sense of self-worth wrought by the abuse has remained for many years in Jackie's unconscious mind. As this difficult process continues to unfold, she frequently expresses a need for my support and encouragement to be assured she is not going crazy.*

Fig. 9   "THE FATHER-WOUND: ALTAR OF SACRIFICE"

Now the amnesia-facade of a happy childhood has crumbled. Now innocent Child can see: she remembers the sexual violations of the father. Now life will never be the same again.

Fig. 9 "THE FATHER-WOUND: ALTAR OF SACRIFICE" 9/12/89

An innocent child and two small angels gaze upward. The child's face is surrounded by a golden halo. Above them is the abdomen and thigh of a male body facing right with its genitals exposed. The children are backed by the crumbling ruins of a classical building facade. Between the child and the male body is an open window that creates a dark hole; to the left of the male figure is a vase of flowers and to the right is a goat. The mosaic base of the image forms an altar with flowers on either side and two large candles flank the entire image. Finally, a small white dove, also with halo of gold, flies in from the lower left.

September 14th (continued)

Jackie made this collage to state explicitly that the problem is incest. Gazing up at the man's genitals is a child with a golden halo of innocence who Jackie describes as "detached" *suggesting the psychic dissociation that is often experienced during and after sexual abuse.* She also speaks of how deeply she has been drawn, in recent months, to pictures of buildings in ruins or to real buildings that are being torn down; she says she "*loves*" them.

I reflect on the fact that psychologically, physical ruins symbolize the destruction of internal psychic structures—the very process the flashbacks triggered in Jackie.[30] In keeping with the feeling of ruins, Jackie has been creating these collages on heavy brown packing paper that is roughly torn. That look, she says, is part of the expression of being wounded. The open window just above the child's head creates a dark hole. In this context I read the opening as an unconscious symbol for the vagina, which was also seen in conjunction with symbols of masculine sexuality and power in two earlier collages (not shown).

The flowers are pink *a color often associated with innocent girls or with the feminine deity* and Jackie says the two large candles are intentional phallic symbols. The goat represents herself as "scapegoat," because, she says, she has long felt she was sacrificed as a child *to* her father and *for* her mother, due to her mother's psychological instability. Jackie describes the dove as a "symbol of hope," *which is strikingly positive at this stage of her therapy.*

As Jackie moves deeper into art therapy, she is expressing both graphically and verbally her rage at her father, and says he always told her she was beautiful as he continued to abuse her; and that even now, it is deeply painful for her to receive compliments.

*　　　　　　*　　　　　　*

This week Jackie followed up on her insight that she was projecting negative feelings onto her brother and son. She gives an example of an experience with a family member that brought up wrenching feelings from her childhood. Because she could now recognize the real source of those emotions, she was able to make overtures to both her son and brother that were positively received. As a result of this new understanding of her behavior, she is able to respond to present family situations without a volatile overlay from her past.

---

[30] J.E. Cirlot. *A Dictionary of Symbols.* Philosophical Library: New York, 1962. 2nd ed. 1983, p. 276.
This association between buildings in ruins <u>and</u> internal psychic destruction or physical mutilation is well articulated in this reference volume.

This week Jackie created four more collages including Figs. 8, 9, and 10 (*The fourth is not shown.*) These collages are explicit visual statements of her experience and in creating them she has found the courage to put the abuse outside of herself where others can witness it. Jackie has few words to explain the combination of pictures she put together, saying simply: "They just felt right."[31]

This week she also went for food allergy testing, had several chiropractic adjustments, and made an appointment for a massage. As Jackie continues to feel good about herself she is even considering the possibility of some casual dating, and has begun to wear make-up again, but with a much lighter touch.

Several years before we met, Jackie created a ritual in which she "buried Alfred." In doing this she renounced all male control in her life and vowed to take care of herself. She says this act is what triggered the flashbacks of all the years of incest that propelled her into therapy. At that point, she went to see a therapist but then stopped after several months and dropped into depression for three years. After that time of desolation, she determined to try once again to heal her wounds. She has found that art therapy is a more compatible way for her to do the inner work and has been able to make many changes. She has courageously confronted her traumatic memories, is feeling increasingly positive about herself as a woman, has minimized the critical, internalized voice of her father, realigned with her positive internal male, Charles, and now is able to make significant and tangible changes in her everyday life.

Jackie shows me a book by the Jungian analyst, Sylvia Brinton Perera, entitled *Descent to the Goddess*. She says that long before she came upon this book, she always referred to her depression and despair as "the abyss" and was encouraged when she found this volume that uses the same term. Perera was speaking of the psychological suffering a person goes through when in the Underworld or the dark night of the soul. Jackie says two sentences moved her profoundly because they let her know she was not alone. She reads them to me now: "Yet here suffering is a primal way.... It suggests presence at its darkest level—a sense of loss of all, even the capacity for action, a loss so deep nothing matters, 'pitched past pitch of grief.'...We can only endure, barely conscious, barely surviving the pain and powerlessness, suspended out of life, stuck, until and if, some act of grace with some new wisdom arrives." Jackie tells me with deep emotion that these words perfectly express how she has felt during the past three years.

Perera elucidates the ways in which the characters in the myth of Inanna symbolize various aspects of an individual's psyche. Her discussion focuses on the process of allowing a constricted aspect of oneself to "die," that is, be transformed, in order that something more vital may be born. Jackie's new insights and the appointments she has made this week to take better care of herself represent just that kind of change and are the beginning of a new direction for her life.

*   *   *

---

[31] *"They just felt right." As an art therapist I know the elements in these collages have come from deep in Jackie's psyche, and reflect the mythic realm with its dream-like archetypal symbols. These universal images are helpful because they place her individual emotional experiences in a larger context that feels supportive to her. The artwork also enables her to express her feelings without any initial need for words. Once the collages have been made, our discussion of them brings the inner meaning more clearly into conscious awareness.*

Fig. 10 "THE BACCHUS SLAUGHTER"

Rage has run amok in the cathedral cemetery. There are dismembered arms and decapitations of both man and girl, abuser and abused. Great mythical lions, guardians at the gates of hell, look on; and smiling mother holds Child as if nothing were wrong.

Fig. 10 "THE BACCHUS SLAUGHTER" 9/13/89

This collage has three main sections. On the left and right are stone animals, each on a black base with a lavender background and vertical column of blue water above them. The central section has three parts. On top is a mother-daughter photograph, and below that is a mosaic image of Christ accompanied by several apostles and angels. Beneath them are a jumble of tombstones; an upside-down grinning head of Bacchus; two strong but dismembered male arms. At bottom lies a diagonally-placed figure of a girl who is covered in blood, having been decapitated and dismembered.

September 14ᵗʰ (continued)

As we move on, Jackie describes the third of the four collages she brought in today. This image is more complex than the others and invites a detailed exploration. I see she has again incorporated religious images into her expression of rage. *The ferocious animals on either side are Buddhist sculptures called "Foo Dogs," symbolic guards of temples and other sacred buildings.* However, referring to her childhood home, Jackie says they represent "guardians at the gates of hell." She reminds me that the lavender color represents rage at her mother; and the blue water, placed vertically above the lions, is an intentional paternal phallic symbol.

The central section rises out of a black base, split in two. *This may unconsciously relate to the fact that she was abused by both parents. The diverse aspects of this part of the collage reveal both her dream of motherly love and protection, and the harsh reality of her childhood and early adolescence.* At the pinnacle of the altar is a photograph of herself as a young girl on the lap of her smiling mother. To all appearances, a lovely Madonna and Child, again enshrined in the safety of a cathedral sanctuary. Jackie says this photograph is deceptive in that it suggests the loving and normal family life she always wished for, but never had. *All three of today's collages are replete with religious symbols. I believe these images reflect the dichotomy of her early home life in which she and her siblings were required to go to church weekly, yet her parents never went to church services.*

Supporting that image is a lighter section: a mosaic scene with Christ in the center, surrounded by angels and male disciples. *This paradigm of the good, even divine, male appears to be not only small in relation to the whole image, but also somewhat imprisoned by the series of pillars and arches around him. Yet, the fact that an image of the good male is present at all reflects the recent tentative shift in Jackie's feelings about men.*

Dominating this collage is the lower central portion, which is a complex combination of dark, demonic elements. Directly below the Christ image is a close-knit jumble of old tombstones, which Jackie also describes as phallic. In the midst of them is a man's head placed upside-down: it is a medieval rendering of a bearded Bacchus. Jackie says she chose the image because of the expression on his face. She hadn't noticed the signature grapes and grape leaves crowning his head, yet the choice of this figure is relevant. I mention to her that in mythology, Bacchus has a dual nature.[32] As god of the vine, he brings warmth and merriment to the hearts of mankind, but his shadow side fosters drunken debauchery and orgiastic sexual excesses known as the "Bacchanal." Jackie says that in this collage the disembodied Bacchus head has the latter connotation (Alfred).

---

[32] Edith Hamilton. *Mythology, Timeless Tales of Gods and Heroes.* 1940. (A Mentor Book, The New American Library; Little, Brown & Company, 14ᵗʰ printing, 1961.) *According to Hamilton, Bacchus initially had both positive and negative sides to his nature. However, in later times, the shadow side of Bacchus was transformed and he became known as Dionysus, who in many specific ways prefigures the character of Christ. Both Christ and Dionysus are present in this collage.*

Below the head of Bacchus are two muscular male arms with hands she feels are still very alive and controlling. Jackie has projected her childhood rage into this image, as she tells me how strong was her inner need, even after all these years, to symbolically sever those overpowering arms from their body in this collage—and how satisfying it was to do it. *This is another example of the power of symbolic images.*

Jackie has placed the most poignant element at the bottom. Extending toward the lower left from between the two arms is the figure of a young girl. I find it difficult to understand this image until I realize Jackie has placed the picture upside down and cut off the child's head, *replaying the theme of decapitation, first seen in the pharaonic head in Fig. 7.* Victim and perpetrator are joined by blood streaming from the child's neck, over the male arms, and around the Bacchus head.

I am still having difficulty understanding the image of the girl until I see that Jackie has cut off the child's right arm and then repositioned it lower on the body, so it now extends from her genital area. Jackie says she doesn't remember doing it, nor does she know why she connected it to that part of the body. She says simply: **"It just went there."** *It is as though that penetrating phallus is still enjoined to the wounded child within her. Also, the fact that it is the child's own arm suggests to me feelings of guilt she may have about the experience, although she hasn't yet expressed such feelings.*[33]

I am amazed by the potency of the collages Jackie has been bringing in. In creating these symbolic images, she is sublimating the intense emotions that have surfaced in her drawings, dreams, and through the energy work. I feel it is the latter, in particular, that has opened the gates to her unconscious and stimulated this out-pouring of creative work for her healing.

It may seem ironic that, just as Jackie is developing a sense of self-worth, she is producing such raging images. Actually, the myth of Inanna has given her a universal context for this experience, and seeing that others have trod this healing path before her has diminished her sense of isolation and given her the ego strength to move out of the stagnation of depression by creating these symbolic images, which are contributing to her more positive sense of self.

*   *   *

---

[33] *Jackie's mutilation of the picture of the young girl illustrates how brutally the abuse affected her, and the magnitude of self-loathing and rage it engendered. Her images repeatedly express the psychic split between her head consisting of memory, consciousness, and understanding, and her body, holding emotions and sensations. In her artwork Jackie is experiencing a degree of dissociation that is paralleling her years of amnesia about the abuse, as witnessed by her lack of awareness of how she has violently altered some images. It is frequently reported in the therapeutic literature that this dissociative condition is a common defense against the memory of incest, considered by many to be the ultimate taboo.*

Fig. 11   "THE ALL-SEEING EYE"

In her imagination Child snuggles into the arms of a loving mother, always longed for, but ever absent. As if looking into her past, she remembers the controlling and destructive acts of the father. Ambivalent red flowers speak of both passion and rage.

Fig. 11 "THE ALL-SEEING EYE" 9/17/89

The uppermost image in this collage is a Madonna and Child sculpture by Michelangelo. Immediately below them is a golden eagle clutching its prey. It is perched on the branch of a dead tree, which rises out of a black base. Central to the image is the side of a house, split into two sections by a red line; there is one large eye filling the lower half of a window. To the left is a cascade of red flowers and a bust of Lincoln.

September 21ˢᵗ

Today Jackie has brought in this collage that illustrates the patriarchal domination of her childhood home. In the upper right is a Madonna and Child. The expression on the mother's face seems sad as she looks down at the enormous eagle just below them. Her child leans in close and holds onto her hand, as if seeking appropriate refuge and security. What the child sees is a strong, fierce eagle clutching its prey - a rabbit, now dead and decapitated *by Jackie* with its blood splashed about. The eagle's open beak is dangerously close to the child's right ear, as if whispering a threat of what could happen if her secret were to be revealed.[34]

To the left is a cascade of fiery-red flowers and a bust of Lincoln. Jackie comments that the lighting has given the face of this revered and trustworthy father-figure a very "ominous expression." She says he represents her father and, rather than expressing love, the deep red flowers signify her rage at him. Jackie chose the central picture to symbolize her childhood home because the house is framed with siding, just as her family's was. She split it into two sections with red paint for blood because once again "that just felt right." The "all-seeing eye" that fills the lower half of the window (*reminiscent of the window in her first collage: Fig. 7*), is Jackie's way of showing the feeling of her father's omnipresent scrupulous observation of her every move. She says the images of the Madonna, the home, Lincoln, and the rose all represent "everything you thought you could trust, but now can't." The entire background for this collage has been painted lavender, and again the rough torn edge of the paper signifies the way she was treated at home.

*   *   *

---

[34] *Jackie tells me she was not aware of any specific symbolism of the eagle, yet it has been important in many cultures throughout time, and is relevant in her situation. Cirlot states that the eagle represents the spiritual principle in general as well as signifying "father." In addition he says "The ability to fly and fulminate, to rise so as to dominate and destroy baser forces, is doubtless the essential characteristic of all eagle-symbolism...In many emblems, symbols and allegories, the eagle is depicted carrying a victim. This is always an allusion to the sacrifice of lower beings, forces, instincts, and to the victory of the higher powers." When used as an insignia carried into war to dominate others, eagle corresponds to the negative aspect of the father principle. As to the eagle's prey, "scared rabbit" is an American colloquialism signifying fear. In this way Jackie's image of the fierce eagle clutching a decapitated rabbit in its talons perfectly expresses the theme of patriarchal domination and sacrificed victim, as she experienced it with her father.*

Fig. 12 "AT THE THRESHOLD OF THE UNDERWORLD"

An innocent young woman has arrived at the threshold of the Underworld. Bacchus is the gatekeeper; skull and bones his crest. She kneels on the blue water wherein lies her hope of cleansing and healing. However, in order to accomplish this, she must travel through the red of her rage and the enormous black of her depression.

Fig. 12 "AT THE THRESHOLD OF THE UNDERWORLD" 9/18/89

A nun, dressed in a long brown robe and white veil is praying. She kneels in water that is surrounded by an area of red, which in turn, is on a black background. Above her, hanging from a lavender arch, is a medieval brass cross with the head of a man superimposed on it. Suspended from a peg on the arch is a net containing a human skull and bones, and to the left is a long-necked bottle with an iridescent gold finish.

September 21ˢᵗ

This collage is bold and simplified, with three large painted areas. I comment that this is Jackie's fullest use of painting thus far; and also, that working so directly in that way is the most personally involved she has been in expressing her emotions.[35]

A nun has arrived at the gate to the Underworld. *I see this celibate figure as representing Jackie's original childhood innocence.* She kneels in blue water of cleansing and renewal. However, in order to effect that healing, she must move through the intense red of her rage, and the ubiquitous black of her depression. On the left is an ancient long-necked bottle with a beautiful iridescent gold finish for which Jackie has no explanation. *In this context it suggests to me a sexual symbol.*

At the central junction of the cross above her, Jackie placed the head of a man whom she feels has a "devilish grimace." Clearly, this is not the Christ figure one would expect there; rather, close inspection reveals bunches of grapes in his hair: Bacchus again, the shadow side of Christ. Jackie says she hadn't noticed that the figure is Bacchus; she simply feels "his smile is deceptive," and that "everything is not as it appears." Jackie notes that on either side of the base of the cross are the two sides of a handgun *also a phallic symbol.* Once again this Bacchus head is disembodied, a theme further emphasized in an even more macabre way by the human skull and bones hanging from a peg on the arch. They provide a chilling warning to this Innocent as she considers crossing the threshold to make her Descent.

*   *   *

---

[35] *In an earlier session Jackie had an experience in which the anguished tears she had begun to cry while drawing with red, were immediately shut down when she switched to black. This experience with the art materials clearly revealed how the black of her depression had sealed away her rage from conscious feeling. The "safe black" has come up repeatedly in our work. She says it symbolizes the isolation and secrecy that, although painful, nonetheless "protected" her from the greater pain of conscious awareness of the abuse, and possible exposure of her secret shame.*

Fig. 13   "THE LAMENT OF THE UNKNOWN KNOWER"

Inner Child, shape-shifted now as Wolf, has long held The Secret of Incest. Now She-wolf wails her grief at the moon for the emotional coldness and abusive patriarchal domination of her childhood home life.

Fig. 13 "THE LAMENT OF THE UNKNOWN KNOWER"   9/27/89

A house, with a single eye filling the lower half of a window, is shrouded in ice and snow. A solitary wolf, sitting on a patch of lavender, bays at a lavender moon.

September 28th

As we begin this session, Jackie shows me a collage she did this week. In it we see the outside of a house and, for the second time, filling the lower section of a curtained window is the all-seeing eye of her domineering father. *It seems significant to me that in both this image and in the collage described on Sept. 21st the single, penetrating eye is placed in the lower portion of the windows. Had it been in the upper section, it could have suggested a feeling of benevolent, even divine, omniscience. In this position, it feels far more ominous to me.*

The house is surrounded by snow and ice, reflecting, Jackie says, the coldness of feeling in both her parents. Her mother is further represented, she tells me, by two painted lavender areas: the moon above and the rectangle beneath the howling wolf. Jackie comments that the wolf is similar in her feelings to the observing child in her first collage (*Fig. 7.*) She says this animal represents to her the "unknown knower" *a phrase used by a Jungian therapist with whom she previously worked* "who knows what's going on in that house." She explains, saying the wolf represents the part of her deep unconscious mind that held the memory of her years of trauma, even when her conscious mind could not bear it. *I believe that what was also repressed along with the memories of abuse was the strong, good core of her spirit, the true Self. That deep level of her being has known all along, and has borne the burden of wailing its lament in years of icy silence.*[36]

I feel the wolf is a perfect symbol for the deepest sadness, for its howl is a poignant, lonely and grieving sound; and once again, there has been a decapitation. In this expression of her anger, Jackie first cut off the wolf's head, but then glued it back on. When I note the severing and repair Jackie is startled—she has no memory of having done that. *This again suggests to me that she was in a somewhat altered state of consciousness while creating this collage. And since the wolf symbolizes an essential aspect of Jackie, I feel that in replacing its head, she has reenacted in her art work the psychological reintegration she is experiencing in this therapeutic process.*

In addition to creating several powerful collages this week, Jackie had a benchmark dream in which she was making love to her daughter. In the dream *she* felt neutral about the experience, but *her daughter enjoyed it. Jackie has courageously reported the dream to me despite the fact that the incestuous implication of the image in relation to her real daughter is embarrassing and has made her anxious.*

Previously, Jackie had mentioned to me that when she sees her daughter in dreams, she generally interprets the image as representing herself as a child. Taking that as a clue, I tentatively suggest that even as an infant, the body naturally responds to touch with pleasure, and so I wonder if the dream might be

---

[36] *In her book,* Women Who Run with the Wolves *(Ballantine Books, New York, 1962), Jungian analyst Clarissa Pinkola Estes says that the archetype of wolf represents that part of the psyche that "knows." Her book was published three years after Jackie created this collage and made that same association. What Jung called the "collective unconscious" refers to a deep level of knowing that is common in humankind, and is the realm of universal images and archetypal symbols. This is another example of how, in the course of her healing process, Jackie often touched into that collective unconscious and chose images to express her personal feelings that had a similar universal symbolism of which she was unaware.*

saying that as a child she had experienced some measure of sexual gratification in her father's touch, and curiosity at first, about his advances. I assure her that in any case, it was her father's behavior that was totally inappropriate, not hers.

Acknowledging that she did experience pleasure, Jackie says she has carried a heavy burden of guilt about it for years. In fact, she tells me she has had a pervasive feeling of guilt and of being bad all her life—even before the incest memories became conscious. She also tells me that twice before when other therapists asked her if she had experienced any pleasure in her father's touch, she had denied it because it felt too shameful. However, now that this aspect of her experience has arisen symbolically and spontaneously in her own dream, and she can see it in a new light, she has been able to own it on a conscious level, thus releasing herself from that old emotional burden.

In the myth, Inanna, goddess of light and life was stripped of her royal robes (that symbolize her illusions of being only good and powerful) and descended through seven gates into the deadly Underworld. In the difficult process of owning her feelings of guilt about the incest, I feel that Jackie has just passed through another of the gates to the psyche's Underworld, which many survivors traverse on the healing descent into their wounded past.

Jackie relates a second important dream she had this week. In it, she saw herself in her house; a couple came, and Jackie was enraged at the woman. She began jumping up and down on her, trying to crush the woman's face with her foot, thinking that her excessive weight would help to destroy the woman. However, this tactic didn't work, so Jackie drove away feeling afraid they would follow her. Jackie says the day before she had this dream she was feeling that perhaps she doesn't need the extra weight she's carrying any more. *Her dream that night clearly indicated that while she thought her excessive weight could be used as a weapon, it turned out to not be an effective emotional defense.*

In light of these two dreams about her weight and feelings of guilt, Jackie is feeling pretty raw and is in great need of support. I assure her this intense and sustained inner work is important for as long as she chooses to pursue it, in order to reach her goal of a life liberated from the domination of her history. *A great deal of violence has been manifesting in Jackie's dreams, fantasies, and collages. In addition, Jackie reports that several times she has been having suicidal thoughts. We discuss her feelings until I am confident she is safe to continue. I am also aware she is seeing a psychiatrist for anti-depression medication.*

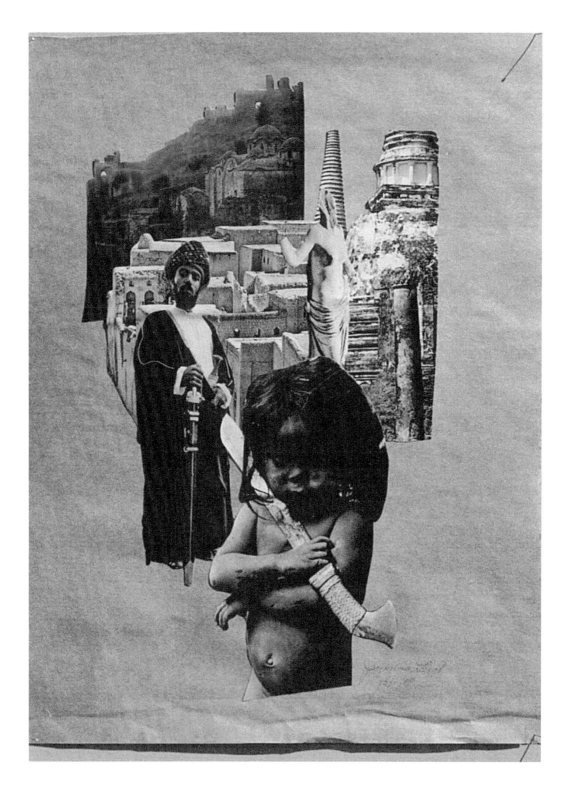

Fig. 14 "THE DECAPITATION OF THE GODDESS"

The destructive effect of the sexual violation of Child has carried over and permeated the experience of Woman. The goddess is partially disrobed and has lost her head and hands, rendering her unconscious and powerless.

Fig. 14 "THE DECAPITATION OF THE GODDESS" 10/1/89

Central to this collage is the image of a naked young girl who is holding a machete across her chest and right next to her throat. Behind her is an Eastern nobleman, a goddess statue without head or hands, and various old buildings.

October 5ᵗʰ

As Jackie and I explore this collage, I see she has created a cogent expression of both the cause and effect of her incest experience. The young girl in this image has dark skin, disheveled hair, and deeply haunting eyes that look directly into ours. Her appearance suggests to me a battered child in that her eyes are sad, her face dirty, her arm bloody, and she has no clothes on. Most startlingly, with arms crossed, she holds against her chest and right next to her neck a sharp and dangerous machete.

Against a backdrop of old crumbling buildings, stands a middle-eastern man in a white shirt, long black caftan, and red turban. Although there is no overt negative implication about this figure, it evokes in Jackie the feeling of a domineering, arrogant man. Protruding up and out from the front of his robe at waist level is the brown hilt of a large dagger, clearly suggestive of an erect phallus. His right hand grips the handle of a sword whose red-tipped sheath touches the ground. Jackie sees this man as symbolizing a controlling male in his most potent and threatening stance.

To the right of this man and just above the child, stands the statue of a goddess who has neither head nor hands, and is draped only on her lower body. Jackie says this goddess figure *felt* right in the collage, but until now she was not at all conscious of how perfectly it symbolizes both her loss of control (*hands*) and the loss of memory (*head*) because of her incest experience.[37]

Adding to the potency of this primal image is a large (*phallic*) column to the right of the goddess and another screw-like column that rises up behind the goddess at shoulder level, suggesting to me how and why she lost her head /memory. In taking a closer look at this picture, Jackie says she realizes now that if the child were to cut off her own head on the angle at which she is holding the machete, it would be the same angle that the goddess's head is broken off. *This image is a curious synchronicity reflecting that what happened to the child did, indeed, get carried over into the experience of the adult.*

This week Jackie also tells me of a dream she had that suggests she may now be having some ambivalent feelings toward her father. In the dream he was making a very beautiful and strong new door for her house. This is the positive aspect in that its beauty seems to honor her, and the door can provide both protection and an opening to the wider world outside herself. Conversely, the negative aspect was that he was also selling her dining room table, which is where she does her collaging, and so represents her creativity and healing.

---

[37] *This therapeutic process of a Descent into the depths of the unconscious generally requires those who tread this challenging path to consciously examine their psychological defenses, their ego's self-image, their beliefs, and assumptions. Additionally, it is most helpful when that person is willing, as Jackie is, to allow the wisdom of the inner dynamism to lead, rather than their conscious ego.*

In this collage having no hands symbolizes a lack of ability to have conscious control of a situation, and once again there is a decapitation—this time of the goddess who I see as a symbol of the beauty of Jackie's own feminine core. This mutilated goddess can be seen to represent that psychological stripping-down aspect of an in-depth therapeutic process that is a contemporary parallel to the ancient myth of the goddess Inanna who was stripped of all her royal raiment as she made her descent.

This partly positive dream suggests to me that there is now a chink in the armor Jackie has had around herself to protect against any further relationship with her father.

Since I will be away on vacation during the coming week, I ask Jackie if she would like the phone number of another therapist who has agreed to cover for me while I am away. Jackie declines, saying she doesn't think anything will come up that can't wait a week.

*   *   *

A letter from Jackie dated October 8, 1989

When I return from vacation, a letter from Jackie awaits me. In it she reminds me she didn't think she would need coverage by another therapist while I was away because she thought nothing troubling would come up; however, this was not the case at all. She had a powerful dream and also a flashback of her mother trying to drown her. The feeling, she says, is just like when the incest memories erupted into consciousness and once again, this intense experience makes Jackie feel she is going crazy. She writes that she also feels deeply depressed with suicidal thoughts.

A few days later she added an addendum to the letter saying she had a day when she was feeling better, but now she is withdrawing into depression again.

Jackie has used letter writing to stay in touch with me, to express what has happened and the emotions she's feeling, even though she knows I won't receive it until I return. Her growing ego-strength has enabled her to do what she can to process her emotions on her own while I am away.

*   *   *

Fig. 15   "THE END OF INNOCENCE"

Child is about to enter a "school" from which she will emerge forever changed. The lessons here will be about brute instincts, domination and control of others, and abusive, self-centered gratification. One could be devoured by such primal forces.

Fig. 15   "THE END OF INNOCENCE"   10/9/89

A young girl, striding up several steps with hands clasped behind her back, is about to enter the high, arched doorway of a windowless old building. Behind her is an elaborate sarcophagus and in the foreground is a crocodile with enormous gaping jaws. Swooping down from above is an eagle with a head clenched in its powerful beak.

October 19ᵗʰ

We begin this session by discussing what transpired for Jackie last week, triggered by her unexpectedly feeling abandoned when I went away, then having that intensely vivid flashback of her mother's violent aggression toward her, which in turn resulted in her feeling suicidal again. She is filled with emotion as she relates these experiences. Yet in spite of it all she managed to get through the crisis, and expresses relief that we can meet again today. Jackie also describes several powerful dreams of being chased by men, of herself trying to get rid of an old woman, and other dreams and violent fantasies that were expressing her rage and fears. We discuss these things at length until she feels ready to move on to the exploration of the two collages she did during that turbulent time.

We begin with this one that she entitled "The End of Innocence." Jackie describes the girl in the photograph as "a happy, joyful child who is entering school." "But," she says, "when this girl has passed through that portal, she will never be the same," *suggesting how the experience of incest destroyed everything she had ever believed in and trusted, the very thing she told me when she began her art therapy about eight months ago.*

She tells me the sarcophagus, in the left foreground, symbolizes to her the death of the child's naïveté. *A relevant synchronicity, which Jackie says she did not realize when she made this collage, is that the sarcophagus is that of Napoleon–a powerful, military dictator, which I feel is an apt analogy for her father.*

Flying down from above the "school," a bald eagle holds in its beak the severed head of her father *a photo here masked for confidentiality,* and looking up from below is an enormous crocodile which Jackie says is waiting to devour the head of her father within its great maw.³⁸ I ask Jackie what the crocodile represents to her, but she is not aware of any particular relevance, saying simply, as usual, that it just "felt right" and that is enough.

It appears to me there is a face inside the crocodile's mouth. This is actually only an illusion of light and shadow, but it does mirror Jackie's description of the crocodile waiting to devour someone. Because of its placement in the overall image, I felt the crocodile was about to devour the child as well. This great reptile also suggests to me that these feelings of rage have long been held by Jackie in the most primal, pre-verbal depths of the "reptilian" brain, an area located at the top of the brain stem in humans. This part of the brain has the function of processing and holding the memory of emotional reactions.

---

³⁸ *The ferocity of Jackie's rage about the death of her childhood innocence is unmistakably illustrated by the bald eagle and the crocodile. As noted previously, eagle is often depicted carrying a victim, representing higher forces overcoming lower ones. In this case, the eagle's victim is Jackie's father, and so, seen here in its positive aspect, eagle represents how the work of healing, in which Jackie is engaged, is overcoming her father's hurtful influence in her life.*

In addition, as Cirlot puts it, because of the crocodile's strength and ferociousness, it represents vicious, destructive power, and at the same time, because it lives in the water and mud, symbolizes female fecundity, mother, and the goddess. Although not conscious of the symbolism of these two animals, Jackie's use of them has powerfully illustrated her primal rage about the destructive influence of both her parents.

Cirlot also tells us that in ancient Egypt, the dead were pictured as transformed "into crocodiles of knowledge and that this powerful reptile is, thus, seen to symbolize the Inversion Principle." This principle states that in passing through what is dark, constricted, and deadly, we move into light, expansiveness and psychological rebirth - precisely the process of the "dark night" of the therapeutic journey.

Fig. 16   "THE CHILD TOO SOON GROWN UP"

Child's dark eyes pierce us with the depth of her sadness and with her unspoken accusation of the male for his exploitation of her vulnerability and violation of her innocence.

Fig. 16 "THE CHILD TOO SOON GROWN UP"   10/14/89

On the left, a woman in a long, elegant evening gown walks beside a nude man. In the center, a man and woman are facing each other; while on the right we see the back of a woman, the top of whose head has been cut off. Above them all is a child, looking older than her years.

October 19ᵗʰ (continued)

In addition to the previous collage, Jackie also brings this image into today's art therapy session. She describes how each individual and couple in this composite image express a different and important aspect of her experience and feelings. *The child and the women are dressed in black. This color is traditionally associated with mourning in our culture, and Jackie has frequently used it in previous collages to express her depression that repressed her grief and rage about the abuse inflicted on her.*

Jackie says the uppermost figure represents "the child too soon grown up" because she feels the girl's dress, makeup, and sad expression make her look older than her years, and suggest to Jackie that the child is being used sexually.

According to Jackie the woman on the left, with her hands covering her mouth looks startled or shocked as she walks beside a nude man.

In regard to the man and woman in the center, Jackie says that while the woman looks adoringly at the man, he looks right past her. These attitudes, she feels, are typical of both men and women, generally, and they make her angry.

Finally, on the right side we see a woman from behind–her sophisticated evening gown exposes her back through a nearly invisible sheer fabric. In addition, Jackie has cut off the upper portion of the woman's head, perhaps suggesting that her amnesia about the incest was an unconscious mechanism of survival. This woman feels very vulnerable to Jackie.

Thus, in this one simple collage Jackie has expressed five major issues for her:

1) having had to grow up too soon due to abusive, premature sexual experiences,
2) being shocked by the inappropriate nude male presence,
3) what she feels is the lack of capacity in men for genuine emotional connection,
4) women's tendency to look to men as the strong ones on whom they are overly dependent, and
5) the vulnerability of females.

         *   *   *

Fig. 17 "MY AMERICAN GOTHIC"

The eyes of the smiling bride are open: she thinks she is making a conscious choice of a relationship she wants, but her incestuous past–dangerous because it is unconscious–rears its poisonous head, overshadowing her marriage. Memory of her abuse will destroy what she thinks she remembers, and bring up that which has been forgotten. It is her own primitive terror and rage that she is married to; it is this that seeks her vow of commitment to healing.

Fig. 17 "MY AMERICAN GOTHIC"   10/22/89

Here Jackie has partnered a photograph of herself as a bride with a male figure in tribal dress. On either side of this couple are panels of black, each with a mosaic icon of a Madonna. Rising up behind them is the broad fan of a cobra prepared to strike, and superimposed on the head of the viper is a photo of Jackie's father (masked for confidentiality). In the foreground is a bottle of alcohol. (Jackie's title is a reference to the famous painting, "American Gothic" by Grant Wood, in which a very severe looking couple is seen in front of a farmhouse that has a simple pointed Gothic arch window. In that painting the husband holds a sharp pitchfork between them.)

October 26th

Today Jackie talks more about what a difficult time she had when I was away two weeks ago. She says that, while I was gone, she began to wonder if I would come back, and this reminded her of feelings she'd had as a child when she feared her dad would go away or not return from work. This anxiety was based on the fact that actually her father was the more stable of her two parents; and her mother, due to her serious chronic depression, was never available to Jackie emotionally. She tells me there was never a feeling of warmth or connection with her mother; yet the intimacy with her father, while confusing, nonetheless gave her some feeling of being loved. Jackie tells me that on the way to today's session, she wondered if she is angry at me; and also wondered if she is confusing me with her mother. *A negative transference now.*[39]

Jackie shows me two collages she did this week. The first one she entitled "My American Gothic." As we begin to examine the components of this image, Jackie immediately becomes fearful and says she feels like she can't breathe *which indicates to me just how powerfully these images affect her emotionally.* In order to release this constriction, I suggest she do some drawing with the materials I keep set up on the table. She begins drawing very aggressively to vent more of her rage at her parents, husband, and presumably, me. Once this tension has been safely vented, she is able to return to an exploration of her artwork.

This collage is singular in that it is the only expression I have seen so far of her anger about her marriage, and about how the experience of incest affected it. Jackie has used a photograph of herself as a bride, looking youthful, beautiful, and naively optimistic, and has contrasted that image with a man in his tribal ceremonial attire.

The clothing of the figure beside her suggests station or royalty. The meaning of his costume is unknown outside the context of his culture, but Jackie uses this figure as an embodiment of primitive power. Holding a long, phallic drum with its red, pincer-like end as a symbol of authority, she says he simply represents to her what she considers the male nature to be, that is, "primitive" with an unevolved, disparaging connotation. He is related, in Jackie's feelings, to the male she described as "arrogant" in Fig. 14.

---

[39] *The word "transference" in therapy refers to those times when the client projects feelings or beliefs they have about someone else in their life, onto the therapist. Typically, this is an important person in their experience and when these feelings arise in the therapeutic setting, it provides an opportunity to examine those emotions and beliefs consciously. I have mentioned how Jackie has several times expressed her caring for me, and that I felt she was seeing me as "the good mother" she never had. Her comment today indicates she is conscious of confusing me with her mother, and also with her father in a negative way, when she felt abandoned while I was away.*

The black panels on either side with their sacred icons once again suggest the themes of "altar" and "sacrifice" and convey two feelings to me. First, the sense that mourning is the appropriate feeling for this marriage and second, the depression Jackie experienced throughout those years, especially due to the loss of her sense of an internal spiritual center to guide her life.

The bottle, she says, signifies the alcoholism of her husband, with which she had to contend for many years. Jackie comments that the cobra represents the way in which her father's presence overshadowed her marriage. She now knows with certainty that the years of incest had a profoundly negative effect on her marriage on a deep unconscious level, long before she ever regained conscious memory of what had happened. For instance, Jackie has previously spoken of a vivid memory she had of her father forcing her to perform oral sex on him when she was young, and how her unconscious rage about that had triggered violent fantasies toward her husband when he wanted sexual intercourse and she did not. She felt intense pressure at those times, and once even fantasized killing her husband with a knife. *(Fig. 5: "Red is for Rage.")*

From a Jungian perspective, this collage could also be read like a dream in which each element is understood to be a part of the dreamer's psyche. The man would represent the negative side of her internal masculine aspect (the animus), and as Jackie described him—a "primitive" part of herself. The cobra with a picture of her father's head would symbolize the unconscious Secret of paternal incest that overshadowed her marriage. And finally her spiritual dimension represented here by the sacred icons, was suppressed by the bottle, and also by her addictive eating.[40]

In my experience I have seen that in dreams a light-skinned person will often see a dark-skinned person as a symbolic reference to something they feel is dangerous. In this context, the focus is not on racial implications, rather it is a symbol for that which is "dark" or dangerous <u>*in the dreamer.*</u>

This image can also be seen from an alternative, Freudian, point of view.[41]

Sigmund Freud defined the personality as having three aspects: the "id," "ego," and "superego." I believe this collage can also be seen from his personality theory. In this way the bride may be seen to represent Jackie's conscious, civilized "ego," while the tribal man who is married to this domesticated innocent could symbolize the dark, hidden "id" of her earthy power, aggression, and sexuality. Finally, the over-shadowing dominance of the cobra with her father's face illustrates the unconscious controlling parental influence of the past that she has introjected, which is referred to as the "superego."

It is precisely because this image and all of Jackie's collages have been made spontaneously without any such conscious conceptualizations, that they serve to illustrate so well those psychological constructs.

---

[40] Jung, C.G. *Aion, Collected Works*, Vol. 9.ii, para. 1-42. *This collage is rich and complex and presents us with a fascinating image of the various aspects of a person's personality (as distinct from the deeper soul level). From a Jungian perspective there is the union of the masculine and feminine elements of a person, what Jung termed the "coniunctionis," i.e., the marriage of opposites.*

What Jung termed the "animus" is the unconscious masculine aspect in women (and conversely, the "anima" is the unconscious feminine aspect in men). Many people mistakenly think the Shadow is only the hidden, repressed, often guilt-ridden aspects of the personality that are denied and repressed into the unconscious. More accurately, Jung conceived of Shadow as being made up of all that is in an individual's unconscious, and thus may also include positive qualities such as a sense of humor or creativity, which simply have not yet been developed consciously.

[41] Freud, S. "The Ego and the Id," in *The Standard Edition of The Complete Psychological Works of Sigmund Freud,* Vol.19 (1893-1899), *Early Psycho-Analytic Publications*, James Strachey (trans. & ed.), W.W. Norton and Company, New York, New York, 1961

Fig. 18 "THE WOUNDED CHILD: BEYOND WORDS, BEYOND COMPREHENSION"

Fig. 18 "THE WOUNDED CHILD: BEYOND WORDS, BEYOND COMPREHENSION"   10/25/89

Backed by four black panels, a naked young girl squats and looks directly into our eyes. Below her left knee she holds a broken red poppy. A long sword is lancing her heart from behind, and red paint signifies blood flowing freely from the wound.

October 26th (continued)

Here we see a young girl who is dirty and unkempt and has no clothes on. Most shockingly, her heart has been pierced by a sword from behind. She looks sad and is bleeding profusely. Jackie says the flower's stem looks to her like a severed umbilical cord.

The association Jackie has just made suggests to me that in this collage she may be saying that the birth process not only separated her from her mother physically, but also severed any potential emotional connection they might have had. And because the number of items seen in art therapy drawings frequently has an unconscious significance to the artist/client, I wonder about the four black panels: possibly having to do with the age the incest began, but I have no way of knowing this for sure. Jackie said she was very young, perhaps even less than four.

As I look at this second collage Jackie brought in today, I am startled by the devastating power and simplicity with which she has expressed the pain of the wounded child within her. I am reminded of the term "deflowered" meaning to sexually violate and deprive a female of her virginity. I see the broken flower as a symbol of Jackie's incest experience, and the resulting remnants of what was once the pure love in this child's heart. Finally, it occurs to me that when a physical wound becomes infected and festers, it must be lanced to release the toxins that have built up within. Piercing this child's heart symbolizes to me both her pain and the fact that psychological wounds also need to be "lanced" in order to heal.

When I ask what the child might be saying. Jackie gets very choked up and says in a whispered voice, "Why did you hurt me? Why did you hurt me?" expressing so poignantly the incredulity of an emotionally abused and sexually exploited child.

Earlier in the session Jackie did some artwork to vent her anger and fear. However, still feeling a great deal of intense emotions, she asks to do some energy work once again. In the same way as when we did the Vibrational Healing in previous sessions, we start by Jackie lying down on the couch cushions as I sit beside her. I use my voice to do toning that focuses vibrations into her body in order to help her release tension and disturbing emotions.

Shortly after we begin, Jackie says she feels as if she is falling into a black hole and dying; she tells me she wants to die "so it'll all be over."

I think back to a collage done eleven days ago which Jackie entitled "A Child Too Soon Grown Up" (Fig. 16) in which she included a picture of a woman whose back was exposed, and commented that the woman was "vulnerable." Now comes this powerful image of the naked child whose heart has been lanced from behind, and Jackie is expressing how desperately she wants the pain she feels to be over.

Having witnessed the ego-strength Jackie has exhibited in doing this level of therapy, and trusting as I do her deep wish to heal, I tell her I believe those feelings and images of dying that keep coming up recently do not portend suicide. Rather, since death is the ultimate change we know of, I see these thoughts as symbols from the depths of her psyche that indicate her need and longing to move through an "inner death;" that is, to release some painful aspect of her past so it will no longer have power over her. I tell her this process involves entering fully into one's painful memories and the associated feelings of rage, shame, guilt, and so on, and has the effect of defusing the psychic charge of the old wounds.

Over the years, I have found in my experience of healing my own wounds, as well as in my work with clients, that re-experiencing one's pain on the emotional level where it was first imprinted, is the most effective way to break through an entrenched depression. However, in order to avoid a simple re-wounding as a result of re-experiencing the trauma, a deeper level of healing work is needed to effect a genuine transformation and psychological rebirth. In my experience this involves finding one's own spiritual center, as Jung spoke of.

Again, I assure Jackie that in doing the energy healing work she is in no physical danger, and she can move through this psychological "death" with me as support and guide. Because Jackie has experienced the Vibrational Healing as powerful and helpful several times before and has come to trust me in this work, she immediately begins to cry and allows herself to fully feel her emotional pain and experiences a sense of dying on an internal level in her imagination. This experience lasts approximately 15 minutes and when the inner process has naturally come to an end, she says she then feels "safe" once again. Jackie has just moved through a profound and crucial step in the healing process, and I acknowledge her courage.

See Appendix #3 on Depression and Suicidal Ideation

*   *   *

Fig. 19   "PARTNERS IN CRIME"

The hands of those who have abused and exploited the innocent, vulnerable Child are bloody, and all can see it is they who have committed the crimes. Now, their former victim claims her power and has given them their just punishment: symbolically putting them behind bars.

Fig. 19 "PARTNERS IN CRIME"   11/1/89

Central to this collage is a photograph of Jackie's parents (masked for confidentiality), taken at her wedding banquet many years before. Their picture is framed in hot florescent orange with painted stripes of lavender forming the bars that now imprison them. Their hands are painted red.

Early November phone conversation:

Throughout the past week, Jackie has been in profound distress and it is clear she is approaching a critical point in this cathartic process. She phoned me several times this week, which she has rarely done before. Tonight Jackie contacts me again and the emotional turmoil she is experiencing is obvious in her voice. She describes a collage she has just completed (*Fig. 19*) and tells me that in creating the image, she began feeling tremendous emotional pain and agitation, and knew she had to call me once again for help.

In recent months Jackie has been experiencing violent and suicidal feelings and fantasies that are also being played out in her drawings and collages. My sense of the situation is that she may have arrived at the very threshold of the core of her pain, because her suicidal feelings indicate to me that she would rather die than try to move through it.

Jackie tells me she entitled this work "Partners in Crime." In it she symbolically put her parents behind bars, and has painted their hands red to symbolize they are dripping with the blood of their innocent child (bride) victim.

The psychological significance of what happened is that in creating this image of punishing her parents, Jackie has reached the point of reclaiming her personal power. This is a first, and taking such an action has terrified her. There is an unconscious irony in this image. Even as her parents sit at the banquet table smiling, there is before them a basket filled with loaves of bread and behind it a goblet of wine (nearly hidden by one bar). I feel she has created one final altar of sacrifice.

As we talk on the phone, I share with Jackie an awareness I gained in the course of my own healing work, which is that although making images of my anger and confusion had been truly cathartic and aided my healing process, at a certain point I found that drawing pictures of the pain I was experiencing so intensely during the days, had begun to hold my consciousness and feelings in that place of trauma.

On the other hand, at night I was frequently having dreams that were explaining the purpose of going through the "dark night of the soul." So when I began drawing pictures of my healing dreams instead of drawing my pain and rage, my attention was necessarily on the positive images directly in front of me and so the art process quickly moved me into a healthier state of mind. Even more than doing the drawings of my anguish, this positive focus helped me in a more effective, long-term way by changing my perspective and feelings. In doing those drawings I took a step forward and rose above the level of my crisis. I experienced the truth of some wisdom passed on to me by a therapist many years ago as I was doing my own healing work and that is from Einstein: "You cannot solve a problem from the same consciousness that created it. You must learn to see the world anew."

I also tell Jackie that as I alternated for a time between drawing my rage, pain, and confusion *and* drawing the healing images from deep within me, the undeniable lesson was that whatever I put my attention on is what would grow in my feelings—either positive or negative.

In our phone conversation, I remind Jackie of how powerfully she has expressed a full spectrum of difficult emotions in her artwork and suggest that, if it feels right to her, she might try making a collage now of how she would *like* to feel. As we end this conversation, she agrees to try what I have proposed; and because she is in such a critical state, I insist she call me anytime, if she begins to feel overwhelmed again.

Fig. 20 *"IN MEMORIAM"*

Now that the perpetrators have been "punished," Child is lovingly commemorated with pink flowers. Her childhood dreams of growing up into a creative, mature woman have begun to be revived, although there is still a defensive moat around her feelings.

Fig. 20 *"IN MEMORIAM"* 11/1/89

The innocent child is here commemorated by a small picture of her in the center that is banked by pink poppies. A seductive woman stands to the left of the child, and a regal woman to the right; above them is a castle surrounded by its moat. There are two panels painted in a free and colorful manner.

November 2nd

Jackie arrives for our session in a much more positive mood and tells me that, after our phone conversation, she decided to follow my suggestion. Having just made the "Partners in Crime" image, she then created this collage in which she shows three aspects of the feminine that are important to her.

In the center is a picture of herself when she was young, banked by large pink poppies with black centers, "*in memoriam* for the child," she says, to honor the fact that she had survived such a traumatic early life. *I feel the choice of these poppies is perfect as I recall the wounded child in Fig. 18 who was holding a nearly destroyed poppy that scarcely had any petals left. Now there are three flowers (a number suggesting both creativity and the sacred). In addition, they are in full bloom and they are pink - the color frequently associated with the feminine. Synchronistically, I see their black centers as corresponding to Jackie's core wound.*

Jackie describes the various elements she has put into this collage in the following ways. To the left of the child is "the seductress," indicating her wish to reclaim a healthy sexuality (although she says she has some discomfort in seeing herself as seductive at this time). To the right of the child is "the regal queen" dressed in a full-length red gown and cape, an image with which she now asserts her dignity, strength, and self-esteem. The two women are backed by loosely painted areas of red, pink, and blue that Jackie says indicate a readiness to return to a more light-hearted artistic expression.

Above them all is a castle and, although it is still surrounded by its defensive moat, it is nonetheless intact and not crumbling into ruins as the previous ones had been. Jackie says this strong castle symbolizes the possibility of reestablishing the positive dreams of her life. This represents a truly significant change in her intention and feelings. She also says the process of creating this more hopeful image just after the "Partners in Crime" collage, immediately had the effect I had hoped for—shifting her out of that desperately victimized and despairing state of mind. This positive effect of working with images cannot be overestimated.

Jackie tells me that recently, whenever she has been watching violent movies or reading the newspaper, she wonders why she is doing that - why she is putting so much of her time and attention on the great pain in the world. She's aware that doing that repeatedly draws up her anger, as well as her memories and projections based on her own experience of abuse. At this point, because of what Jackie has just said about how the artwork at home immediately helped her shift from deep fear to this positive, forward-looking image, I ask her to examine her therapy process in the same way. That is, is it still serving a useful purpose for her to keep creating images of the early trauma, the memory of which will always be with her in any case? Or is it possible to begin shifting emphasis away from expressing her rage and pain, and toward creating a positive self-image of what she *wants* to become in her life, as she has just begun to do with this collage? I tell her she can always process painful dreams or memories whenever they may surface spontaneously, but perhaps she no longer needs to deliberately elicit them. Jackie seems to respond well to this idea.

It's possible that these last two collages, "Partners in Crime" and "In Memoriam," both done on the same night, may form a benchmark, a turning point in Jackie's healing journey. After all the work she has done to express her pain, in choosing now to make a positive statement about herself and focusing on how she wants to shape her future, she has made an essential shift, set a new direction for our work, and thereby may be embarking on her Return to the Upperworld of Life. However, a healing journey is never a straight progression from anger and pain to health and happiness, and so I anticipate there are likely to be continued ups and downs.

*   *   *

POSTCARD OF 11/3/89:

In thinking about the intense depression she experienced in that recent turning-point crisis, Jackie writes me a brief note in which she says, "A thought: Maybe I got sucked down into the negative again—or part of the reason, anyway—is because I'm more comfortable with it—maybe it's safer in some way. You know, like the seductress image in the collage & my discomfort with it—and the castle."

*   *   *

November 9ᵗʰ

Jackie is very much in touch with her emotions now and so, fortunately, she is able to express her feelings of anger at me from time to time, which makes this a safe place to have an authentic exchange.

In this session, after experiencing the cathartic turning point in her crisis last week, Jackie tells me that when I have spoken of integrating the dark, shadow side of ones feelings and moving toward the light, *meaning to begin feeling better about one's self again,* she feels "irate." For although I have told her I do honor each person's timing, she feels I am reprimanding her for not being farther along the path of healing than she is.

Jackie is still struggling with letting go of her rage, which does not happen in one moment, but rather over a period of time. I recognize this, but also know that, at some point, letting go of "old baggage" is necessary if she is ever to feel lighter and happier within herself.

I tell Jackie that, of course, it is essential for her to take as much time as she needs to do her healing work. But as her therapist, it is always my intention to keep in mind that we are moving toward her empowerment. I have no interest in keeping her in the place of the victimized child, nor in making her dependent upon me.

The metaphor that occurs to me is that of a lighthouse keeper. I speak to Jackie about my deep conviction that it is the central function of the therapist to be, on the psychological level, the "keeper of the light at land's end." That is, as one's client launches out into the deepest waters of the psyche's unconscious and encounters dark and turbulent seas—at times fog-bound with all sense of direction obscured—and confronts all the monsters there-below, that the therapist's presence and words will be a beacon of hope. And the hope is: effective change and transformation are indeed possible in this process of owning and balancing and integrating the dark and light dimensions of ourselves. Without this beacon of light, one could surely get lost on the "night sea journey."

*   *   *

I have been away this week for a professional conference, so Jackie wrote me a letter dated 11/13/89: In the letter she tells me she has had a confrontation with her father over a financial situation and how, after sending him a letter, she reverted to a state of total panic and began to dissociate from her body. Jackie quickly reversed that old pattern, called a friend and was able to calm "the kid" in herself and then, with her newly developing self-confidence, she contacted her lawyer and began to seriously consider taking legal action against her father. Jackie says she was then enjoying the feeling of being empowered and not afraid of her father anymore.

*   *   *

Fig. 21 "LEAVING THE PAST BEHIND"

The time has come to move on. Having fully expressed her rage, it can now recede into the background as Woman surveys the road she has traveled and what she is leaving behind. Now she is reunited with a healthy inner-child and is moving into her future with vitality, joy, and genuine self-esteem.

Fig. 21 "LEAVING THE PAST BEHIND" 11/23/89

The primary image in this collage is that of a woman with her head thrown back in laughter. Beneath her is another radiantly happy woman holding up a smiling young child. In the upper right is a picture of the side of a mobile home and the road it has traveled. Around and above the child's head is a panel of vibrant red.

November 23rd

As we begin, Jackie tells me that the past two weeks since our last session have been difficult for her. First of all, in seeing a movie about a good mother-daughter relationship, she says she again plunged into a deep well of grief, realizing ever more acutely how much she has always missed having a loving and protective mom.

In addition, since our last session, her mother had a stroke. In sharing with me her feelings about it, she had to examine the possibility that her mother might die. As she thought about what that might be like, she says she would want her mother to ask for her in the hospital. I am deeply touched when she also tells me she can't imagine saying anything to her mother except: "Why didn't you love me?" Jackie says that for a while this past week, she again felt consumed with anger at her parents. Yet, the roller-coaster nature of her emotions at this time is witnessed by the fact that not only is she feeling a lot of anger and fear in regard to them, but her growing self-esteem has given rise to this joyful and optimistic collage.

In the face of such graphic evidence, I have no doubt that Jackie is genuinely beginning to feel good about herself, as it would have been virtually impossible for her to create such an image, even a short time ago, when she was experiencing only deep depression and a wish for vengeance on her abusers.

In this collage a very happy woman holds up a nude male toddler - her cheek is pressed against his lower abdomen and genitals. The boy's arm with fisted hand is held up in a position of power. Jackie has made no comment about the significance of this picture, but I
can think of several possible meanings: 1) the woman is mature now and the external dominating male is reduced to a child who is no longer a threat, 2) woman's inner male aspect (the animus) has a newly developing strength, suggested by the boy's gesture, or 3) woman is at peace with her inner child.

Jackie has used the color red in previous collages to express her wounding and the resulting anger. Here there is a wide band of red that now adjoins both the child and one woman. This image suggests to me that having fully acknowledged her childhood rage, Jackie is now able to accept the reality of anger as a normal emotion, certainly appropriate in a situation such as abuse, but she is no longer dominated by it. Jackie has expressed her childhood rage—both non-verbally in her art work, and vocally in the energy work, in our conversations, and in her recent interactions with her father.

Finally, both women have open, expressive smiles, and mother and child make direct eye contact with us. This body language tells me there is a new openness in Jackie, and an exuberant release of joy previously buried beneath her depression. Now, as her self-esteem continues to increase, Jackie tells me she had a dream this week in which she took a love letter out of the freezer. I feel this is a monumental dream heralding a significant change in Jackie. She says she has now begun to consider the possibility of an intimate relationship with a man in the future. *The picture of the woman holding the boy suggests to me these early inclinations to be with a man once again.*

* * *

November 30ᵗʰ

There is a crucial moment in today's session: Jackie tells me she feels she has, at last, dealt with all her incest issues as much as she needs to. She says, although the memories of her painful experience will always be part of her, she can now put them aside and get on with her life.

Jackie mentioned to me some time ago that she has long dreamed of selling her home and moving to England for a time. Now she is able to envision that goal as more imminent: in April. She is beginning to see a light at the end of this long, dark, therapeutic tunnel. Jackie speaks of the picture she put in the upper right of the last collage and says again that the view out the window of a mobile home and of the road it has traveled symbolize what she is now ready to leave behind.

Suddenly Jackie realizes how hard it's going to be to leave her children and friends. I tell her she also needs to consider seriously how much time she wants to give to processing the conclusion of our therapeutic relationship, because after nearly a year of deep, intensive work many feelings will come up about our separation. Jackie says she hadn't thought of that at all, and it makes her feel worse just to consider it.

*Jackie's comment reveals her affection for me and how meaningful this work has been for her. The feeling is mutual, and I am determined that our separation will have good closure. I do not want the ending of our work to add, any more than necessary, to the overall difficulty for her of this major transition she is approaching.*⁴²
Feeling a deep need for closeness and support, Jackie asks for a hug before leaving. It is a poignant moment for both of us.

*   *   *

December 7ᵗʰ

As a first step toward concluding our work together, Jackie brought into this session all of the collages she has done in order that we might see the path she has trod, as it has been revealed in these powerful composite images. In addition to her early drawings, there are now twenty collages; the first was done last July. What a prolific outpouring of creative and healing work this has been.

Considering the sadness Jackie expressed last week about the possibility of our work coming to an end, I am amazed she has spontaneously brought in all her collages for us to look at together. Having such a visual record of the twists and turns of the healing journey is a very helpful part of the termination process, and is unique to art therapy or any modality that incorporates visual images.

---

⁴² *Termination is an essential aspect of the therapeutic process. I have observed over the years in several settings that this crucial element is not always given sufficient time and attention for a variety of reasons. Especially when the work has been as deep and intense as Jackie's, there are complex issues and feelings that are engendered in the client by the process of separation. In addition, when a therapist does this level of work with a heart that is open to the other's pain, and with an awareness that the learning in this experience is always mutual, then both client and therapist need time to process their feelings, although in different ways and at different times. For example, therapists may need to examine their feelings in supervision or their own therapy.*

We spend the entire session reviewing this body of work and it is obvious there has been a significant change in the content of the last several collages *(not all shown here)*. It is eminently clear that Jackie has, indeed, moved through a fundamental turning point. Her artwork has shifted away from expressing her old pain and rage regarding the abuse and now is revealing beautiful and positive images of the new dimensions that are developing within her. Jackie hasn't done any more collages in the last several weeks, which suggests to me that her psyche is already beginning to slow down this process in preparation for bringing it to a close.

*   *   *

Fig. 22   "ENCOUNTERING THE GODDESS"

Beneath the emerging feminine crescent moon, a graceful goddess in flowing robes reveals herself as the reflection of Woman's own inner beauty. Having regained her head signifies a return of memory and consciousness, but the goddess still lacks the full empowerment that two hands provide.

Fig. 22 "ENCOUNTERING THE GODDESS" 12/13/89

Beneath a crescent moon an attractive woman in sophisticated attire faces the goddess in her flowing robes. Here the goddess has a head, but still only one arm and no hands. The two women are connected by a band of deep indigo blue.

December 14ᵗʰ

Jackie begins today's session by explaining that in order to express the change in her feelings since the "turning point" when she symbolically put her parents behind bars, she has been going to the grocery store to pick up current women's magazines in order to find pictures of active, contemporary, forward-looking women who feel good about themselves. She says these kinds of images express her new, more positive feelings of self-worth in a way the earlier pictures of religious, primitive, and classical themes could not. Those were more suited to expressing her rage, shame, and guilt.

In this simple and elegant image Jackie meets the "goddess," which, from the point of view of Jungian art therapy, is actually a reflection or symbol of her own inner beauty. With an expression that is at once open and direct, this woman faces right *(often seen in art therapy as signifying the future)* and gazes slightly upward at the goddess who stands below a newly emerging *(feminine)* crescent moon.

I note that the black Jackie has always used to symbolize her depression, is now changing. The woman is dressed chicly in black, and the black panel holds both a crescent moon and a beautiful goddess.

I feel it is significant that Jackie has joined the woman and the goddess at the genital level. Again, she says she was not conscious of how relevant that is in her situation. This image stands in sharp contrast to Jackie's dream many months ago in which she was jumping up and down on a woman's head, using all her weight in an effort to destroy her (in the text with Fig. 13). I saw that dream as representing an unconscious effort in Jackie to destroy all memory of her deeply wounded feminine nature or as an expression of her rage against her mother.

In contrast to previous collages, the goddess has now regained her head, signifying the return of Jackie's memory, and therefore no longer any unconscious denial of her dark experience. The fact that the goddess is not yet fully embodied suggests to me that this new state of affairs is still a work in progress. For example, an arm may represent the fact that Jackie is feeling more personal strength in her life, yet the fact that there is only one arm suggests it's likely there is more work to be done.

Reiterating what she said last month, Jackie speaks of her openness to the possibility of once again having an intimate relationship. *I recognize what a major shift this represents!* However, she says she is struggling with the notions of commitment versus freedom, and so even *the idea* of marriage is inconceivable to her at this point.

We talk briefly about her going to England in a few months. Once again I see Jackie's ambivalence, because having spontaneously brought in all her collages to review in a recent session, she now emphatically states that she does *not* want to talk about the termination of our work and of our therapeutic relationship. I tell her that, for at least the last month, we should taper off to every other week, so the ending will not be so abrupt. Jackie says she does not want to taper off at all, and certainly not sooner than the last month.

*   *   *

Fig. 23   "THE INNER CHILD TRANSFORMED"

Child is free at last. No longer intimidated, dominated, nor exploited by the phallus, she now meets the vipers eye to eye with confidence.

Fig. 23 "THE INNER CHILD TRANSFORMED"   12/20/89

In this image, a healthy and happy young girl smiles as she gazes, eye to eye, at four cobras. Wide bands of black are on either side of her, and there is a narrow one of red. She wears a red and white polka-dot shirt, with red and black ribbons braided into her hair.

December 21ˢᵗ

Once again Jackie has created an eloquently simple visual statement of her feelings. Just one week after her encounter with the goddess, she has brought in this image of the "inner child," now transformed, renewed, and fearless.

In discussing this collage, Jackie and I can see that the large black panels, which in the past signified her depression, have parted to reveal a smiling child and four snakes.[43] On the far left, a narrow band of red "peeks out," she says, from behind the black indicating she has not forgotten her rage, but it is no longer dominant. Now, neither the rage nor the depression constrain her as they did for so many years.

The young girl smiles as she looks directly at four cobras—the same snakes that had previously represented the poisonous influence of Jackie's father on her marriage (Fig. 17). Not only are the snakes no longer a threat, she seems to have even made friends with them. An important universal symbolism of snake is that because it sheds its skin and continues to live, it represents rebirth or transformation.

I feel this collage illustrates powerfully Jackie's newly acquired ability to confront the men in her life, represented by the snakes, knowing herself to be their equal. For example, in recent interactions with her father, she did not yield to his demands and self-serving manipulations regarding a financial matter. She says she was able to use her anger in that situation to speak up for herself and she felt justifiably proud about being able to do that. With the resolution of that issue, Jackie again says she feels she has completed the healing she needed to do regarding the incest.

I tell Jackie her action in that situation is an important use of the energy of anger. She did not attack her father; nor did she collapse into a victim stance and turn her anger against herself. Rather, she recognized the emotion and used its energy to assert herself in a way that protected her integrity. Another major growth step.

---

[43] *Throughout recorded history in the mythologies of the world, snakes have been imbued with a wide variety of meanings. Not only have they been seen to symbolize the goddess and both male and female sexuality, they are also commonly viewed as a representation of spiritual transformation because they shed their skins (the past) and keep on living. The ancient Romans considered snakes to represent wisdom, as used in the Caduceus, the medical symbol of healing; and there are numerous other meanings, as well.*

There is a similar multiplicity of meanings associated with the number "four." Jung has shown us that in many cultures this number is seen to represent wholeness or completion, for example, four seasons, four directions, or the four sides of a square. In addition, in the ancient study of numbers known as "Numerology" one aspect of the number four that is relevant to Jackie is that it represents being boxed in. Both the snakes and the fact that there are four of them in this image suggest to me that we are nearing completion of the healing of her deep incest wound. Both meanings of "four" (being boxed in and completion) and the sexual and transformative symbolisms of snake, are implied in this collage.

I feel it is important to note, once again, that Jackie has been creating these collages from a place deep within, which she always says "just feels right." She is not deliberately contriving to make a picture that illustrates a conscious idea; but as we discuss these composite images, it becomes clear to me how perfectly and specifically her spontaneous collages are expressing her inner process.

Both Jackie's rage and the depression that she experienced as The Abyss (Fig. 4) have now been integrated into her consciousness. I see this as symbolized by the red and black ribbons that are intertwined in the child's hair. I am fascinated to see how the color and patterning of the snake skin, and their placement, seem perfectly woven into her braids. In addition, there is red around her neck as there was in the "The Bacchus Slaughter," (Fig. 10) but it is not the red blood of the decapitated child, rather it is a vibrant and playful red and white polka-dot shirt.

This image of the joyful, healed child stands in dramatic contrast to the Wounded Child in Fig. 18. And although the healing work may be an on-going life process for any of us, it is clear that Jackie has come a long way on her inner journey of transformation. I know that in the case of a wound as primal as sexual abuse, healing typically happens in stages and cycles, so it will remain to be seen if this issue comes up again. Her father's denial of any incestuous behavior suggests to me either a total unwillingness to take responsibility for his actions; or that he, too, out of shame, may have repressed the memory of those years in amnesia, just as Jackie did. In all likelihood, she will never know which it is. Perhaps it is both.

Jackie brings in an important dream in this regard. In it she is committing minor incestuous acts with her two children, but then stops herself, realizing that even a little such behavior (in the dream) had violated their trust.[44]

Jackie and I talk about how there is the potential in all of us to experience the entire spectrum of human behavior. At times we may be to some degree: victim, healer, or victimizer. I tell her it is my belief that in order to heal, we need to honestly own the times we have hurt others and, in feeling genuine remorse for those acts, ask forgiveness or do anything we can to heal the wound we have inflicted. On the other hand, when we are the injured party, we may need to go through the crucible of healing and transforming our own wounds if we are to genuinely live in contact with our true Self, or spiritual essence. The process may then become a transpersonal experience, for when we are able to do that work there arises within us a deep feeling of compassion for everyone else in other cultures and times who have had traumatic experiences.

Further, I tell Jackie that in my years of experience as a therapist, it has become clear to me that when someone hurts another person, the abusive one may be able to physically overpower the other, but that action does not come from inner strength of character; rather, it comes from a wounded place in the abuser that has never been healed. Predatory behavior arises out of feelings of insecurity and inadequacy: a feeling, basically, of being unloved. These feelings in the perpetrator give rise to a need to take control and dominate or humiliate others in a misguided attempt to feel strong and competent. When those who have been victimized have done enough of their own healing work, they begin to recognize the wounded child in that abusing adult, and perceive that person's deep feelings of inadequacy, rather than continuing to view them as all-powerful.

It is in this honest place, deep within the healed heart, that true compassion is engendered.

Jackie has now been experiencing art therapy for ten months. She has graphically and viscerally expressed her rage about the incest; has allowed the equally painful memories of her psychologically sick and abusive mother to surface; has

---

[44] *Incest, or even a "lesser" degree of sexual molestation, can have a devastating effect on the ability of the abused child to trust others. If the early wound is not healed, that effect will last a lifetime and may seriously impair the abused person's capacity for genuine relationship (as was seen to happen in Jackie's marriage).*

struggled with the meaning of "forgiveness" and the possibility of that being a part of her healing. She then symbolically put her parents behind bars which initiated the diminution of her self-loathing and an increasing sense of empowerment. In owning her feelings of guilt about the incestuous relationship, her negative attitude toward men gradually became one of greater openness toward them. And as she was increasingly feeling more positive about herself as a woman, there arose even the possibility of a relationship in the future. In addition, recent images (some not shown) showed her leaving the past behind, having a joyful reunion with the child within, encountering the goddess within herself and feeling "at peace." Finally, yesterday we saw the happy child confidently confronting the four snakes of transformation.

In the <u>Dictionary of Symbols</u>, Cirlot speaks of the philosophical/spiritual side of medieval Alchemy in this way: "Alchemical evolution is epitomized, then, in the formula Solve et Coagula (that is to say: 'analyze all the elements in yourself, dissolve all that is inferior in you, even though you may break in doing so; then, with the strength acquired from the preceding operation, congeal')." I believe this is fundamentally the same experience as the process of in-depth psychotherapy, such as Jackie is experiencing here.

This has been an extraordinarily transformative passage to have witnessed.

*   *   *

Fig. 24   "RETURN TO THE UPPERWORLD"

While there is memory of the pain and shame of her Descent into the dark and terrifying depths of the Underworld, now Woman also experiences a resurgence of joy and is moving actively toward the future.

Fig. 24 "RETURN TO THE UPPERWORLD"   12/27/89

The central figure of this collage is a woman sitting on a small stool with her back to the viewer. To her right is a deeply wooded area with a low stone entrance to an underground chamber, which is backed by two wide panels of red. On top a woman is wrapped in a wind-blown sheet; this picture also has a red panel on the left. The final picture, lower left, is an overlay of two views of a woman.

December 28th

As Jackie prepares for her journey to Europe, she has brought in this collage that suggests something about where she's been and also where she's going.

The woman on the stool is nude from the waist up and her head is bent so low it cannot be seen, suggesting Jackie's former feelings of vulnerability and shame. A low stone post-and-lintel entrance to an ancient underground burial chamber deep in the woods represents with simple, earthy eloquence, the portal to the dark Underworld of psyche from which Jackie has now re-emerged.

Uppermost in the collage is a beautiful woman who looks radiantly happy, wrapped in a wind-swept sheet with her long hair flowing out behind her. Jackie says she especially loves this picture which illustrates so wonderfully the lovely rebirth of feminine energies in her. *Considering that the primary issue has been incest, I find it interesting that this ecstatically happy woman is wrapped lightly in a bed sheet.*

The final picture is an overlay of two views of a woman. In the smaller insert, she is running energetically towards the right (future) wearing a red shirt; in the larger view we see only a profile of her head facing left (past). It is always interesting to note the changes in Jackie's use of red.

Today as we review this collage Jackie says she feels "all that old stuff is done now."

A structural process that began at the critical time of the turning point with Fig. 20 "In Memoriam" has continued. That is, instead of the pictures all being carefully cut out and interwoven, Jackie has been retaining the simple rectangular form of most of the pictures, just as they come from the magazines.

*   *   *   *

IT IS 1990

January 4th

Jackie talks about many troubling dreams she has been having. Generally, the themes are of being in the house where she lived while she was married; of not trusting her own judgment; of needing to get home to care for a baby so it won't feel abandoned; and of sexual fears regarding her father. She describes intensely fearful emotions surfacing as she prepares for her imminent move to England.

At the same time, Jackie tells me she is also experiencing some very positive feelings and brings in several more collages that have optimistic images: active, positive, and/or seductive women, as well as images of her dream to go to England. I tell her something I have noticed repeatedly in my years of working as an art therapist. That is, often those with whom I worked would create an image spontaneously that was much more positive than they were feeling on a conscious level at that time. This surprised them because it was not done deliberately as a mask or defense against feeling painful emotions. What I observed is that this apparently premature lightness is actually a herald of increasingly positive feelings that began to be manifested in them soon after.

Jackie tells me yesterday she said to the universe: "Let me be open to that again," referring to a relationship with a man. She had a dream of a very large snake biting her. In the dream she was afraid the snake-bite would kill her, but it didn't even hurt.

The snake bite is a powerful sexual symbol. It is significant that actually in the dream she was in no danger.

*   *   *

January 11th

In discussing her trip to England, Jackie tells me she is planning to take all her collages with her. This outpouring of artwork, which has become a symbolic record of the intense passage she is making, is such a precious part of her that she does not want to be separated from it as yet. I suggest she might consider taking photographs of them instead and leave the originals safe at home. Jackie decides this is a prudent idea and plans to ask her brother to photograph them for her.

Once again, not wanting the end of our work together to suddenly come upon us unprepared, I remind Jackie that, based on the date she has chosen to leave for England, we have about three and a half months left to complete any work she needs to do: this includes our work here, as well as all her other separations. As I suspected, she did not want to discuss the end of our working relationship, but now as she recognizes the reality of the situation, she reluctantly agrees.

I am particularly aware of the importance of attending to this termination process because, when our work is done, Jackie will not only be going through the usual emotions associated with ending a long and intense therapeutic relationship. She will also be leaving behind her children, all her friends, her work, and will be selling the home she has lived in for many years. This promises to be a major experience of letting-go: a stepping off the edge of her familiar life into a great new and unknown phase.

We will prepare for this as best we can.

*   *   *

Fig. 25   "LEAVING HOME"

As the end of this cycle of healing draws near, the process of separation has begun. It is fully acknowledged by Woman, although she feels a great deal of ambivalence about it.

Fig. 25 "LEAVING HOME"   1/18/90

This collage is done on two separate pieces of brown paper. On the left panel is a black silhouette of a figure running toward the left; on the right one are three figures facing the first one. They are connected across the chasm by white bands.

January 18ᵗʰ

This week at work, Jackie was asked to train to do a different job. She says the hardest part was that she had to move out of the safe and familiar boundaries of her "cubicle." In her new space there are no walls around her desk, and that leaves her feeling vulnerable on a deep emotional level. Jackie says that despite her discomfort, she recognizes that somehow this change is a kind of gift from the universe to help her begin to let go of all that feels safe and familiar prior to her move. *I am gratified she has this insight.*

I see that in the context of leaving home, and even departing for a new continent, the structure of this collage graphically conveys its meaning. This image is unique in several ways: first, it is done on two separate pieces of the roughly torn brown paper she always works on, and in addition, it is the only one in which Jackie has cut out silhouettes from construction paper, rather than finding figures in a magazine. Although the single figure is facing left/past, Jackie says the figure is running "to" the future, not away from anything nor back to the past. *Over the years I have observed that spontaneous images convey a condition that is not always recognized by the client who did the artwork. In this case, given the anxiety Jackie is already experiencing in regard to this great transition, it seems likely this image of the figure running to the left belies her denial of any fear.*

The white laces, Jackie says, connect her to her loved ones "heart to heart." We both note that the shape and position of the arms on the silhouette cut-outs of those she is leaving behind appear strangely phallic *(only one with that shape can be seen in this photo)*. She had noticed that when she cut them out, but made a conscious decision not to change them. *Because Jackie did not feel a need to somehow destroy the phallic symbols, it suggests to me that what she is mainly leaving behind is the way in which the early sexual abuse has ruled her life.*

*   *   *

January 25ᵗʰ

Jackie tells me she has decided not to ask her brother to photograph the collages. As yet, her feelings about this body of work are so fresh and raw, she feels self-conscious about having him see them. I tell her I refrained from mentioning this last week because I did not want to interfere in her plans with her brother; however, since she has changed her mind about asking him, I now feel free to offer to photograph her artwork, as I have often done with my own. My offer evokes Jackie's tears.

She says three or four times this week she felt strongly what a gift I have been in her life, escorting her through this intensely difficult healing journey, and how much she'll miss me when we part.⁴⁵

---

⁴⁵ *My approach to this work is not that of the classically neutral, totally non-self-disclosing stance of some schools of therapy. For example, in classical Freudian analysis there is not even eye contact between analyst and analysand during a session. There are, of course, specific reasons for this, designed to bring up the client's issues in the transference. And while I am aware that transference is always a part of the process and needs to be carefully attended to, a completely non-disclosing formality is simply not a compatible way for me to work.*

In this moment I choose to express my own feelings of caring for Jackie, trusting that a genuine, heartfelt response is appropriate. I let her know I will miss her, too, and will always be interested in knowing how she is doing, if she ever wishes to contact me. However, I also tell her that as her therapist, it will not be appropriate for me to contact her because it would likely have the effect of fostering continued dependence on me, which would undermine the very independence and freedom of spirit she has been working so hard to attain.

*   *   *

February 1ˢᵗ

In an image, titled "A Survivor Resting" (not shown) a kneeling woman, partially draped, is leaning against some boulders. Her expression and appearance suggest someone who is exhausted and possibly grieving. The figure is at the intersection of two wide black bars that form a truncated cross.

With simplicity and power, we are shown the emotional exhaustion of the survivor who has finally come to a resting place. Having returned from the Underworld, there is a period of transition in which both the old pain and a new appreciation of herself are being experienced.

At this point in her therapy, Jackie again states she is experiencing considerable ambivalence in her feelings. She describes alternately being aware of the deep pain she has moved through for so long, and then her new feelings of self-esteem and enthusiasm for life.

A dream Jackie had this week helps her realize that the process of protecting herself from any further vulnerability has given her a hard edge in some respects. In the dream three women: a teenager, a 30ish married woman, and an older single woman, are all telling her that "her angry and aggressive feminist attitude and way of speaking have been keeping her from having a relationship with a man." *Since this recognition arose from Jackie's own deep wisdom, it is far more acceptable to her than if someone had tried to point it out.*

Jackie tells me that since October she has been eating more carefully and exercising and is beginning to feel a weight loss, and that this is the first time she hasn't immediately reversed it. *I am not surprised when I remember that it was October when she experienced the critical "turning point."*

In another aspect of her life, Jackie is having an unexpected problem. She says recently she is aware that because she is leaving, three of her friends have been withdrawing from her "as if I were dead." She

---

In my experience, the very process of art therapy lends itself to more informal interactions in a creative setting in which the client may be moving around, choosing various media to work with, asking for help with a process, and cleaning up. In addition, my approach has always been influenced strongly by the ground-breaking insights of C.G. Jung, who believed it is essential for a person to reconnect with their own deep spiritual center in order to heal and to use any of the arts in that quest. In my opinion, that level of work is not done in an interpersonal vacuum. I have also been influenced by Carl Rogers' "Client-Centered" approach, by the interactive processes of Gestalt Therapy, as well as by subtle Energy Healing work. And so it is my firm belief that at times it is of great benefit to the wounded person, who is in a process of healing their heart and spirit, to receive a genuine expression of caring from the one who serves as escort and guide on their inner journey.

At the same time, when the work has been completed, with proper attention taken to the process of termination, the appropriate professional stance in most cases is for the therapist to not initiate further contact with the client, which could have a regressive effect.

realizes that in the face of this, she too, has shut down emotionally and hasn't expressed her hurt or anger to those friends about their reaction. I suggest her friends may be shutting down because they also do not want to feel their pain at her leaving.

This is an enormously important passage for Jackie: it is her experience of the classic archetype of the death of an old pattern of life and the subsequent rebirth into something new but as yet, unknown. I encourage her to move through it as consciously as she is able—like natural childbirth. The recent move from her safe cubicle at work helped her see the value of trying out new experiences before her move to England so she would not be overly disoriented. I believe there is a parallel on a psychological level: this experience of leaving her children and friends is giving her an opportunity to examine other aspects of her life that could come up as a result of the separation. This may include issues such as: 1) examining the importance of various relationships, 2) the way in which past experiences have affected her beliefs and feelings, 3) the occasional necessity of letting go of what is held dear, or 4) the finality of some endings.

Fig. 26   "BACCHUS TRANSFORMED"

Woman-as-Victim has become Woman, the Survivor. Even as she remembers her old pain and her cry for help, she is now able to anticipate a future life in which her feelings toward men are truly transformed.

Fig. 26 "BACCHUS TRANSFORMED"   2/7/90

In the lower-center picture, a woman looks askance at a courthouse building as she holds a newspaper with the word "help" visible from the want ads. Above her is an aerial photograph in which the shadow of a jet plane, like an arrow, is pointing the way to, and just touching, a large English castle. To the left, a beautiful woman is about to kiss a classic statue of a god; and to the right, the woman is cheek to cheek with a man who is alive.

February 8ᵗʰ

In this latest collage, Jackie offers two associations to the courthouse: 1) the divorce from her husband, and 2) the legal action she is considering taking against her father. They are the two primary male figures in her life and with both of them she has felt vulnerable, deeply wounded, and in need of help. Now that word "HELP" in the newspaper brings up all those old feelings and she begins to weep.

When the emotion of that association has ebbed, we move on to consideration of the other elements in this collage. Above the courthouse is a picture of an English castle, which is beautiful and intact and no longer has a defensive moat around it. That is to say, the crumbling castles which she earlier said represented the ruined dreams of her childhood, have now taken on new life with verdant growth all around, even as the image also anticipates her upcoming departure for England. The shadow of the plane on the ground just touches the castle, hinting she is about to reach that dream. It also creates the suggestion of a phallic projection, which is now tentatively, but increasingly positive in her feelings.

On the left, a beautiful woman is about to kiss a classic statue of a god; she is alive, but he is cold stone. Close inspection reveals bunches of grapes in his hair: it is Bacchus returned, this time not at all malevolent, but more like an Adonis. In the picture on the right, it appears that the woman's kiss has had the effect of bringing the god to life in a configuration that is similar to the balance of opposites in the yin/yang symbol. I comment that it is rather like a reversal of the classic Sleeping Beauty tale; in this case, the woman's kiss has brought the man to life.[46]

Another measure of the reality of the inner changes taking place in Jackie throughout this year is that it is now increasingly noticeable that she is actively working to lose weight.

As we talk, Jackie again cries at the thought of separating from me because, she says, that to come to the art therapy sessions "feels like home," that is, the caring, nurturing home she never had. Just as before, when she expresses her caring for me, I respond in kind. I encourage Jackie to allow herself to experience this grieving, and to know that her ability to feel this bonded to me is a measure of the good work she has done in opening her heart again. Our mutually-caring therapeutic relationship has opened for her the possibility of developing other loving, trusting relationships.

---

[46] *What a graphic illustration this is of the change in Jackie's feelings when compared to the first collage in which the severed head of the pharaonic god-king was about to be exhumed from his long entombment—Fig. 7. In this series of collages, I have noted three images of Bacchus. The first and second represented his dark aspect of debauchery or, specifically for Jackie, incest, and in this third one he is seen as transformed into the positive animus. It is worth noting that while all this has been perfectly relevant to the changes going on in Jackie, she was only aware of the first one, Fig.10, being Bacchus. The second was Fig.12.*

As the therapeutic process moves forward, I notice that Jackie's collages keep getting larger, spontaneously reflecting the growing expansiveness in her feelings. This one is several times larger than the earlier ones done before The Turning. On the other hand, although aesthetics is not a primary concern in art therapy, from that standpoint I feel, but do not mention it, that in using simple block images, this collage is arguably the least interesting composition of all she has done so far.

*   *   *

February 15th

Jackie arrives for this session despite freezing rain "because Louise is here, and I don't want to miss time with Louise." There are now thirty collages and she has brought them all for me to photograph. In giving me her artwork, Jackie says she feels like crying because parting with them is difficult. As an art therapist, I know they are a very personal extension of herself and I assure her that I will treat them accordingly.

Today Jackie closed on the sale of her house and she needs to move out in less than two weeks. Thoughts of her brother and sister have come often this week as she anticipates this move and other up-coming changes in her life. Jackie decides to draw in this session. In her drawing, the feeling of "leaving home" turned out to be leaving her parents' home where she grew up. It was done all in red; she wonders aloud why this is so before concluding that it's anger. As she begins this drawing Jackie finally really breaks down and sobs—deeply feeling the pain of "leaving home" on many levels. I rest my hands gently on her shoulders to support and encourage this emotional release. *The color red suggests to me she is also leaving behind more of the anger associated with her childhood home.*

*   *   *

February 22nd

Today Jackie and I talk about how hard it is sometimes to let go of pain and allow joy to fill that space in our lives. She says that although it is her choice, going to England feels like dying; she doesn't yet know who she will be when she's there.
I feel that what is dying is her image of herself as a wounded and angry victim.

A difficult issue comes up in regard to Jackie's sister. Several years ago when Jackie told her about the abrupt and unexpected flashbacks, her sister didn't believe any of it had happened. This hurt Jackie deeply and caused an estrangement between them. Now she has received a Valentine card from her sister acknowledging past differences and wanting to make up. Jackie is angry and maintains she can never forgive her. She says her sister is like a board: hard and unbending. I suggest her comment could be a projection of her own rigidity in rejecting her sister's request for forgiveness, healing, and reconciliation. Jackie winces at that.

Two works of mixed media incorporating a few pieces of paper with very free brush strokes of black ink are also brought into this session *(not shown)*. They are distinctly different from any others Jackie has done, in that they are totally abstract in black and white, and the line-drawing aspect of them is so loose as to feel scattered to me. This dynamic, but disjointed quality is not surprising, given the fact that Jackie moved out of her house this week. These two pieces unequivocally suggest the upheaval she is experiencing.

I give Jackie the first few photos I have taken of her artwork. She is moved to tears and pats them to her heart saying "They're mine." *It is clear that this extraordinary body of work has been a birthing process, bringing forth an entirely new sense of herself that in recent years Jackie thought would never be possible, and which she now values deeply.*

        *   *   *

"CLOUD NINE"   2/28/90 (not shown)

A healthy, attractive, and independent woman sits alone on a bed of soft, puffy clouds. Her expression is one of great joy. She holds one hand on the back of her neck.

March 1ˢᵗ

Once again, Jackie reiterates that throughout the three-year hiatus between the flashbacks of incest and the resumption of the therapeutic process, she was so filled with rage, shame, guilt, and grief, she thought she would never again feel good about herself. Clearly, the change in her attitude is well-illustrated by this very simple collage. It is the largest one she has done.

This image of being up in the clouds also has a contrary meaning for Jackie. She says that all week, since her move, she has felt very "spaced out." It's an uncomfortable and unfamiliar sense of being in a "time warp," as if it's been a long time since she's seen me or seen a friend of hers. Actually, it has only been about a week.

In her descent into the dark Underworld of repressed pain, Jackie has confronted her Shadow and submitted to the death of her former self-image and is now reintegrating the parts of herself that had been split off and lost to her. For example, she now has the ability to genuinely feel all her emotions: joy and self-esteem as well as pain and anger. Because of this Jackie is no longer trapped in The Abyss of repressed emotions that caused her depression; she can speak up for herself and protect her own personal boundaries. The goddess has indeed regained her head. Her ascent to the Upperworld of daily life, with the possibility of a full range of emotions and relationships, is now well underway.

It is worth noting that since the crisis I call "The Turning," Jackie has not experienced any further suicidal thoughts. It's also been interesting for me to see that before that critical point in the process, Jackie's images were mostly dark and angry, with only a few positive ones. Since that time, they have been mostly light and forward-looking, with just a few reflecting her darker emotions. Even as we see our time of working together nearing its conclusion, Jackie's inner processing continues to be full and rich including potent dreams, important issues and experiences.

The ongoing legal issue with her father, which came up in early February, is painful but has helped her to complete some unfinished emotional business. Specifically, in a recent financial transaction, her father asked something of her she did not want to do, but she had acquiesced. She says that afterward, she regretted having done it and felt her father had "f....d" her again. Jackie says due to that experience, she now recognizes more clearly than ever before that she had complied with her father's sexual demands when she was young, and she still feels profoundly guilty about it. I suggest this present legal interaction with her father may be providing her with an opportunity to heal that emotion.

What is important is that the experience brought up the guilt about her childhood relationship with him. As an adult, it would be helpful for her to recognize that when she was young her father destroyed any trust she might have had in him. In addition, as a child—helpless, dependent, and lacking any awareness of its aberration—she could not refuse his demands. Now if she could consciously choose to stop blaming herself for the incestuous relationship, she would finally be released from the guilt. Jackie agrees and says this perspective makes her feel better about the recent encounter with her father because now she can find meaning in it.

In my experience I have seen that whenever clients feel guilty for having done something they feel is wrong, they need to forgive themselves. This letting go of an old burden is internally healing.

Jackie says the deepest feelings of rage she has about her father are getting through to her consciousness more fully now. She has always been aware of her anger at her mother, but with her father there was always some kind of "buffer" that mitigated her anger somewhat, despite all the rage she has expressed verbally and in her artwork. Now her anger at him for abusing her as a child and robbing her of her innocence is clear and fully present to her.

- *In a great step forward Jackie says she understands why she is now able to fully feel her rage at her father. She tells me the reason is that she has owned her own feelings of guilt regarding her participation in the incest. Her father bears responsibility for having repeatedly used his innocent daughter for the satisfaction of his own lust; but she says she then began to feel pleasure in his touch and so complied with his demands. In experiencing her enormous feelings of guilt about that pleasure, and feeling that she, too, was in the wrong, she then realized she could not lay all the blame on her father, nor could she allow herself to feel the enormity of her rage. Now, in consciously owning the pleasure she experienced, Jackie is able to move beyond projecting all her guilt onto her father. By acknowledging the feelings of which she was so ashamed, that emotional "buffer" is gone and Jackie can now fully feel her outrage at her father for initiating and perpetuating the abusive relationship.*

I am profoundly moved by the integrity of this insight Jackie has come to on her own. I believe it is the single most crucial step in her healing to date, and it has taken an enormous amount of courage to acknowledge those feelings so completely.

Jackie says she has been thinking of something I said some time ago: that it is conceivable her father may also have dissociated from any awareness of incestuous behavior in order to maintain some sense of self-worth. She says she can now consider that as a possibility.

I remember that several months ago Jackie first expressed feeling personal guilt about the incest (Sept. 28ᵗʰ - Fig 13). It came up when she described a dream in which she was making love to her daughter. As often happens in the spiraling process of therapy, this issue has come around again, and as I hear her words, I am aware that the healing of that emotion has now gone to a deeper level. I believe whether or not her father had repressed all memory of any incestuous actions, her ability to view his denial from this perspective represents a measure of objectivity and greater conscious insight that can only come from an increasingly healed heart.

Over the years, I have seen that the experience of children who have been sexually abused varies widely. As noted previously, sexual touch in incest is sometimes the only approximation of love and acceptance a child in an abusive home ever experiences. Often abuse survivors have expressed to me feeling guilt about pleasurable sensations, just as Jackie did; but many others experience only terror, pain, and shame. Jackie's profound sense of guilt about the incest is certainly also a crucial factor that contributed to her repression of this experience in amnesia.

After talking about the dissolving of the buffer between herself and her rage, Jackie says she is aware she has been eating a lot more this week since that encounter with her father. She tells me she recognizes this is what she has been doing for many years—eating to cover and pacify her feelings of rage and guilt. Jackie's daughter, who is living with her at this time, had dinner one night this week with Jackie's parents. Jackie's father sent her daughter home with some leftovers and said he would also send them some sharp knives *an odd and unexplained offer*. Jackie does not take this as a good-hearted gesture; rather, her response is one of fury because both the food and knives are things she associates painfully with the incest.

After discussing these issues, Jackie decides she'd like to do some energy work. As she drops into a deeper awareness of her body, she can feel she is holding a lot of tension in her stomach and in the back of her neck *where the woman in this collage is holding her hand*. Jackie says that the back of her neck feels connected to her incest experiences of oral sex and the feeling of being told to "hold still."

It is a powerful session.

*   *   *

March 8th

As usual, Jackie brings up many important feelings and issues in this session. In one collage, there is a house on a mountain. She emphatically states "the mountain is safe, but the house is not." We both see that for her the mountain symbolizes strong and stable feminine energy. Jackie says she *is* the mountain and that she can take her safety with her; it is within her now in her strong sense of self-worth. Prior to her trip to England, Jackie has settled into her new home and says she is surprised at how relieved she feels to be out of her old house.

We discuss several important dreams she had this week. In the first, Jackie is making "penis stew" by putting a penis in a pot to simmer on the back burner until tender. Jackie says that just talking about this dream makes her feel itchy, but only on her right (masculine) side. *I see this as one of those wonderful visual puns that sometimes come in dreams. The implication I see is that her old issue with male sexuality can now be "put on the back burner." She can give priority to other issues in her life while her relationship with the masculine gets more "tender."*

In a second dream, a black man steals Jackie's purse. He did not take her wallet, but still she is incensed by this violation. She chases and catches him, knocks him down, puts her foot on his throat, and retrieves her purse. He then changed into a white policeman.
As noted earlier, "black" and "white" in a dream do not necessarily refer to racial characteristics, but rather are more likely to be symbols for what is either dark and unknown or what is light and positive, within the dreamer. For example, the Black man in this dream may represent either Jackie's own dark side of guilt, or her father (who was Caucasian). In fact, Jackie remembers that as a child she wondered if her father might be Black because of how dark he would get in the sun and yet the palms of his hands remained light. In a similar way, gender can be transposed in a dream. In this case, the White policeman does not necessarily refer to a male, but may be seen to represent Jackie's own sense of strength and authority now—the positive animus.

Jackie often refers to her large purse as "my life" because she has such a file of important papers and other valuables in it. In this dream, the Black man/father robbed her of her purse/life (signifying the "incesting" of the body). But he did not get her wallet with her identification and her money (representing what is most valuable to her, that is, her soul-Self.) Most important, as she is able to express her outrage and take action, it enables her to reclaim her life, and in that process, her image of men is transformed from one who violates personal boundaries to one who represents safety and good authority. This dream is reminiscent of her earlier experience of Active Imagination in which Alfred spontaneously yielded to Charles. That shift is being seen more and more now in collages and dreams indicating it has happened on a very deep level of her psyche.

Jackie tells me her most recent collage did not turn out at all as she had first intended; yet in describing it in words, she can see it expresses another, deeper level of feeling. She says her collages "speak to her," *an experience common to artists, particularly if the work arises spontaneously from a deep emotional level, rather than being self-consciously pre-planned.*

Jackie also says that her sense of being in a time-warp continues, though she really does feel much better in her new house. She still hasn't responded to her sister, and recently in a dream she understood that the reason for her lack of trust in her sister is that she really doesn't believe anything her sister says. This remains a sore point for her. *Jackie's attunement to her dreams is such an active aspect of this therapy, frequently bringing her clear insights about the deeper levels of her emotions. Because she pays attention to the dreams and is willing to examine them with me, even when she is embarrassed by their content, they have been tremendously helpful in this work.*

March 15th

Today Jackie tells me that on five separate occasions in the past several weeks she has forgotten to sign her name to something important. This is a clear indication of the stress that is mounting in her. At the same time, Jackie notes that now she is more accepting of all her feelings, including the feminist ones. She says this week she felt "happy as a pig in sh...."

An image comes to me of a balloon, and I comment that if you squeeze one side of it that would represent the negative feelings, it will get smaller, and then the other side—the positive emotions—will necessarily expand. Jackie says "yes!" and that, in fact, she had just bought a balloon this week. *A lovely synchronicity.*

In a second dream, Jackie is standing in a swimming pool, only ankle deep in water, and she is singing at the top of her lungs. She feels this dream image indicates she has overcome the negative feelings surrounding her memory of her mother trying to drown her. Again, Jackie says she is feeling happier about herself than ever before in her life and that she's really enjoying this feeling.

I have been reconsidering what I have been saying to Jackie recently about the need to taper off our work as it nears an end. She really doesn't want to do that, and I realize again what an unusual circumstance this is. She will be experiencing so many different separations at the same time, and is already feeling much anxiety about them. I have decided it is important to empower her as much as possible, and so I tell Jackie to consider the pros and cons for a week, and then *she* should make the decision about how much tapering off she honestly feels would best serve her needs at this time. Jackie seems to appreciate this.

*   *   *

Fig. 27   "THE POIGNANCY OF SEPARATION"

Woman prepares for a sojourn in the English countryside. Along with enthusiasm for this adventure in the near future, she experiences anxiety about the unknown, and especially, grief at leaving home and loved ones behind.

Fig. 27 "THE POIGNANCY OF SEPARATION" 3/20/90

Central to this collage is a picture of a woman whose expression is wistful, far away, and deeply sad. She is bordered by images of woods with blue spruce.

March 22nd

This is one of four collages Jackie has brought in today that express various emotions about her upcoming move to Europe. The emphasis here is on her sadness regarding so many central aspects of her life that she is about to leave behind.

A related collage (not shown) features a picture of this same woman. In that one, she is surrounded by images of the English seaside, a cozy country cottage, and flowers. There is also a picture of a man holding a bouquet of roses. Although the English scenes represent what Jackie wants at this time, the woman's wistful expression reveals to me better than words how Jackie is feeling about the many separations she is about to make. She tells me the man with the flowers represents Charles and the possibility of having an intimate relationship once again. These pictures are bordered by either red or turquoise and Jackie says that red, for her, has now taken on its positive connotation of the vitality of life. It seems appropriate to me, that the way in which she has put red brackets at the top and bottom of the man and the cottage images, suggests magnets and what she is now open to drawing to herself.

Previously Jackie had learned the color turquoise is considered in many cultures to symbolize healing. She says she chose to put it around two of the English scenes because her journey there represents the healing and growth she has achieved. I add that I learned some years ago that in some Native American traditions there is what is known as the Turquoise Woman. Her function is different from that of the Medicine Man; she is a nurturing person who will listen compassionately when someone has a problem, and acts as a counselor.

In the third collage of the day, a woman is holding a cat (often seen to symbolize the feminine). She is wearing white slacks and a long elegant black coat that has blown open revealing a beautiful red satin lining. Again I think of the colors symbolizing essential transformation in Alchemy and suggest a possible interpretation of the image. That is, the black of her depression that previously enveloped her, has now opened wide to reveal vitality and passion inside, and the white pants may be seen to signify her pure center or true Self. After a full year of such intense work to heal her depression and rage, my reading of this image brings tears to Jackie's eyes.

*   *   *

Fig. 28   "ONE LAST GLANCE BEFORE MOVING ON"

Woman is free to go now, and she gives one last glance back at her past, even as she embarks on the path to her future. She is ready to launch into her new life and she says that this is the year of letting go.

Fig. 28 "ONE LAST GLANCE BEFORE MOVING ON" 3/20/90

In this image a woman is walking away from the viewer and is looking toward the left. Above her is a rainbow-colored kite, and below it is the year "1990" in black and red. The bottom picture shows a hand holding a model plane facing right.

March 22nd *(continued)*

March 22nd (continued)

In another collage Jackie brought in today, she describes the woman as giving one last look at the past as she strides down the path toward her future. She is now determined to make this break from her painful history even though she is experiencing much anxiety, grief, and trepidation about separating from her loved ones.

It seems appropriate to me that the bold numbers of the date are black and red. These are the crucial colors with which she began this journey (Fig. 4 "The Abyss" and Fig. 5 "Red is for Rage"), and this date of 1990 marks the time when she is able to chart a new path. Her collage tells me she will not forget the past, but will no longer allow it to rule her life.

Above her, as a symbol of freedom, is a beautiful, multi-colored kite. *Once again, I think of the tiny spots of primary colors that were barely visible in her first drawing (Fig. 4 "The Abyss") and can see they have now spread wings and soared into a clear, blue sky.* **In describing the airplane, Jackie says "it's ready to be launched, and this is the year of letting go."**

In talking about this transition she is making into the unknown—both the new, emerging aspects of herself and the unfamiliar place to which she is going—Jackie again begins to cry, which, as always, is a deep release for her tension and anxiety. As we part, I tell her I am witness to the enormity of this passage for her, and I give her a supportive hug. I also express my feeling that, because we are all connected by the subtle energies of spirit, in doing this healing work Jackie may be helping others let go of their painful histories, too, in ways she may never know.

Jackie again brings up the difficult situation with her sister. It is obvious from her expression and demeanor that their estranged relationship is very painful for her. I tell her that I hope they may come to some good resolution, possibly before she leaves for England. I also suggest, if it feels right to her, that she might respond to the valentine card she received last month in which her sister expressed hope of a reconciliation between them. Jackie says she'll consider it.

After thinking about my offer last week to let her decide whether or not to taper off our sessions in the last month, Jackie has decided she wants my support weekly until the end, and I agree to that.

*   *   *

Fig. 29   "...and the cheese stands alone"

As the work of healing draws to a close and separation is imminent, Woman experiences new feelings toward her escort on the journey. Angry and defiant, but also strong and independent, Woman stands alone. She embodies both the feminine and masculine aspects of her being.

Fig. 29   "...and the cheese stands alone"   3/28/90

With a strong stance and a defiant expression this androgynous figure stands with hands clasped behind her/his back, on legs that taper to sharp points instead of feet.

March 29ᵗʰ

Two days ago I received a scorchingly angry letter from Jackie, dated March 25th. In it she says for the past two days she has been feeling "suicidal, depressed, angry, like never seeing or speaking to anyone ever again, like never going to therapy again...and writing to my sister was not worth it!!!" Also, she's angry at me "because I feel like you want these tidy little, nice little endings and that isn't how things are." She continues: "the scab got scraped off the wound" by which she means that writing to her sister, who doesn't believe Jackie's incest memories, has caused her to question all her experience and, once again, makes her feel she is crazy.

When Jackie first talked to her about the flashbacks that arose so abruptly several years ago, her sister's refusal to believe that it happened resulted in their estrangement. During the week, Jackie followed up on my suggestion that she respond to her sister's request for reconciliation; but from Jackie's point of view, reconciliation required that her sister believe her memories. When that didn't happen she felt victimized once again and enraged about it.

I see this intense combination of rage and suicidal feelings, together with doing this artwork and the letter she wrote to me as all being parts of a transitional stage in her therapy process that has both positive and negative aspects. Because this intensely painful experience came up between her therapy sessions, and she could not express her outrage at me directly, her initial regressive reaction was to turn her anger against herself and feel suicidal. The unspoken question within her was "Will claiming my anger, and expressing it directly to the person who triggered it, be acceptable?" This is the voice of her inner child, fearful that if she speaks up for herself, dire consequences will result. On the positive side, even though she was alone at home, Jackie's decision to use art and writing to express her anger at me was a healthy choice in order to vent her painful emotions until we could meet directly. I believe her ability to once again make that shift from passive inaction to an active use of creative work within three days represents significant growth in her.

In addition to her letter, Jackie has clearly expressed her anger at me in the solitary, independent figure she created in this collage, which she entitled "...and the cheese stands alone." *The collage implies two things to me. First, since the title comes from a nursery rhyme, "The Farmer in the Dell," it suggests a protection for her inner child who fears she may be abandoned by me. Second, when everything else has been taken away, as an adult she feels strong in her anger, and she will still be able to stand on her own and take care of herself.*

The legs for this figure are cut out of a photograph of blue spruce trees. Jackie says the evergreens felt feminine to her when she was making the collage and she is surprised to learn they are considered to have that symbolism.

The expression, being able to "stand on your own two feet" conveys the idea of inner strength, independence, and stability. Jackie tells me that the pointed legs represent her considerable anger at me, and that she feels quite stable on those points. *This indicates that on a conscious level she is getting stronger in being able to express feelings that previously left her feeling vulnerable, but the image of having no feet suggests to me there is still an inner ambivalence that belies her outer expression of confidence.*

In working to vent her anger at home during the past week, Jackie did many drawings and has brought them into today's session. She shows me pages of jagged scribbles including a dagger once again, expressing her anger at me. She says she feels I am "expecting too much good feeling" from her. I apologize for forgetting to honor her timing, as I always try to do. My response brings up tears in Jackie. She expresses gratitude to me for validating her feelings. Jackie indicates an immediate lifting of the dark cloud of suicidal feelings. *How patently clear it is to me in this moment that suicidal feelings are often anger at another that remains unexpressed and is then turned in upon oneself–and also how quickly those emotions can change when one's feelings are witnessed and honored.*

As Jackie's level of trust has increased and she feels safe enough to express her anger at me even as our separation nears, it seems significant that the figure in this collage should appear to be androgynous. In symbolic Jungian terms, the androgyny (embodying both male female qualities) represents the true, whole Self. I ask if this person has a name and Jackie spontaneously and emphatically replies "Judith!" She says she hadn't thought of naming this figure before, but in this moment that is simply what occurs to her, and she has no particular association with the name.[47]

Last November, when Jackie first spoke of selling her house and moving to England for a time, her original plan was to leave in early April. It is now late March and she has changed the departure date twice for various reasons. Noting these repeated delays, I feel a transference dependency on me may be unconsciously compounding her difficulty in making this major break. I decide it is necessary to address this issue directly.

In order to provide Jackie with a clear structure in this time of transition-chaos, I tell her we must *decide together on a firm date* for ending our work. I know there is always more inner growth work that can be done by anyone in therapy. However, Jackie has already stated unambiguously that her work on the incest issue is complete as far as she knows; she has sold her house, and has made her plans to go to England,

---

[47] *The New English Bible, with the Apocrypha,* Oxford Study Edition, (Oxford University Press, New York, 1972). *Subsequent to the last session, Jackie and I each independently did some research to see if the name "Judith," which she spontaneously gave to this androgynous figure, would have any particular significance for her. In consulting a numerologist friend, Jackie was told that the name corresponds to the number "9" symbolizing with perfect relevance the completion of a cycle, preparation for a new beginning, and the balance of both the feminine and masculine aspects of the self.*

For my part, I was aware there is a "Book of Judith" in the Old Testament. In the early centuries of the Christian era, this and other texts were excluded from the Bible and set aside in a book known as the Apocrypha. Having no specific knowledge of this ancient figure, I decided to look her up in order to see if this reference might have any bearing on Jackie's inner journey. Having seen countless relevancies in this body of work of which Jackie was unaware, I have begun to assume this may be so about anything that arises spontaneously, as this name did.

What I learned is that Judith was an exceptionally beautiful and devout Hebrew woman who singlehandedly overcame the ravaging hordes of Nebuchadnezzar's army who were about to destroy ancient Israel. She did this heroic feat, without losing her honor, by seducing Holophernes, the commander-in-chief, into a drunken stupor and then (of course) cutting off his head! Jackie says that like me, she had no knowledge of this story. It is yet another striking instance of how she is able to draw up, from the deepest levels of the collective unconscious, images that can perfectly relate to her feelings and help her express what she needs to release.

The theme of decapitation—of severing rational control and understanding from the primal affects of the body—has been the single most effective motif to tell her story and embody her rage in an image.

and so we need to bring this process to a healthy and timely conclusion. We agree to complete our work at the end of May, just before her departure at the beginning of June. My hope is that this mutual agreement will form a helpful framework in which we can do the important work of termination and separation.

*   *   *

Fig. 30   "CHURNING SEAS: TERMINATION ANGER"

Solitary Woman maintains her defiant stance, even as the "angry" churning sea and the old "safe black" of The Abyss loom behind her. There is also a touch of sadness in her expression as she holds a crucifix close to her heart for protection.

Fig. 30 "CHURNING SEAS: TERMINATION ANGER" 4/4/90

This collage is composed of three black and white pieces. The central picture is of a woman standing in the stubble of a harvested cornfield. In her crossed arms she clutches a wooden crucifix and looks directly at us with an expression that is both angry and sad. On the left side, ocean waves crash against the granite boulders of the shore and on the right is a solid black area.

April 5ᵗʰ

Jackie arrives at this session still very angry with me, and says she is once again postponing our final session another 10 days from the last week of May until the end of the first week in June. I am startled to hear her decision to do this for a third time, considering our mutual agreement last week on a firm date for termination at the end of May.

I tell Jackie in order to support her healthy decision to leave and not get derailed by her anxiety about it, I feel it is essential we complete our work with a review of the entire process and then terminate our therapeutic relationship within the time frame we have already agreed on. In addition, even if she again moves her departure date further away, I will not meet with her for any more art therapy sessions after the end of May. Jackie is upset to hear this non-negotiable stand I am taking. Despite the fact we had agreed together on this date in our previous session, she feels I am abandoning her in the very last week. She says this is *her* therapy and the ending date should be *her* choice. She feels that for some reason I am doing this for myself.

There is a degree of truth in what she says, but not that I am doing this for my own convenience. Rather, that my experience has taught me how essential it is for therapists to provide their clients with a clear structure for ending the work. In this way both client and therapist can move through the stages of separation that are the essence of a good termination process. Therefore, after several previous postponements by Jackie, I feel it is imperative we adhere to the ending date we agreed upon last week.

Sensing control of the situation has been taken from her, Jackie says she feels like screaming and stamping her feet. *Her inner child is having a temper tantrum because this triggers the feelings of powerlessness that stem from her childhood.* I take these feelings seriously and offer a way for her to actively express her anger at me. Since we have been working to bring all her feelings into awareness and to have an open and honest expression of them, I suggest that she could vent her anger by pushing her hands against mine as I push back. Jackie says "pushing away" is okay, but touching my hands to "join with" is not acceptable. She thus states a rather universal sentiment that it is okay for her as client to decide to leave me and to set the time, but my making those decisions is not alright. *I silently empathize with this sentiment.* With our hands together, we press hard against each other for a minute or so, and it has the desired effect of venting her anger in a direct, yet safe and effective way.

Jackie says she was afraid to express her anger at me again for fear I would abandon her. I tell her I support her decision to embark on this momentous passage and welcome the expression of all her feelings in these last two months. I assure Jackie I will be with her until the last session, and that we may have phone contact in that final week, if she would like. *In my experience, this is precisely what the process of termination is for and, when done well, requires the therapist's full presence and openness to whatever the client may bring.*[48]

We now turn our attention to this collage, which like the last one, is entirely a statement of her anger at me. Jackie describes the harvested cornfield in which the woman is standing as "barren," which reflects her feelings at this time. *I see the fact that the woman clutches a crucifix as a throwback to the early collages with their themes of altars, victims, and sacrifice.*
More positively, spirituality is the core of deep healing.

The ocean waves that crash violently against the immovable granite boulders of the shore clearly suggest the powerful turbulence of her churning feelings. *I feel the unyielding boulders may likely refer to me.* **The way Jackie has cut around the figure of this woman has given the picture a distinctly penile shape, which makes me feel she is saying, "F__ you"— an implicit, but graphic expression of her anger at me. She tells me she cut it in that shape deliberately—I got the message!**

In contrast to the raging sea on the left is the area of solid black on the right, which represents the regressive temptation Jackie feels to escape to The Abyss of repressed emotions that are not felt consciously. She referred to that as the "safe black" in her first chalk drawing fourteen months ago (Fig. 4). Thinking back, I realize that since The Turning four months ago, the "safe black" has been seen in only two collages; they expressed either her anger or painful exhaustion. Jackie's image tells me there is a part of her that would like to return to that oblivion now due to her intense anxiety.

In this collage Jackie has simply and powerfully expressed both her anger at me, her therapist, and what she has previously known as the only safe thing to do with her rage, that is, repress it in self-contained depression. In this image the two aspects are about equally balanced, and if anything, the active anger of the turbulent sea is making inroads into the lifeless dark of depression.

Once again, Jackie's anger at feeling abandoned has been directly and consciously embodied in the full figure of this woman in her artwork. She has cut off the bottom half of this woman's feet, but she has left part of them, which suggests to me she is now on somewhat more solid grounding in expressing her anger directly. I feel this has been a great "step" forward for her, although internally her anger was difficult for me to receive.

As previously noted, I feel strongly that the ending of Jackie's in-depth therapy should be clearly defined and worked toward consciously. I do not want to enable her to delay this crucial separation by lingering here longer than necessary. If Jackie does that, she may backslide into depression where she will feel "safe" temporarily, but it will not serve her larger need to take that strong and independent stance as "Judith" in her life. The result could likely be that the fearful "child" in her would rule, and her adult self would feel resentful at being kept infantalized in the wounded child/victim state. As

---

[48] *When clients have done a deep level of personal examination of their inner world over an extended period of time, as Jackie has, the process of separation from the therapist to whom they have entrusted their soul's journey, will necessarily bring up a wide range of emotions. This can be a time to examine issues of interpersonal loss, which are difficult for most people. These feelings may not have come up earlier in the therapy, and so the client has time to explore a whole new level of emotions, which very likely will have a resonance with other losses they have experienced throughout their life. Sufficient time is needed to process the ending of this important relationship. In art therapy, a review of all the artwork will enable clients to see and internalize what they have learned and healed. They will recognize their increased level of personal strength and integration and will leave the work with a feeling of wholeness, knowing the loss of the therapist's physical presence will not leave them feeling excessively vulnerable, for what was the therapist's support is now within them.*

Jackie's therapist, it is my intention that she now be fully empowered as the adult woman she is, which is in keeping with her own expressed wishes.

For me, this has been a rich experience of escorting this woman on her Descent into the dark, chaotic, terrifying depths of psyche, and then watching as she has been re-emerging into the light. Consequently, I, too, am experiencing a grief in having our relationship draw to a close, but this is my own inner process to deal with personally or in supervision and not to be shared with my client because it could easily confuse the issue for her.

Internally, I feel upset by Jackie's anger at me. I am trying to serve her highest interests in the best way I know from my training and experience, and it hurts to feel she thinks I am being callous about her feelings. I am well aware that this particular termination process is triggering major countertransference in me in regard to the issue of how an intense therapeutic journey is ended. In the session I remain quietly firm and non-defensive about my decision, knowing this is an important issue for me to take up in my supervision, especially since I am a relatively new art therapist.[49]

*   *   *

April 12ᵗʰ

Jackie comes into today's session depressed and irritated with everyone she knows. She feels no one is going to miss her—only she will miss us. I ask what she is doing in thinking this way. Is she the only one who is sensitive and caring and hurt by loss? What does that kind of thinking do for her? Jackie says perhaps it allows her to be angry at others, and I agree. I also note that this makes her feel less vulnerable and, thereby, allows her to more easily leave those she loves. *It is likely this was an unconscious aspect of the rage she expressed toward me in her last two collages.*

I ask Jackie what she wants to do in the session today. She decides on energy work, but first she has brought in a dream to process. In it, a "Charles-like" man is trying to talk with her, but he is unable to

---

[49] *In any type of therapy, it is best to have a supervisor who is trained in the same mode as the therapist who is being supervised. In this case there was no other art therapist available, so I received supervision from the director of the counseling center where I did this work. He was a marriage and family therapist with many years of experience, and a keen sensitivity to the arts and their therapeutic value. In my next supervision session, he provided valuable guidance that helped me process my counter-transference issues. He asked me to consider, "What does maintaining the intensity of weekly sessions ask of me, and is that okay?" We examined my need to start the termination process early enough so my client would have time to address all her feelings and issues that would come up in the process of ending this work. In addition, we also looked at my need to taper off more gradually, rather than have an abrupt ending.*

Suggestions made in supervision will also help me assist Jackie in looking at some very practical considerations in the remaining time she has before embarking on her journey to England. For example: she might try some ways to explore unknown territories while she is still here in the States and begin to get used to being in unfamiliar places. Also, she needs to look at issues such as: will she work there? or perhaps go to school? Can she explore some of those possibilities before leaving? What does my defining the end point of our work together stir in her? Does it feel like I am leaving her? And when have others left her?

Those of us who are involved in the therapeutic process may at times experience, either in our own healing work or when we are professionally assisting our clients, that terminations are not always what we would like them to be, despite all our best efforts. This dilemma can be painful and confusing at times, but a broad, transpersonal perspective has been of great help to me. This view allows me to trust that when, as therapists, we act with integrity, in fact, everything will unfold exactly as it needs to for the growth of all parties concerned. This is true even when, at the time, we cannot see the whole picture that would make this unquestionably clear.

communicate except through drawings. I suggest the positive male communicating with her through drawings, is a part of her—the animus. Images are the language of the unconscious; we dream primarily in images, not words. In this dream, an unconscious aspect of Jackie is able to communicate best with her conscious mind through her artwork. She says again that her drawings and collages "speak" to her and often the final result is not what she intended when she began. The notion that Charles is speaking to her conscious feminine mind through her images feels good to her.

After discussing the dream, we shift into energy work. After a few minutes of relaxation with her eyes closed, the first thing Jackie sees is an image of a penis that is shooting out of her right hip like a rocket, moving up and away from her. The image suggests to her that she is releasing from her energy field the residue of her experiences with inappropriate male sexual behavior, and she feels good about this spontaneous happening.

As part of the energy process, I touch her right shoulder lightly. Jackie immediately gets the feeling of her mother holding her down and wants to push her away. Taking the part of her mother, I invite her to push against me, but when she does I resist and won't be pushed away. *I do this in order to take her deeper into that feeling and see what emotion will arise.* Jackie is surprised at how angry she feels and how powerfully she is pushing back (*against her mother*).

After a few moments, her solution is to turn away from me; then, of course, I stop pushing. This feels good because the insight that arises in her is that if she stops pushing against her mother in her feelings, the old battle will stop because her mother will have nothing to push against. Jackie then tells me she recognizes it is *her* choice to stop the battle she has been waging internally ever since the flashbacks began four years ago in 1986.

*   *   *

April 19th

As we begin today's session Jackie says she is often procrastinating or forgetting things, and recognizes this is caused by the anxiety and stress she is feeling about leaving. I tell her this is precisely the reason I am trying to help by providing a clear framework for termination. She responds saying she now understands why I have been so firm in that decision and is no longer angry about it.

Once again Jackie talks about her two internal male images. As she previously mentioned, Alfred was a symbol for the constantly criticizing voice of her father that she had internalized, which made her feel she was always doing things in the wrong way. On the other hand, the positive male first came into her awareness spontaneously during a meditation about eight years before we met. In a dream-like manner he came with a full name, Charles Andrews, and although she doesn't understand it, she senses he is somehow connected with her feelings of being drawn to the English countryside.

Jackie tells me she has decided she wants to share her artwork in order to show other survivors that, even with this magnitude of pain, it is possible to work through their early wounds and regain an authentic sense of self-worth. I am deeply moved by this because I feel her openness to share her painful process is a measure of the degree of healing she has achieved. In order to do this, she wants to have an exhibit of some of her collages. However, because the rough, torn edges of the heavy brown paper are a deliberate and important part of the expression of her deep pain, she asks me how the collages might be mounted so those edges would not be covered up. There is a lot of the brown paper around the photos that would need to be trimmed if they were framed, and matting would certainly cover those edges, so I suggest she talk with someone at a framing store to find the best way to do it.

Jackie says she is not sure she would be willing to identify this process as having to do specifically with incest—that still feels too embarrassing to own. She says this body of work could illustrate the process of working through any early wound. I agree that the non-verbal images can be universally understood to be the record of a healing journey, and there are very few that would specifically suggest incest. *In particular Figs. 1, 6, 9, 10, 11, 15, 16.*

I tell Jackie I would like to use our session next week to review the work we've done by looking at all the photos I've taken of the collages and also talk specifically about our separation. Jackie gets tearful, knowing we will have only six more sessions.

In keeping with my supervisor's suggestions, I encourage her to drive to unfamiliar areas of the state she lives in, allowing herself to get lost and feel playful about finding her way home again. I also suggest it could be helpful for her to do more research about England and begin to shape a positive image of what she will be going to—not simply being aware of all she is leaving behind. Jackie is planning to fly first to Germany with a friend who lives there and spend some time with her as a transition to being on her own in England. She is interested in Tragering,[50] a particular type of massage therapy and is looking into the possibility of studying it while there.

*   *   *

April 26ᵗʰ

As we begin this session, Jackie tells me she had been with her brother this week and how his hug really communicated something very different than she had ever felt from him before. She says he is also in therapy now, and that it is probably by getting in touch with his own pain that he has been able to have more empathy with hers.

"High anxiety" is the way Jackie describes her feelings of the past week. She took several steps to prepare for her departure, for example, getting an international driver's license and information on studying Tragering. Originally, her friend from Germany was going to come to the States in May, and they planned to fly back together. Now her friend is not coming, and Jackie will have to fly there alone. Because of this, she is experiencing many questions, doubts, and fears.

Once again, I encourage her not to deny her feelings of loss, fear, and so on, but rather to acknowledge them consciously. At the same time, it's best not to dwell solely on those painful feelings, but also to keep planning and preparing for the future in positive ways in order to keep from getting swamped by her anxiety.

We then begin our review of the collages by laying out the photos on the long coffee table in front of the couches where we have usually sat, except when she was drawing at the larger table. This provides an

---

[50] Trager, Milton, M.D. *Trager Mentastics, Movement as a Way to Agelessness*, with Cathy Guadagno, Ph.D., Station Hill Press, Barrytown, NY, 1987.

excellent way for us to view all of them at once. It's obvious to both of us that, had we been looking at the originals, we would have had to do it outside on the parking lot in order to have enough space. There are about 130 in all.

Jackie says she knows, deep in her feelings, that these images truly reflect far more of herself than she could ever recognize consciously or define verbally. Once again she says, "they just feel right." She tells me that several times in the past week she thought of making a collage, but then decided she really didn't want to. *What a change this represents; her deep psyche is really beginning to close down the active inner exploration.*

*   *   *

May 3ʳᵈ

We continue our review of the collages. In observing her artwork, Jackie reaffirms her feelings of completion. She says in the past week she has gotten little sleep and has been very distracted and daydreaming a lot at work—often simply feeling blank. It's clear that an intense internal process is going on. No new collages again this week, but in the midst of our review, another tender expression of affection for me.

Looking back, I realize I entered into this process at the very beginning, just as Jackie was about to confront her parents with a letter she had already written about her memories. Now, like a story contained between bookends, she has completed the cycle and her therapy is drawing to its natural conclusion. It has been deeply gratifying for me to witness the comprehensiveness of the change in Jackie's feelings.

*   *   *

May 11ᵗʰ

I have forgotten the photographs of her artwork which we had planned to continue reviewing! This, of course, is an unconscious indication that it is also difficult for me to bring to an end our time together. I shall miss Jackie.

This week, Jackie went to a movie with a friend. In the film, a man had an affair, and Jackie's friend did not trust his motives. In a shift of attitude that I feel is significant, Jackie says for the first time in years it didn't even occur to her to doubt the man's motives. She says that no "creep alarm" went off in her head this time, and she feels this is a bad sign, as if she is letting down her guard too much. I tell her my feeling about that experience is much more positive. I see this as a clear indication from her deep unconscious mind that there has been a profound (instinctual and, therefore, true) change in her level of trust in men. This new attitude creates the possibility for the relationship she says she wants. She responds that my interpretation is shocking and scary to her, but I feel it is in keeping with her experience of the spontaneous diminution of Alfred, the rise of Charles, and the dramatic change in the content of her collages.

Regarding her imminent departure, Jackie says her daughter refuses to think about it; her son says he will miss her, but is glad she is doing this for herself; and her friends are now dealing with it directly. They have been able to express their feelings of anger that she is leaving, but Jackie says it's okay now that she's able to receive their feelings without collapsing or feeling intimidated.

This week Jackie was reviewing difficulties she's had with some friends she's known for thirty years. She found herself wanting to dismember a doll, paint blood on it, place it in some building ruins, and then photograph it—a throwback to the early collages, except this time she would be creating a three dimensional assemblage. The life review triggered those old raging feelings. She tells me she knew she did not have to stay with those emotions any more, and was able to avoid getting caught in depression.

This past week, Jackie was even more scattered and distracted at work. She has been talking about making this move for two years; now that it is happening, there is an air of unreality about it. Again she comments about what a dark, suicidal time that was and how she thought she would never again feel good about herself. She sees that dealing with all her emotions directly has brought resolution and a genuine sense of self-worth. The work has taken enormous amounts of courage, but she says that persevering through the process has been worth it.

Jackie mentions that it has been nearly two years since she changed her last name, which resulted in her feeling relieved, cleansed, and freed of both her husband and father. *This was done nearly a year before she began the art therapy work with me. I feel that on a deep level of her psyche, she had already begun at that time to create a new, non-victim identity for herself.*

*   *   *

May 17th

As we begin, Jackie tells me her best friend since childhood has always been her hero. Today she says she is her own hero now. *I love it.*

Nonetheless, she begins to cry as we move into the session because she feels she cannot do this: cannot make this total transition she has set up for herself.

We continue our review of all her collages. Knowing the importance of the termination process, and also how much Jackie values personal, meaningful rituals, I suggest she might think about creating a ritual of closure for our last session. She likes the idea and will think about it.

*   *   *

May 24ᵗʰ Our Second-To-Last Session:

Today Jackie has arrived with several parting gifts for me: 2 photographs she took and a book, *The Great Cosmic Mother: Rediscovering the Religion of the Earth.*[51] Jackie inscribed the book to "Louise, my great 'psyche' mother." *I am deeply touched.*

Our work today has to do with the difficulties her two children (late teens, early twenties) are having regarding her imminent departure. I encourage her to spend as much time as possible with each of them individually and help them express their concerns.

We then talk more about her feelings in regard to leaving both me and this inner process that has been so intense and meaningful for her. We take time to complete our review of her journey by looking at the remaining collage-photos. There has been such a flow of artwork for the past fifteen months that it has taken us three sessions to review it all. [52]

Since her second expression of anger at me in early April, Jackie has done only one more collage. It was a very forward-looking one, done in mid-April (not shown). It has been surprising and interesting for me to observe how this collage-making process that has been so rich and vital and therapeutic for Jackie has tapered off in the last six weeks of our work. Clearly, her psyche is just naturally shutting down the intensity of her involvement with these images.

Following the suggestion that I made last week, Jackie has been thinking about how she would like to have our final session structured. She wants us to somehow create a circle that we could both be in, and then to do some artwork together. She leaves the specifics for me to work out. I suggest that, since she has used this medium so well to express both the high and low points of her inner journey, at this time it might be helpful for her to create some kind of summary of her pilgrimage in collage, as part of her termination. "Interesting;" she'll think about it. The feeling of everything being somehow unreal has continued. Jackie says she has even felt a bit dissociated from her body at times. I remind her to breathe in a deep and relaxed manner whenever that happens in order to maintain a conscious connection with her body in the present, and to stay aware of what emotions are arising.

---

[51] *Monica Sjoo & Barbara Mor, The Great Cosmic Mother, Rediscovering the Religion of the Earth, Harper & Row, Publishers, San Francisco, 1987.*
[52] *I find that having photographs of the artwork is a particularly powerful way to review what has been accomplished. Images elicit the emotions that were being experienced in the course of the process, as well as more specific details than would come up in just thinking about the past.*

"TOGETHER WE JOURNEYED"   5/31/90 *(not shown)*

May 31, 1990   Final Session:

Jackie arrives for our last session carrying an enormous collage that is not only a synopsis of the work done, but also another parting gift for me. She entitled it "Together We Journeyed." Many words accompany the images, each of which has specific relevance for her.

What had been locked for so long in the stony silence of the unconscious because of amnesia has finally, through the mediation of images, been given conscious articulation in words.

In this summarizing collage *(not shown)*, both words and images begin on the left where they express the pain Jackie experienced in the past. In the center they have to do with the positive, healing aspects of our therapeutic relationship in the present. Finally, those on the right anticipate her next step into the future.

On the left the pictures are of a headless woman riding a bicycle through water and the head of the ancient Roman monster Medusa whose mouth is open. Below her float a sea of words: "pain," "secrets finally revealed," "a father's deed," "mother love: lessons in lunacy," "madame," "evil," "to drown us," and "archaic-barbaric."

The pictures in the central section include a globe in a blue-green circle Jackie says represents the cosmos or the totality of everything, and her sense of completion. Above that sphere in the center of the entire piece is a sculpture of a female nude, walking to the left and smiling as she looks over her shoulder at the viewer. The naturalness of her form and the softness of the lighting seem to suggest that the goddess who was disrobed, beheaded, and lost her hands in her Descent, and who then began to be reintegrated, is now beginning to come alive as a real and warm woman. I ask Jackie about that progressive dismemberment and then reintegration of the goddess images, and she reaffirms that those changes happened without premeditation on her part. In their various states, they simply reflected accurately how she was feeling at those times. The same is true of the sequence of changes in the castles.

Above this goddess, top center, is a picture Jackie took of me at a recent session. She has bordered it with turquoise and roses. The words in this area are: "our work," "we know," "lifeline," "changes," "repair," "woman," "center," and "my heart." This last word was intentionally cut apart between the "e" and the "a" in a jagged way that indicates the heart had broken in two or perhaps been struck by lightning. Only after doing that did Jackie see its other uniquely relevant implication: "he/art" also suggests her use of art to heal the wound of male violation.

The photo on the right is of a large old tree in a peaceful English garden. Jackie's intention with this image is to indicate that her wounded "inner children," who she had always visualized beneath a great tree, are now experiencing peace and beauty. The largest of the pictures in this collage is of a field of beautiful wild flowers, which Jackie says she is very drawn to at this time. *This is yet another measure of the change in her: ruins and rubble have yielded to wild flowers.*

Below the tree and flowers she placed a picture of herself smiling happily. She deliberately backed the left side with red, and the right with turquoise. Connected to her is a picture of a woman's lower leg and foot taking a step toward the future, as her hands hold a passport near her ankle. The foot is stepping into "1990," which Jackie recently said was, "the year of letting go." In this future section the words are: "burden: you can't take it with you," "passage," "isle of me," "1990," and just above her signature: "love."

Finally, in the center-right there is a relevant quote from C.G. Jung about his personal experience of the therapeutic value of images to help him work through and understand his emotions.

> *To the extent that I managed to translate the emotions into images—that is to say, to find the images which were concealed in the emotions—I was inwardly calmed and reassured. Had I left those images hidden in the emotions, I might have been torn to pieces by them. There is a chance that I might have succeeded in splitting them off; but in that case I would inexorably have fallen into a neurosis and so been ultimately destroyed by them anyhow. As a result of my experiment I learned how helpful it can be, from the therapeutic point of view, to find the particular images which lie behind emotions.*[53]

Jackie included this quote because Jung's words perfectly express her feelings of how therapeutic and profoundly satisfying it has been to make these powerful collages—even when she had no rational, conscious understanding of, nor explanation for, the images and symbols she chose.

Jackie and I talk about the simple block form of her collages since The Turning. Although the symbolism remained potent, aesthetically they have been much less interesting. Jackie says she thinks this happened because the feelings of self-esteem are so new to her it has been disorienting. *It is as if, at this point, she really does not know how to put together "the pieces" of her life and will need time to integrate all the changes.*

To honor Jackie's idea about the circle, I suggest that we try a collaborative project I recently learned about. Jackie agrees. First, we create a 12" diameter ring of clay. Next, we each make symbols that represent important aspects of her healing process and attach them to the ring. Finally, we make a clay bridge from one side to the other with clay flowers placed on the top. Jackie is very pleased with this. Our shared creative involvement has been a reflective and satisfying experience for both of us, and Jackie has the clay piece as a remembrance of our work together.

And so Jackie's journey has come to an end. As she prepares to leave, we embrace and acknowledge the value of the healing work we have done.

*   *   *

---

[53] C.G. Jung, *Memories, Dreams, Reflections,* Recorded and Edited by Aniela Jaffe, trans. from German by Richard and Clara Winston, (Pantheon Books, div. of Random House, New York, c. 1961, final revised ed. 1973), p. 177.

INTERIM

JOURNEY TO EUROPE AND RETURN TO THE ABYSS

(6 MONTHS)

*"It is Fool who has chosen to blow the wind
        that fills the sails,
        and has set the boat on its course."*

June 12, 1990   First letter from Europe:

Jackie left about a week ago, and I've just received a letter from her. She's at the home of her friend who has lived in Germany for five years. She plans to stay there temporarily as a transition until she gets her bearings, and then go on to England where she expects to stay for about a year. Jackie writes that she has been crying for the first three days, feels deep anguish, does not know why she felt such a need to make this trip, misses her kids, her friends, and her apartment. She has tapped into a very painful memory of when she was eleven years old. Her parents had put her on a train by herself to stay with a relative in Maine for an entire summer. She says she didn't want to go, felt miserable the entire time, and now wonders what was going on that they did that. She's surprised her father would let her be away from him that long.

Jackie says she feels a real need to continue collaging and will get herself some materials so her creative work can continue. She makes an interesting comment: she doesn't want *to think*, but she does want *to collage*. She says this art process is very familiar—like when she is sleeping. *This comment corroborates my observation that her collages are often very dreamlike. Both her dreams and her collages arise out of the non-rational or "primary process" aspect of the brain.*

*   *   *

While in Germany, Jackie has been limited to making small, notecard sized collages; these have generally incorporated words with images. She has sent me a number of her collage-cards, but now is worried that perhaps she should not do that. She does not want to keep me in the role of therapist, but then she decides this is simply our way of communicating, and she needs to communicate with me. It's fine with me; I'm glad to know how she's doing.

*   *   *

June 20, 1990   Second letter:

Jackie writes to tell me that, as she listens to her friend talk about how hard it has been as a foreigner to get work with reasonable pay and other difficulties in living there, she's having second thoughts about her whole plan. When they visited a castle together, her friend began to cry and said how wonderful it is to have a friend with whom she can talk. Jackie says she does not want that kind of isolation for herself, and now thinks she may just visit as many different countries as possible and then return home in late September, near her birthday. She confides that if she returns home so much sooner than she had planned, she feels she will be "wimping out" and doesn't like that about herself.

Jackie heard a report on television that a bill has been introduced into the United States Congress to make physical abuse of women a civil rights violation. She says "...about time. They should do that before making an amendment about flag burning. Life is so cockeyed!"

She then writes about a trip she and her friend made to the fallen Berlin wall. "By 12 p.m. Sat. the place was mobbed. Tour buses, trailers, bikes, cars. Vendors lining the way—table after table of people selling pieces of the wall, uniforms, military hats, etc. looked like a flea market. We brought a hammer and pick, but, boy, you really needed a jackhammer—that wall is <u>HARD</u>. Got a few slivers though. I wrote my name on the wall with an eye-liner pencil and took pictures of it. We're going to go back next weekend, and I'm going to paint on it and take more pictures."

Jackie says she is dreaming a lot about her family members but cannot remember the dreams when she awakens. *This is unusual for her.* One exception has been that, right after she got to Germany, Jackie dreamed that her father was dead, and she was telling her sister and mother they had to take care of the arrangements but they were totally unresponsive. *Although her father is alive, the dream suggests he no longer has power over her, and she has no intention of being responsible for whatever emotional debris he has left behind.*

In an effort to occupy her mind and get more comfortable so far away from her loved ones, Jackie is learning from her friend how to develop her own film. She also says that putting on the exercise tape she had been using at home is giving her a feeling of something familiar.

*   *   *

June 23, 1990   Third letter:

What Jackie describes in this letter is the most difficult to explain, but speaks to the deep unconscious feelings that have drawn her to England.

Her letter describes an experience she had on a solitary drive through the Cotswolds in southwestern England. Jackie stopped and walked to the top of a hill where she saw a vista that touched her deeply. Off to the left was a castle; opposite that, on a hill to the right stood a very large tree; and between them a river was running through the valley. Jackie says that in seeing this bucolic scene, she welled up with tears. It looked exactly like the internal image she has had for many years. The castle is where she imagined being with Charles. The large tree was the safe haven to which her two "inner children" always retreated when they/she felt scared. *The picture of the large tree in her final collage, "Together We Journeyed," referred to this internal place that, on this day, she saw physically before her.* Finally, she tells me that in her visualizations the river was where she always went with the adolescent part of herself to "dump the guilt" she felt.

Jackie has no words of explanation nor any insight about this experience—she simply comments that the entire scene moved her to the depths of her soul. She says it reminds her of a small collage she made for me, which she included in this letter. The image is of a single puzzle piece missing from the whole, and the words are "The Search. Power. Play." Jackie says this landscape feels like that missing piece for her because it seems to give some objective reality to the internal images she has had for so long. Those visualizations have been essential aspects of her inner life as she struggled to find refuge from her painful experience of shame.

Jackie says it feels as if—in some other time-space dimension—she has been with a Charles Andrews in England, in a place with a castle and a great tree for safety, and a river for cleansing. And who is to say? Somehow, it seems to speak to the fact that our minds work in mysterious ways, and at times the unconscious is able to tap into other dimensions of which our conscious mind has little or no awareness. (A similar phenomenon might be a precognitive dream in which one experiences something while dreaming that is later experienced in exactly the same way in their waking life.) I've had this experience several times. I've dated and recorded in my dream journal, a situation or location that I had dreamed, and then weeks or months later, saw precisely the same situation in my waking day. This is not an uncommon experience and some people feel it is an explanation for "deja vu."

This trip to England Jackie made alone, without her friend in Germany, and a small note added to her letter says: "There's no one here to really laugh with—a great void."

*   *   *

June 27, 1990   Fourth letter:

On one of her tours, Jackie had time to observe a couple at length. She says while the husband was very attentive, the wife was extremely controlled and tight in both her dress and manner. At one point, Jackie tried to engage this woman in conversation and got only a very brief response. Looking into her eyes, Jackie sensed the woman was "dead" in her feelings; that nothing animated her. Jackie says this made her very sad, and she kept thinking this woman would have a big story to tell.

In a dream that was related to that experience, Jackie saw a woman who was a "neat freak." Jackie commented to someone else in the dream that she used to be that way, but now she is sloppy and she loves it; and she started laughing. *Both this dream and Jackie's sensitivity to the woman on the tour suggest how much she has loosened up in her feelings, and also how compassionate and understanding she has become about others who are in the Abyss of emotional numbness. She can relate to that woman from her own experience.*

Jackie also describes in detail a dream in which she and two young children, a boy and a girl, were in a room with numerous "big fat brown snakes" that look like slugs. Jackie was very frightened and rushed out of the house. She then remembered the children and ran back in to save them. She tells me she was aware of saving only the little girl and now she wonders if, in this dream, she was "rehashing the discovery of the incest and saving the little girl" in herself.

*   *   *

July 9, 1990   Fifth letter:

"I wish I could describe this trip and do it justice. Words don't hit it exactly. It's kind of like one of my collages. The words are on the top, but there's volumes underneath. At 9 am Saturday we did a boat tour of Lake Constance, in Lucerne. The boat's name was 'Charles' and along the shore, off in the distance, was a round sign like a bull's-eye with the number 10 inside it." *Both the name and the number have significance for Jackie.* I said to myself—'O.K.' - and wondered what was going to happen that day.

"I knew that on this trip was a chairlift ride up a mountain. Ann *(the friend she's staying with)* is the tour guide and said she would go with me, and told me about a couple of men she took, who were terrified also, but wrote to her later and said how glad they were that they did it. I decided that I would do it solely on the basis of pushing through barriers. Step ladders made me scared!

"Throughout the morning I kept seeing myself going up in a chairlift, and felt overwhelming fear when I did. Right up until almost the last minute, I gave myself the chance to change my mind, but I thought of you, when you did your firewalk, and said to myself, if you could do that, I could do this—and I wouldn't die—BUT, if I did, it was my time. *Previously, I had told her about my experience of confronting and moving through my fears by participating in firewalks.*

"The chairlift has 2 separate seats hitched together, a canvas top that comes down, like a flap, on one side. I told Ann I had to have that wall. The chairlift started and I asked myself what the hell I was doing!

I held on for dear life—I was petrified. We were going up a mountain that faced the north side of the Eiger Mountain that was in the movie 'The Eiger Sanction.' It was so beautiful, but I was too scared to move, to take my camera out.

"After about seven minutes, I relaxed, I loosened my grip on the post between the chairs, and looked out at the mountains, and absorbed it in my soul. You can hear the silence, Louise. It felt very healing and soothing. I started to cry and then to sob—and it wasn't fear. It felt like something breaking—I kept having an image of a wall tumbling down. I enjoyed the rest of the ride, which lasted about 20 minutes altogether—although I still didn't look down or through the flap or in back of me.

"We stayed on the mountain about 2 hours. It's about 6,000 feet up and it was incredible! I wished I could have stayed there. I also thought if Kathy (*her friend since childhood*) could come just for this one day, it would be worth it.

"On the trip back down, I moved that flap, looked over the side, in back of me, <u>and</u> took pictures. And when we came to places that really made me aware of the height, and I felt scared, I looked right at it and took a picture. I walked into the fear. It was wonderful! I got off that lift and felt like I could do anything. I also knew, without a doubt, that if I came home, it would be because I wanted to and not because I was too scared to try and stay here.

Ann tells me that there is a glacier train that goes to a cave inside an iceberg. Icebergs, for me, are beyond terror. Also there's a cable car ride that goes higher and ends up at a restaurant carved out in an iceberg. I want to do at least one of those things before I leave here."

I feel moved to tears as I read of Jackie's courage in confronting her terror. She has sent several small collages with this letter. One is of a statue of a woman bending forward and the photography creates a blur behind her that gives the impression she is moving very fast to the right. The words Jackie has used are: "Many things are built around a strong center."

In this letter, Jackie goes on to say that her son recently told her he will be getting married next year. She has found herself obsessing about how awkward it would be to be with the family with none of them talking to each other, and so on. Then she kept thinking about the incest, her parents, and all her painful history, and she hated that she was thinking about it.

Another small collage says "The Secret Invitation," and the image is of an old stone wall that has an opening with stairs leading up into a place one cannot see. This has the same sexual implication of some of her early collages. A third collage simply says, "Express Truth." Jackie says she doesn't want to think about any of that anymore, and after her experience on the mountain, all those old fears simply pale by comparison. She says now she can think about the awkwardness in the family and simply say, "So what?"

Several months ago, just before our termination, Jackie said she wanted to exhibit some of her collages in order to encourage others to do their healing work. In this letter, Jackie also informs me that she recently received word there will be an exhibit of artwork done by survivors of sexual abuse, illustrating how art can be an important aspect of recovery. It will take place next Fall at a rape crisis center near her home in the States. Jackie says she has applied and been accepted as an exhibitor. So this will be her first opportunity to share her work. She has decided that the collages she will enter will be Figs. 8, 14, and 16. Then she wonders if she should also submit Fig. 20 as an illustration of having regained her self-esteem.

I am deeply moved by the openness Jackie has expressed—her compassion for the suffering of others, her wish to help them by sharing her own suffering, and the healing process with which she has steadfastly engaged.

*   *   *

July 14, 1990   Sixth Letter:

Jackie has written to thank me for a letter I wrote her. She describes, in her letter, a trip she made to Bavaria. She says that being in the Alps made her feel like crying. This gut response surprised her until she remembered a collage she did many months ago in which a small house was banked up against a snowy mountain. At that time she commented that the house did not feel safe, but the mountain did. Now in the physical presence of these great pinnacles, her feelings are touched deeply.

Jackie sends a collage. The image is of two native men who are dancing, covered in mud and leaves. They have flat, rectangular masks over their faces, with crude holes cut out for eyes and mouths. The words are "On Edge Outfront—Culture Crash."

Another crucial piece: On the way back from that trip to Bavaria, Jackie's tour stopped at a Nazi concentration camp. Again, her words: "Today we stopped at Dachau on the way home. Another place I will never forget. I kept feeling myself putting the brakes on my feelings—it was quite overwhelming. It's one thing to see movies made about what happened there—quite another to <u>be</u> there and also to see a documentary film of actual footage filmed there during its operation.

"The visit there made me feel hopeless for the world—it brought me to The Abyss again. In the film they showed the prisoners (some of them) standing there while some army person made a speech. A young girl in a prison uniform was just crying and it made me think of how I get when I realize what I've survived. I also understood Israel in a whole new way—why they're so hard-line about their borders, etc. It was so clear to me. It's just like me with my family and in trusting other people in other ways. There's a monument there that says it all: 'NEVER AGAIN!'

"And there's a very long walkway—lined with trees on both sides—the trees were planted by the prisoners—these were the things they held onto. I thought of all the places in the world that brutality goes on. If more people don't start owning their dark sides, nothing will change." *And, feeling overwhelmed by this magnitude of man's inhumanity to man, Jackie adds,* "And maybe nothing would, even if they did."

Her letter concludes: "Some prisoners died from the shock of being set free. The Red Cross went right in to give them warm clothes, food, blankets, etc., and they (the prisoners) couldn't handle it. So the Red Cross backed off and let them come to it, in their own time. I walked out of there knowing that I was one of those trees." *It is this experience, in particular, that has touched Jackie's feelings about being a survivor of any kind of abuse, and her emotions have been stirred deeply. She has begun a profound questioning of the nature of good and evil and has decided it's about time to come home.*

*   *   *

July 30, 1990   Seventh Letter:

This letter is accompanied by several more collages that I see truly reflect her feelings at this time. One large one says: "Laying, the Blame...think...How...yesterday I... Discover...Lethal Weapon....The Pleasure Principle." In this last letter from Germany, Jackie describes how uncomfortable she has often been there and how awkward and judgmental she felt in relation to her friend and her friend's live-in boyfriend. She was afraid she was intruding on their space, and her own response was to become aloof and withdrawn. Jackie says her "dark side has been on its high horse." She adds, "I'M SO GLAD I'M COMING HOME!!!" and "I also keep thinking of my brown paper—I'll have access to my brown paper."[54] Another collage has a large colorful image of a shuttle rocket blasting off on bright yellow paper that says: "A woman...severing the cord." A third says: "My life as a woman—worth its wait" with bright colors around it.

And finally there is a second large collage with very bright colors around a young woman on a bike with a wide open smile. The words are: "Healthy people play." "Laugh." "Being silly is a life skill." And finally, "To be frivolous is to look straight into the weight of the world, put your thumbs in your ears, wiggle your fingers and say 'nayah, nyah, nyah.'"

And so Jackie's trip has come to an end after only two months, rather than a year as she originally planned. I have learned from her letters that although she was mostly uncomfortable while there, she also experienced several very important breakthroughs in regard to her inner images, fear, tyranny, and compassion. The first was her feeling of physically being in the same place she had often imaged internally with "Charles" and her "inner children." The second was the enormous breakthrough of her terror on the mountain, and the third was her experience of empathy with the survivors at Dachau. She also had time to review and get some distance and perspective on her family situation and all the healing work she has done. And finally, she is about to begin to share her artwork as an encouragement to others. My sense is that, although her time in Europe was cut short, Jackie really has accomplished the purpose of her journey.

---

[54] *Jackie is referring to the heavy brown paper with its torn edges that she has used for the ground of her collages. In order to get a closer focus on the images, often large areas of the brown paper around them have been cropped in these photographs. Unfortunately, in many of the collages this required a sacrifice of the torn edges that Jackie said were part of the expression of her wound.*

Fig. 31 "ISOLATION: CUTTING THE TIES"

Solitary Woman is running toward the left indicating a regression into the dark depression—back into the familiar Abyss. In that place there are no connections to loved ones: she has cut her own lifelines.

Fig. 31   "ISOLATION: CUTTING THE TIES"

This is the same collage that was seen earlier as Fig. 25 ("Leaving Home"), except that Jackie has now cut the ties that connected her to her children and friends. She did this sometime between returning to the States in September 1990 and resuming art therapy in March 1991.

Before Jackie left, my supervisor made a comment which proved to be prophetic. He said if Jackie were to go to England without a specific, forward-looking, plan (for example, enrolling in school) going away from all her familiar supports could become a very painful, regressive experience. Clearly she needed to plan more substantially because this is exactly what happened. He said that in that situation she would feel a deep need for the love and nurturance she never got as a child and so her unconscious would manipulate the situation so she would want those close to her, including me, to provide that support. If that happened, he said, she would very likely be back in the States in a few months.

Jackie did return early with a plan to go back to school to study either painting, photography, or language (which she discovered she has an ear for). However, instead she slipped back into depression and began to isolate herself from her friends. This continued for some months until she recognized she had more inner work to do. She contacted me and asked if she could return to therapy.

In art therapy we always have two aspects to take into consideration: the work of art and the process which involves both verbal discussion and the relationship with the therapist. There are many examples in Jackie's work that show clearly how the process of art therapy, that is, the physical act of creating something, can be therapeutic. A few examples will demonstrate this. First: Fig. 10, "The Bacchus Slaughter." Jackie said it was a powerfully satisfying experience for her to cut the strong controlling arms off the male in the photograph. It was as if, in that way, she was able to sublimate her raging wish to do grave physical harm to the abusive male in her life.

Second: Fig 19, "Partners in Crime." In creating that collage Jackie put her abusive parents behind bars and, through that action, claimed the right to her anger and had the strength to punish them. Doing this even "just" symbolically, shook Jackie to her core with fear. However, in having the strength and will to take that action on her own behalf, Jackie's need for vengeance was satisfied without hurting anyone. That was The Turning at which point she was able to shift her focus away from internalized rage and begin the process of constructing a new life for herself.

Finally, this collage Fig. 31, "Isolation: Cutting the Ties." When Jackie returned from Europe and again dropped into depression, she went to her portfolios and got out this collage, which she had done about six months before. She then altered it in a significant way by cutting the ties that connected her to loved ones and found that action to be a deeply meaningful and satisfying way to express her feelings of isolation.

DESCENT AND RETURN

AN INCEST SURVIVOR'S HEALING JOURNEY THROUGH ART THERAPY

PART II

"Storms will be encountered and mythic monsters will rise from the unplumbed depths."

IT IS NOW 1991
March 21st - The first day of Spring

Jackie arrives and begins by saying that for the past several days she's been feeling a lot of fear about resuming this difficult process. She wondered what was coming up and why she felt compelled to examine it, concluding there are three clearly defined areas she needs to address:

1) Spirituality: the loss of any sense of connection to a beneficent God;
2) Mother: her rage and grief about that relationship; and
3) Personal empowerment as a woman.

These are the skeletons in the closet of her psyche that have now arisen and require attention. After addressing a few groundwork issues such as scheduling and fees, we resume our work.

As Jackie moves into this second segment of her art therapy, she tells me she's had a series of "big" dreams in recent weeks (*Jung described dreams with archetypal content as "big."*) **and has felt a lot of fear coming up, but isn't clear what has triggered it. In each dream she was asking herself a major question.**

The most important of these, the third, was about spiritual values. All that was spiritually meaningful to her previously was torn away by flashbacks of the incest. Jackie says at this time she is "nowhere" spiritually and she cries because of the isolation she feels in this inner vacuum. She observes her friends participating in meaningful religious practices from both East and West, and mourns the loss of contact with a central guiding core within herself.[55]

This is the crucial piece I feel we only touched on in our earlier work. I see Jackie is now ready to examine these difficult and profound issues and questions.

*   *   *

---

[55] *C.G. Jung: Letters. Vol. 1, p377, Letter to P.W. Martin, 20 Aug 1945. Selected and edited by Gerhard Adler in collaboration with Aniela Jaffe. Translations from the German by R.F.C. Hull in two volumes. (Bollingen Series xcv:1, Princeton University Press, 1973, Princeton, New Jersey.)*

In his letter to P.W. Martin, Jung states that seeking the spiritual dimension became the core of the work with his patients. He says "You are quite right, the main interest of my work is not concerned with the treatment of neuroses but rather with the approach to the numinous. But the fact is that the approach to the numinous is the real therapy and inasmuch as you attain to the numinous experiences you are released from the curse of pathology. Even the very disease takes on a numinous character."

This view is in contrast to Sigmund Freud who believed sexual dysfunctions or inhibitions were his clients' main problems. I believe spirituality and sexuality are the two essential sides to our human nature, and they both need to be rectified and integrated. Jung also said that after the age of about thirty, the most frequent problem he saw in his clients was they had lost a sense of their own spiritual center, often as a result of trauma. I, too, find that deep healing, as distinct from a physical cure, is spiritual in nature. A person may make a meaningful connection with their sense of God or a "higher power" in various ways, for example, through Jung's work, deep religion, in nature, a 12-Step program, meditation, or therapy. Whatever form it takes, the process essentially involves an individual's journey into the core of their being, where it is discovered that the very fact one is alive is the connection with the Divine energy that is the Source of all life. If there were no connection to that Life, one would simply not exist. The experience of being separate physical entities causes the fear of also being separate spiritually and conceals the truth of the interconnectedness of life on all levels of being, which science has also shown to be true through quantum physics and later developments in recent decades.

A Native American story says that the Great Spirit wanted to hide itself from humans. It tried many possibilities, but realized that in each place wily man would find it. Finally, the perfect hiding place was found. It was deep in the heart of each human because they would never think to look for the Great Spirit within themselves.

March 28th

Jackie speaks of the polarities of good and evil; of moralistic dualism versus cosmic oneness; of how she used to be against capital punishment, but now feels for some crimes it is appropriate. She says she's never read or heard anything about how people cope with or ever resolve the dark/light dichotomy of life, especially after experiencing unmitigated evil—as in the Holocaust (*of which she now has a much deeper awareness since her recent visit to Dachau*).

Jackie is tearful as she says she feels no one can really understand her feelings or the enormity of the questions for which she is struggling to find answers. I suggest a support group for incest survivors might diminish her feelings of aloneness. However, she says she's not interested in that because she thinks members of such a group would most likely be dealing with the specific issues of their incest experience, which is one aspect of her healing work she feels is now complete. She thinks others in such a group would probably not be engaged with the deeper core issues of good and evil, and the meaning of life.

Jackie did a painting this morning: a devil's face to illustrate a figure of evil in a dream she had last night. (*not shown*) *Jackie has gone to a level of awareness where she is not simply absorbed in her own personal experience of abuse and pain, but is also struggling now to understand the larger context in which it is couched. I realize it is crucial for me to simply support her process while she works her way through this morass of pain and confusion until she is able to find her own answers to these fundamental questions.*

Jackie says she's afraid she'll never be able to come to that resolution. I assure her of my conviction that she will do the work she has come to do. She says it means a great deal to her to hear that.

*   *   *

April 4th

While in Europe, Jackie used a lot of words in her small card-collages, and this has carried over into the collages she is doing now. One she did this week reads: "In this hard, hard life, it's hard to imagine being without life's basic necessities. Questions. Answers." The image is a brown moon-like surface with large boulders (*not shown*).

Questions about the meaning of survival and what this life is all about are often coming up for her now. Jackie tells me she saw a report on television of a woman who had been in the concentration camps during World War II and had subsequently repressed the memory of the whole experience for more than twenty years. Jackie says her own experience of amnesia makes clear to her how that can happen.

Another word/image collage says: "Alone. The meaning of survival: what is it?" The image is of a woman walking alone down a tree-lined road (*not shown*). Jackie says she is feeling horrible and overwhelmed. She begins to cry as she again expresses how meaningless life feels without having a sense of real connection with her spiritual center.

She reports a comment her daughter has made about her grandmother (Jackie's mother), who has been sitting for hours at the kitchen table staring out the window in silence, withdrawn and depressed. Her daughter wonders what's wrong. Jackie remembers when she was a child, her mother often sat at the table that way. She realizes that she herself has been doing the same thing in recent months and wonders if there's some connection.

We talk about the possibility of unconscious psychic patterns being handed down, just as physical traits or tendencies to addiction are passed on through our genes. Jackie hates the thought she may be carrying the burden of some of her mother's unresolved issues. She asks, "If I've carried stuff for my mother throughout my life, would or could this be a way of bonding with her—because there was no other way?" *A poignant thought, and perhaps a valuable insight.*

*   *   *

April 11th

Jackie created a collage in which she, represented by a small blue silhouette, is holding out a large red bag of "shit." *(Not shown.)* This symbolizes both what she feels she's received from her mother and her anger about it. She is giving it back to her mother, who is represented by a very large, ominous, black shape. Jackie says she wanted to put a photo of her mother's head on this figure, as she had done in so many previous collages, but she's run out of photographs.

Jackie then tells me of a significant dream she had this week. In it someone stole her money, driver's license, and credit card. She flew into a panic and felt despair; yet, at the same time, another part of her recognized she shouldn't worry and that her panic was disproportionate to the situation.

We discuss this dream image which indicates the ambivalence she is experiencing at this time. On the one hand, she feels robbed of what is most valuable—a sense of self-worth *(symbolized by the money)* and even of her identity—who she thought she was *(driver's license as identification)*. The thief signifies the abusive behavior of her parents who robbed her of a normal childhood. On the other hand, there is another aspect of her psyche—the observing ego that can see the larger picture and is able to reassure the panicked aspect of her that feels violated by the robbery and is afraid.

Dreams are picture-stories that arise from the unconscious and embody truths that our conscious minds defend against. Thus, the calm, observing ego that appears in Jackie's dream reveals a part of her that has developed the capacity to rise above her immediate pain to a level of greater understanding.

Nonetheless, it is the frightened aspect of herself that Jackie is feeling in this session. Her weeping bears witness to the anguish she continues to experience in this spiritual void. As in previous sessions, I encourage her to breathe, to feel all the emotions that are coming up, to acknowledge them, and then let them go. I suggest she use the active imagination process to breathe in light and exhale the tension and fear. Jackie immediately says "Not 'sweetness and light.'" The thought of that makes her "gag." Rather, she envisions the inner light, more accurately, as a powerful energy and she refers to it as "The Force."

As Jackie begins to drop deeper into this breathwork, I speak of her courageous choice to move *through* the Abyss of depression rather than continue to repress her pain. She has been exploring the content of her dreams and allowing herself to inhabit her emotions and release them in her artwork, tears, and other visceral expressions of her outrage. This process has enabled her to clear a space within her entire being that can now embody a new sense of who she is. A full range of emotions will certainly continue to cycle within her throughout life, but as she becomes conscious of what she's feeling, she'll have the capacity to make new choices about how she will respond. At the same time, having released so much of the pain she was identified with, she is experiencing a vacuous sensation that is confusing. The question has become: "If I'm not who I thought I was, who am I?" I tell her that the emptiness she feels is really a receptive space and to remember, as she visualizes inhaling the light, that her deepest core is part of that greater Light and she can choose to align with it at any time.

This has a direct bearing on the longing she has expressed to reconnect with her spiritual center.

Referring back to her dream, I tell Jackie she can keep as a foundation what she valued of her life before the death of her self-image, caused by the flashbacks, and then build for herself a new identity on that base. I encourage her to make some notes to put in key places around her house to remind herself to stand back and observe whatever it is she is feeling. It is a difficult balance: to both feel and witness one's emotions without getting overwhelmed by them. I note that was precisely what she was able to do in her dream.

By the end of the session, it is noticeable that Jackie looks and feels much better. In leaving, she smiles and holds up one arm in an empowered gesture. She says she feels a need to create some kind of sacred altar. I encourage her to follow such intuitive promptings, knowing symbols have the power to affect change within us. *Although the process Jackie has just experienced had nothing to do with any specific religious belief or ritual, her immediate sense of needing to create her own sacred symbol indicates the reality of a meaningful spiritual experience. This is what Carl Jung spoke of: the necessity for an individual to experience a spiritual connection with something larger than oneself in order for healing to be accomplished.*

*   *   *

April 18th

Jackie tells me she really likes what I said last week about how she is now in charge of her life and can choose what her emotional response will be in any situation. I remind her that being conscious enough to choose how one responds is not a superficial decision. Rather, it is an ongoing process in which a person learns to examine, as they rise, issues that have stirred up old, painful experiences. An old pattern of anger may be the initial reaction, but through therapy one gradually learns to more quickly recognize how one's history is influencing their reaction, thereby enabling one to be more present in the current situation.

Jackie then shows me something she brought into the session. It is the paper pattern she made last week to represent herself in the "bag of shit" collage. She says she was somewhat horrified to realize she had unconsciously doodled all over the pattern, filling the entire form (*herself*) with the word "Joy." Her first conscious reaction was "Ugh!" She says last week she also found herself unconsciously doodling hearts.

Jackie describes a dream she had this week: Aliens were taking over people by entering into them etherically, (that is, in some non-physical form or from some dimension above the Earthly realm), which caused the victims to lose their separate identity (*reminiscent of the dream last week in which her wallet was stolen*). One male alien approached her and she stood firm, this time without panic, and said "No" several times. He assured her she would be safe. At first she did not believe him until he handed her a breast plate and shield and said only "Warrior." Then she knew she was safe and strong; the feeling was similar to the empowered stance she had taken just before leaving our last session. Jackie is creating for herself a new, strong, non-victim identity; she says maybe this dream signifies an integration of the masculine and feminine aspects within herself. *I feel Jackie is developing a genuine inner strength.*

A deep emotional shift is bubbling up to the surface, bypassing Jackie's inner censor. At the same time, her conscious mind is suspicious and having difficulty adjusting to a more positive state of mind (just as she was suspicious of the alien in the warrior dream). That creature from outer space who was telling her she is a strong warrior, is an aspect of herself that is truly "alien" to her conscious mind. Jackie has been through this shift once before, i.e., at "The Turning" point in the first segment of her work a year ago; however, having returned to The Abyss, once again it is difficult to make this transition into a positive sense of herself.

*   *   *

April 26th

Today Jackie brings up the Holocaust for the third time. She has been hearing about a Nazi chaser, that is, someone bent on finding Nazi war criminals and bringing them to justice in the international tribunals. She sees that some people want retribution, while others just want to forget and leave their pain behind. Jackie is embroiled in a massive struggle between the part of her that wants to move into love and good feelings (doodling hearts and "joy") and the part that doesn't want to forgive or forget her incest wound.

My feelings are touched as I witness the depth of Jackie's struggle in grappling with this core issue.

*   *   *

May 2nd

Today, for the second time in recent weeks, Jackie says she nearly called to cancel her session. Once again she is feeling she really doesn't need to be here. *As I consider the intensity of the images in her dreams and collages, I suspect this is a bit of self-sabotage from the unconscious.* At Jackie's suggestion we begin with a discussion of trust, particularly of God, but quickly move into processing three dreams she had this past week.

The themes had to do with her rage at the devastation of her family home by the phallus; the need for compassion for the inner aspect of her that nearly died as a child; and a growing ambivalence in her feelings toward her father, that is, they are no longer only rageful. In one dream her father was having a heart attack. Jackie saw his spirit standing outside his body and even the spirit looked dead. She was able to act with compassion as she called for help for him.

This dream is reminiscent of one she described in her second letter from Germany in which her father died and she was trying to get her mother and sister to help, but they were unresponsive. When viewing these other two females in the dream as representing aspects of herself, I can see how these inner images are playing out ambivalent emotions of compassion and indifference that Jackie now feels in regard to her father.

We explore the male and female images in these dreams in more depth. Jackie says the only acceptable male image for her is "Charles." The reason is that she has always imagined him to be outwardly a strong male, but possessing what she feels are the inner feminine qualities of nurturance, non-verbal constancy, and sensitivity to children. We also speak of how obesity can be self-destructive. Jackie wonders why she would be doing that to herself, but at this time she has no answer for her question.

*   *   *

May 9ᵗʰ

Jackie calls the Counseling Center; she is having car trouble and must cancel her session.

*   *   *

May 15ᵗʰ

This week Jackie again cancels the session. I call to check on her because this is very unusual. As I suspected, she says she canceled because she is feeling herself withdrawing into depression again. I tell her perhaps she needs to feel this pain again; perhaps not; she's the only one who can have a sense of that. I remind Jackie that because she has done all this work in therapy—work that she has initiated—she is no longer a victim. She does not have to be ruled by that feeling—she can choose what actions she will take. I tell her to let me know what she wants to do about the next session. She says she is expecting to come next week.

*   *   *

May 23ʳᵈ

When she arrives Jackie tells me that she almost called to cancel again but decided not to.

Since our last session I thought more about what I said on the phone last week about being able to make choices and not being ruled by depression. (*See Appendix # 3 on Depression and Suicidal Ideation.*) Jackie had responded positively when I first broached the idea, yet I've wondered if she might have felt criticized, even though that wasn't the spirit in which I said it. I decide to ask her how she felt about that concept because, in case it made her angry, I want to give her an opportunity to express those feelings. On the contrary, she says, her feeling was one of relief because there was no judgment from me, as she thought there might be. Once again, I tell her I *really* don't know what's right for her at any given time. Perhaps there was something important she would learn from a longer experience of the depression. However, now when she sees she's holding herself back, she can consciously recognize that this *action* is a choice made because she's *feeling* depressed. Again Jackie responds well to this idea, because she senses it is empowering and will help her be more conscious of the connection between her emotions and her actions.

Jackie tells me about many instances when she was growing up in which she felt her mother was in competition with her. She sees how, even now, she often holds herself back rather than shine in comparison to anyone else. She also notes various ways in which she acts like her mother: sitting at the kitchen table, withdrawing into depression, taking an antidepressant recently, and feeling suicidal at times. Here is that insight again. I recall that about 6 weeks ago (April 4ᵗʰ), Jackie made the connection that her depressive symptoms were possibly the only way she could bond with her mother. Now she begins to see that it's imperative for her to do the work needed to separate from those old patterns. She also feels that the need for an anti-depressant medication may be linked to "a change-of-life hormonal shift." *Jackie hasn't mentioned taking medication for a long time.*

*   *   *

May 30ᵗʰ

Jackie relates a dream she had in the past week in which an innocent young woman was killed by her mother. She gasped as she saw the mother's face and recognized an expression of "pure evil." Jackie tells me that she and both her siblings have talked about how they all were aware of what they called "the look" their mother would give them—a kind of "evil eye" expression that her brother said would "go right through you." Jackie says she and her brother would often get blamed for things, but inexplicably, their younger sister was exempt from such treatment.

I ask Jackie if she thinks her mother was aware of the incest. She says it seems likely, but ever since she confronted her parents with those memories, her mother has denied it. In any case, Jackie tells me that she believes her dream of the woman killing her daughter expresses how her mother must have felt about her. Again I speak of how that destructive mother image became integrated into Jackie in the form of self-destructive behaviors, and now by holding herself back in life, in over-eating, and having suicidal thoughts, she seems to be acting out her mother's apparent wish to get rid of her.

Once again, Jackie says she is horrified by the thought she might be "doing the dirty work," so to speak, for her sick mother. I remind her that having brought this into conscious awareness, she can either continue this self-abusive behavior, or begin to value herself and create a joyful, meaningful, and loving life. She says that, in this moment, she feels like crawling into a small, dark place. *The safe black again.* I tell Jackie that she can choose to do so, but I see the fact that she has returned to do more healing as evidence that she has all the courage and strength she needs to create the kind of life she wants: the three issues she articulated for resuming this work. I suggest she put a picture of a giant on her fridge as a reminder of her inner strength.

Jackie says one time, before her flashbacks began, she said to her mother that she felt she had been sacrificed *to* her father and *for* her mother. Her mother had agreed on both accounts, and Jackie found that response to be strange and inexplicable. She believes it's very likely that her mother was jealous of her sexually. *It would appear that, as oldest child, Jackie was the scapegoat of the family, and the sacrifice of her may have protected her younger siblings from such abuse.*

However, Jackie says her sister once told her that she, too, had memories—in her case, of being molested by their mother. She was very young at the time and her memories were understandably vague, yet because of them she never wanted to be around their mother or to be alone with her. However, several years ago, when Jackie revealed *her* memories, she was deeply hurt by her sister's reaction. Her sister did an about-face, saying that her own memories must have been imagined. She repudiated Jackie, began to develop a good relationship with their parents, and to defend them from Jackie's accusations of incest. Jackie has been unable to forgive her sister for this, for it feels like a profound betrayal. *She had referred to the rift between them early in our work.*

*   *   *

June 5ᵗʰ

Jackie brings in a powerful dream image in which her eyes were bleeding. In order to glean her associations to it, I ask her a series of open-ended questions. After a few minutes, Jackie says she hates being questioned this way. I immediately stop and ask what she would like to do instead: breathwork? artwork? talk of something else? She decides to do some breathwork.

We begin with a relaxation process and this immediately takes her to a deeper level of emotion. As we work with the breath, she tells me about a TV show she watched this past week in which the theme was incest. In the story, the mother of the incest victim was aware of what had happened to her daughter but hadn't protected her. The mother later acknowledged her behavior and didn't want to be hated by her daughter due to the inept way in which she had handled that abusive situation. As Jackie relates this story, she gets short of breath as an underlying panic begins to surface and she constricts with fear. She says she didn't feel short of breath while watching the show on TV, and wonders why she is experiencing it now. I suggest the reason is that in this moment it is *her* story, and it's *her* mother.

Jackie says that this week she has felt the magnitude and intensity of her hate for her mother more than she ever has before. She says she's tired of still having to deal with "all this old wounded-child shit." I ask what she would like to do with it. She tells me she would blow it up. I ask how: like a volcano or with dynamite? "Dynamite." Why? She says because then she would have the power and control over when it was done, how powerful to make the explosive, and so on. But, she says, it would be important to have a long fuse so she would not also be blown up. *I feel her comment about the long fuse is very important because it indicates part of her really does not want to hurt herself, even though she says that yesterday she was again feeling suicidal.*

She tells me that during that dark fantasy she had thoughts of driving into on-coming traffic but didn't because she didn't want to hurt others. Jackie says that if she ever has a real accident, she would want her children and friends to know it wasn't suicide. If she were to commit suicide, she's not sure if she would want people to know. I ask what message her suicide would give to her children? She says she thinks that they would feel she killed herself because she didn't think they were worth living for. I suggest this is also the message she is giving to herself: she's abandoning her own life/Self because *she* feels she's not worth it. Jackie's response, in this moment, is that life is not worth it. I tell her: "That's a cop-out; you *are* that life."[56]

*   *   *

June 13th

I begin our session by asking Jackie why my questioning her about her dream last week was so upsetting. She says that a series of questions like that reminded her of her father's constant questioning about the housework she did when she was young. She would do the cleaning in a very meticulous way, as required; then he would come home from work and ask if she had done it. When Jackie would affirm that she had, indeed, completed everything, her father would contradict her, run his hand over the most obscure surfaces as if with a white glove (such as the ledge of woodwork above a doorway) and insist she do everything again. *This kind of domination and control of a child is typical in an abusive family.*

---

[56] *In my years of practice, I have seen the loved ones (particularly children) of persons who commit suicide are often left with the feeling that something is wrong or inadequate about them, for several reasons. They may believe that the person who died did not care enough about them to want to live or that person committed suicide in reaction to something they did or did not do. The survivor may also be left feeling totally inadequate or helpless to have done anything to save the one they loved. I have often seen that many who are bereaved experience the suicide of a loved one, not only as a deep and unresolvable grief, but also as a profound blow to their sense of self-worth, and that loss becomes a burden some carry throughout their lives.*

I then ask how she felt when I immediately stopped asking her questions when she said she was disturbed by them, and let her choose how she wanted to proceed. Jackie says, with emphasis, that she was "*so relieved*" when that process stopped, and that it hadn't occurred to her she could ask. I remind her that this is her therapy and she is in charge; my function is to help her become aware of some possible alternatives and to support her as she finds her way to her own answers. Jackie says both this week and last she has had a migraine headache during the art therapy sessions, indicating she is feeling a lot of tension and anxiety as we proceed with this work, and yet she continues.

*   *   *

June 20th

This week there was a family gathering—a surprise party for Jackie's brother. Jackie spoke with her sister-in-law who told her that Jackie's mother asked why they invited Jackie. Their answer was that they had a relationship with her; her mother's response was: "Why?" *(since they have been estranged since she confronted them with her memories two years ago).* Knowing that Jackie would be there, her parents decided not to attend the party for their son. Jackie had been invited before, but never went because she was uncomfortable knowing her parents would be there. Now as she is feeling a greater degree of self-assurance, she is able to go to the party. She tells me she is glad that this time it is her parents who are uncomfortable, rather than herself. Jackie's sister was at the party, but she says they did not make any eye contact.

Jackie brings in a collage she created yesterday. The main element is a face in the center of a full red rose and she feels the expression on that face is evil. Jackie is surprised when I note it's a woman's face because she had not associated "woman" and "evil" consciously while making this image. Then she says that as a child, she always felt like Cinderella; that is, she was in a cruel family that devalued her and made her do all the housework in a demeaning way. In Jackie's case, the evil step-mother was her own mother. She says the greatest evil she has known is actually in the feminine; that her mother was "malevolent in a way that even my dad's incest wasn't." *As I think about the fairytale Jackie just mentioned, it occurs to me that both she and Cinderella were left unprotected. Although it was the long absence of Cinderella's father that left her vulnerable to the malicious whims of her evil step-mother; by contrast, in Jackie's situation, she was vulnerable to the abuse of both her parents.*

Jackie says if a man had the qualities she always imagined Charles to have, that is, someone who valued her and was supportive and fun-loving, he would be her prince. I ask if she values herself. Her response is "Sometimes, no." I tell her if she doesn't honor her own being, how will "the prince" ever recognize her as kindred and as someone with whom he would like to share his life? *The positive male she has created internally has helped her cope with the destructive influence of her father.* As she gets up to go, Jackie comments that she didn't come with a headache today, but she's leaving with one, and she's able to laugh at herself, recognizing how her body is reflecting the stress she's feeling as she deals with the issue of evil on a personal level.

.

Fig. 32 "LIVING GODDESS IN GOLD"

Woman's inner beauty, previously represented only by cold, lifeless statues, has now come fully to life, and both she and the barren wasteland are a radiant, golden hue. She is becoming aware of the need for balance between the feminine and masculine aspects of her psyche, symbolized by the mountains and sunflower.

Fig. 32 "LIVING GODDESS IN GOLD"   6/25/91

A beautiful woman, in flowing robes, faces the mountains; a mature sunflower full of seeds is above her head and all these elements are bathed in a golden light. Symbolically, sun and sky are often seen to represent the masculine; moon and earth—the feminine. In this image, the sunflower and mountains are of equal size.

June 27th

This morning, Jackie tells me, she began to get a bad headache just after awakening and only then did she remember that her art therapy session would be this afternoon. Jackie also acknowledges that, once again, she almost called last week to cancel her session, but then changed her mind. *A powerful inner conflict: first dealing with the issue of the Shadow side of the feminine nature in general, then to the evil she experienced in her mother, and especially, to the potential for that within herself. In recent weeks, Jackie has sufficiently overcome her resistance so that she was able to get to the art therapy sessions, but that tension is being rerouted into her body, causing headaches.*

This collage is one of eight that Jackie has brought in today. Eight! She comments that she was "a collaging fool" this week! She is no longer incorporating words into her collages, as she had been doing since going to Germany. She says it feels good to be back to images-only, allowing the power of them to stand on their own. *I recall that before Jackie left for Europe, she said she wanted to be part of a survivors' exhibit in order to encourage others to do their own healing work. She then asked how to frame her collages so that the rough, torn edges would not be cut off. Jackie deliberately chose to work on that industrial weight paper with its torn edges to emphasize her pain. Now I note that since resuming her art therapy, Jackie has been creating these collages on fine quality drawing paper. This suggests she is moving away from that wounded victim stance and from the very brown paper for which she was anxious to return home.*

I think it would be beneficial at some time to explore with Jackie what she feels is the significance of her return to images-only. However, because she has brought in so many collages today, we don't have time to pursue that issue.[57]

Feeling "overwhelmed" by the thought of really claiming her own authentic strength and beauty, Jackie tells me that while working on this collage, the urge to decapitate the goddess came to her again. However, she overcame that impulse, and so the radiant woman, representing herself, remains intact. Also while creating this image, Jackie noticed the farthest mountain has a soft, breast-like form, and for that reason she almost cut it out of the picture *another way to express her anger and self-loathing, and to disparage her femininity.* However, she changed her mind and decided to leave it in. The sunflower, representing masculine energies, was a conscious choice, and now she likes its balance with the feminine elements.

I feel that the beautiful golden woman represents Jackie's essential core. Each time she refuses to decapitate or otherwise mutilate the feminine in these symbolic images, as she had done in the early collages, she takes another step toward honoring her Self.

A second collage is all black and white (*not shown*). It includes images of two temples on the acropolis of ancient Greece: the Parthenon, and the Caryatid Porch of another temple in which female figures form

---

[57] *Words are typically a more rational means of expression and, at times, may be used to distance oneself from the impact of emotions. Literature, especially poetry, is generally an exception to this. On the other hand, once a person has gotten in touch with the emotions (often by accessing the inner images), words can then serve to bring those feelings into conscious awareness where they can be integrated.*

the support columns for its roof. On the left of this collage is a line of innocent looking young choir girls, and to their right, a woman who stands facing right, wearing long flowing robes. Her arms are outstretched to each side as she holds a black veil that drapes across her face. Jackie says this woman feels strong and militant to her, reflecting those feelings in herself. In order to non-verbally express a different impression I have of that woman, I stand in the same position with a scarf over my face. In seeing this it becomes clear to Jackie that the woman has taken a very open stance in which she would be vulnerable because she is covering her own face, which would keep her from seeing clearly where she is going or what is happening right in front of her.

The posture of the woman just described is very similar to that of the golden goddess (Fig. 31) except in this collage the woman's face is covered. This difference illustrates a point Jackie feels is important. She says she now realizes how much women, in our time and culture, disown their own uniquely feminine power, and she remembers describing the face of a woman in a previous collage as "evil." I sense there may be a connection between those two observations. That is, if we disparage what is strong and healthy in us, perhaps that is the "evil" we do to ourselves, because that attitude diminishes our sense of self-worth, circumscribes our thinking, and prevents us from sharing our gifts with the world.

Of the many collages Jackie has brought in today, another seems of particular significance. (*This was one of the harder choices of images that cannot be shown due to space limitations*). It is an image of a contemporary house with ancient Greek style ionic columns on either side of the door and a courtyard that has a pool in the center. It is winter, the trees appear dead, and a small window on either side of the doorway has lattice that suggests prison bars. A key figure over the door is a radiant, golden angel who is holding up a barely visible sign that says "Amor—Charitas." Jackie tells me that she had not seen the sign until I mentioned it. In the foreground is a bird of many colors and on the left, dressed in black, a mother holding her son. Jackie has decapitated the mother. She says she almost censored her impulse to do that, wondering what I might say about it, but then went ahead and did it. I tell her I'm glad she created the image in the way she felt to do it, without concern for any opinion of mine.

Jackie has slipped back into self-deprecation in the collage where the woman was draping her own face with black, and in this image her old rage at her mother has again been expressed by the decapitation. At the same time, she was not aware she chose the image of a house where a radiant angel holds a banner of Love above the threshold. Two messages, one conscious: the rage at her mother, one unconscious: a heralding of the love and good feelings she is moving into.

*   *   *

July 4ᵗʰ

Jackie brings in four new collages today but before discussing them she begins by telling me that when her son saw the final collage we discussed last week, he did not seem to notice the mother had no head; however, he said the boy she held should be "put in the water to look like he is floating dead." He did not explain his comment. Her son will be getting married in two weeks and recently has called Jackie several times just to see how she is. Jackie says that she has expressed incredulity to him because this much initiation of contact on his part is unusual. She wants to rein in this reaction so he doesn't become self-conscious and turn away. I agree. His behavior indicates his need for more connection with his mother before getting married.

Jackie remembers how, when her children were young, she would do a modified inspection tour of their chores, similar to what her dad had done with her, and that at times she yelled at her kids a lot. *This is an important and honest acknowledgment. The wounds of the past, when they have not been processed and resolved, may likely get carried forward to the next generation. I wonder if the memory of those inspections are behind her son's comment about the boy in the collage, or if perhaps he is feeling the boy within him is dying now that he's getting married.*

Considering the fact that Jackie equates her own mother with evil, the symbolic decapitation of the mother in last week's collage may have been her way of negating that influence in her life. In that case, the beheading represented a safe and needed expression of anger at someone who wounded her. The positive indications of continued healing include not decapitating the younger golden woman (Fig. 31) who symbolized herself, the pool in the courtyard representing the waters of cleansing and life, and the angel holding a banner proclaiming "love."

Here I see another example of how Jackie's collages spontaneously "speak to her" of things present within her, of which she is often not conscious at the time the images are made.

*   *   *

Fig. 33   "RETURN FROM THE ABYSS"

Balanced rather precariously and appearing androgynous, Woman picks her way back from the barren rock wasteland toward vegetation, color, the Tree of Life, and new growth and psychic integration within herself.

Fig. 33 "RETURN FROM THE ABYSS" 7/2/91

A figure, seen from behind, has short hair and is wearing pants and carries a man's hat and rolled umbrella. However, the coat is that of a woman, so it is unclear if this is a male or female.

July 4th (continued)

In this image, Jackie shows a person carefully traversing a wasteland of boulders, moving toward rolling hills of grass and a golden sky. She associates the tree with her visualizations of a great tree that has always been the safe haven that sheltered her inner children. Jackie comments: "this person is returning to life with masculine and feminine energies more integrated."

How perfectly this image mirrors Jackie's situation as she is now moving out of the depths of her depression, toward a revitalized and more integrated life.

Because the image seems so timely, I ask Jackie if she would stand in the same position as the figure in her collage to see how it feels. She follows my suggestion and says it feels unstable and also a bit like she's bowing. Yes, I sense one must take each step of this return reverently and mindfully. One could so easily fall back into the darkness.

When she resumed her work in art therapy four months ago, one of Jackie's specific goals was to develop a feeling of personal empowerment as a woman, and she talks about that again today. Recently I had said that I felt a lot of potential power, that is, inner strength, in her. During the week she remembered that when she heard those words she had recoiled inwardly, and said to herself: "That's not me." She tells me she now realizes her unspoken thought was another instance of disowning her power or strength of character. She can see how insidious and pervasive is the attitude of disparaging the power of her feminine nature—even within herself.

*   *   *

July 11th

As we begin, Jackie says she's again feeling like a failure because she's slipped back into depression, has had to return to therapy, and needs an antidepressant in order to cope with her emotions. She also realizes her anger is a defense, a protection, and she's afraid if she lets go of it she'll be vulnerable. On the other hand, Jackie says, if she can't release her anger, she'll feel she's weak or even bad. Feeling overwhelmed by her contradictory emotions, she breaks down and sobs.

After a few minutes, when she has regained her composure, we continue and once again, Jackie struggles with the feeling that her own mother is "the embodiment of evil." Then, for the first time, she tells me how her mother had been deeply wounded as a child. *As I hear of those significant early traumas, it occurs to me that Jackie's mother probably experienced what the shamans describe as a "loss of soul" which may result from the abuse, neglect, or abandonment of a child (or even from serious trauma as an adult.) If that were so, it's likely her mother became very angry and depressed because she was cut off from her own emotional and spiritual roots.*

As I listen, Jackie says she can see in my eyes compassion for her mother's childhood pain that contributed to her later illness. She says initially she had also felt compassion for her. However, since the flashbacks and memory of her mother's abuse and lack of protection, she can no longer feel any empathy. Jackie says that recognizing the dark side of the feminine nature "out there, distanced from her own life, is one thing; but it shouldn't be *her mother*."

As the session draws to a close, Jackie makes another important comment in regard to her rage at her mother. Even as she recognizes it has kept her from feeling vulnerable, she says, "But if I can't have compassion on her, can I have compassion on myself?"[58] *We do not have time today to examine what connection Jackie might find between herself and her mother. It seems to me that neither of these women experienced real mothering. But with Jackie's parting comment about compassion, I sense she is getting close to a breakthrough in her healing.*

---

[58] *When a person deliberately and maliciously hurts another, that action always arises from the abuser's own unhealed wounds—out of brute strength and repressed rage, not from any strength of character. Due to abusive childhood experiences, severe depression, and other psychological disturbances, her mother's personality developed in a painfully distorted way. As a result, Jackie's mother did not have the inner strength to be the kind of loving, protective presence that every child needs. In order to heal, Jackie must change that old destructive pattern and begin to love and nurture herself—to give herself what she did not receive in childhood from her parents. If, in the course of her inner work, Jackie comes to genuinely feel compassion for her mother, it will signify that she has come to a place of acceptance of her own Shadow aspect, which would enable her to accept her mother's Shadow.*

The more we learn about the interconnectedness of all life, from the study of quantum physics to learning about the bio-magnetic energy fields in and around all beings, the more we recognize the truth of the Golden Rule: "Do unto others as you would have them do unto you." In fact, the experience of complete oneness with all life that has been reported by mystics and by those who have had near-death experiences, seems to indicate that one could more accurately say: "Whatever you do unto others, you do unto yourself." Through the process of healing old wounds we come to know that it is in our own best interest to behave in a way that is also in the best interest of others.

Fig. 34 "WOMAN'S INNER RAGE"

Woman is pensive and wears a cross around her neck as she considers the next level of work in her healing. Inner Child has been bitterly angry at both God and her mother for not protecting her from the abuse. Now Woman is embarking on a quest to see if she can revitalize her previous connection with her own spiritual core by healing another aspect of her rage.

FIG. 34 "WOMAN'S INNER RAGE" 7/18/91

A woman, whose long hair hangs down over her shoulders, is dressed in peasant clothes with her sleeves rolled up for work. A cross hangs from a cord around her neck. Behind her, protected by medieval armor, is a sculpture of a raging female warrior. This is Athena, goddess of war. On her breast-plate is a small representation of the head of the gorgon Medusa.

July 18th

The woman on the right side of this collage is described by Jackie as "pensive" and the figure behind her as "enraged." Jackie says that, while she was putting this collage together, it was very important for her to make a slight separation between the two, along the top edge. She questions if the angry woman in the collage is a part of herself, or if it represents her mother; and then says perhaps both are true. *Because Jackie does not want to be identified with her mother, her question indicates why she felt a need for at least a little separation between the two figures in the collage. However, the degree to which they are still connected suggests she has more work to do on this essential maternal issue. From my perspective, this collage perfectly symbolizes the need to reflect on and resolve the internalized rage that is "behind" one in the unconscious. When not acknowledged, repressed rage often results in disturbing physical, emotional, mental, or spiritual problems.*

Jackie says she's noticed recently, as we work on her feelings about the feminine Shadow, that she doesn't think about the sessions during the intervening weeks, as she always did when working on the male/incest issues previously. However, her body continues to register emotional and somatic symptoms of her tension including headaches, nausea, clenching teeth during sleep, and crying at the sound of a friend's voice on the phone.

Jackie is now fully engaged in a confrontation with the raging warrior within herself. It involves a conscious examination of her anger and of what purpose it has served. This week she saw a movie that triggered a feeling that a mother's own experience of abuse is no excuse for her not to protect her children from that same trauma. We had spoken of the concept of forgiveness last year. Today she says she's not even considering forgiving her parents.
There are three reasons I can think of that would cause Jackie to feel this way. First, she is still caught in a common misconception that to "forgive" means that the abuse she experienced was acceptable behavior and that the abusers bears no responsibility for their actions. Clearly, this is not true. Second, feeling angry gives her a sense of being strong and invulnerable; and third, she is not yet ready to let go of her rage, which has become a part of her identity.

Jackie wonders why she has always been aware of the dark male energy (Alfred), but except for her mother, she has not otherwise been aware of the dark feminine until recently. I ask her what the difference is between the two. She responds, "their sex," and with that comment she realizes that in seeing only the male as evil, she has distanced it from herself. In her struggle to come to terms with the malevolence of her mother, Jackie now states she feels that disowning her own feminine strength, and also projecting what she sees as "evil" only onto others and not finding the potential for the same within herself, is itself evil. *Another important insight.*

She says perhaps the "dark mother" is the shadow side of the "goddess," in the same way that Alfred is the dark side of Charles. Recognizing the dark and the light as two sides of the same archetypal pattern, she now says, "If I'm going to find the goddess in me, I guess I'll also have to claim the dark mother."

In seeking "the goddess" in herself, Jackie is now ready to acknowledge there is goodness and beauty in her, not just a shamed and raging victim. At the same time, she is also owning her Shadow side: her angry wish for vengeance on her parents. In accepting that both goodness and rage are aspects of herself (like the balance of opposites in the ancient Chinese yin/yang symbol), she is moving out of the state of helpless victim. Now she is entering into an honest and empowered stance in which there is the potential for integration of all aspects of her being and, therefore, authentic healing. Jackie has taken another essential step forward.

I am reminded of her statement at the end of our last session about needing to have compassion for her mother so she could have compassion for herself. I suggest the reverse of that statement might be more appropriate. That is, when she can acknowledge her own weaknesses and aggressive tendencies and have compassion on herself for not being perfect, she will no longer be torn apart by the struggle to deny the aggressive energies of her own human nature. From that place of inner peace there arises a genuine love and respect for one's Self. Her personal experience in this regard will enable her to understand and empathize with the wounded child within any abusing adult, even her mother, who is acting out of fear and covering insecurity with abusive behavior.

Forgiveness is a word charged with many meanings by people with different perspectives and experiences. I find compassion to be a better word, for they both imply a lack of vengeful judgment.

Fig. 35   "THE PINK AND BLUE POLKA-DOT MONSTER"

Woman has a dream; it tells her that the monster from the deep is no longer a threat to her. She is able to move with it through the healing waters of the unconscious deep—and even extend to it some nourishment or a peace offering.

Fig. 35 "THE PINK AND BLUE POLKA-DOT MONSTER"   7/25/91

This drawing illustrates a dream in which a woman is standing on the back of a deep sea monster and is feeding it something. Two concentric circles are to the right.

July 25th

Jackie reports a dream: A woman, dressed in a white flowing toga, is riding confidently on the back of an ocean monster. That fearsome creature is long and snake-like, pink in color with blue spots. Jackie, as observer in the dream, is afraid the woman will be hurt. The monster turns its head to face the woman, and Jackie feels even more terrified, fearing she will surely be eaten. Then the woman feeds it some kind of round white "pill." Jackie says it's neither food, a pain killer, nor a tranquillizer. In fact, she's not sure what it is, but apparently it's something the monster needs. The "pill" has a raised center suggesting to her both sun and womb.

In dreams, the ocean is generally seen to symbolize the unconscious—the vast unplumbed depths beneath the surface of one's psyche. The monster represents the contents of the unconscious.

Jackie draws a picture of her dream, and it immediately becomes apparent that this leviathan from the deep is no longer any real threat. It is childlike: pink with blue polka-dots. Jackie realizes this dream is saying that in her deep, unconscious feelings she is no longer afraid of the snake-like *(sexual)* inner monster that had terrified her when she began the therapy process. In riding on its back and feeding it, she is now in control. *This dream image suggests that, through her therapy, Jackie is now able to own her deepest fears and can nourish that part of herself with confidence and compassion. I mention that the boy/girl colors and her associations of sun and womb are yet more indications of a continued integration of the masculine and feminine aspects within herself. Jackie jokingly says "it pisses her off" that I see meaningful things in her collages that she hadn't recognized in them, and it always surprises her.*

It's interesting to note that while Jackie has generally used food, and also at times an antidepressant, to numb her emotional turmoil, her feeling about this dream is that the woman is giving the monster neither food nor a pain killer. Her associations to it suggest the spiritual realm (sun) or a new beginning within herself (womb). Based in my own history, the small round white object that is being fed to the monster suggests a sacred host. I feel this association is relevant because in my experience, having a meaningful spiritual connection is necessary in any healing process (not necessarily involving a particular religion.)

With a smile, Jackie tells me this week that she got her headache one day early, and so today it's better. She also comments that if this morning's dream really indicates she's made peace with the "monster" within her, maybe she won't get any more headaches in this process.

Another dream she had suggests to her the possibility of a reconciliation with her sister. And a collage done this week *(not shown)* includes pictures of Aboriginal cave paintings including men and women, and women giving birth—*an interesting correspondence with her association to womb in her drawing of the deep sea monster dream.*

August 1ˢᵗ

This week Jackie made a collage (*not shown*). Her comment about a woman in it reflects her increasingly positive feelings about herself: she describes the woman as "content" and as "someone with a strong presence—like she knows something."

Then she relates the following experience to me: while at home alone, Jackie decided to do an Active Imagination process in order to "call forth the goddess," that is, to experience on a deep feeling level, her own beauty and strength. She tells me that in her mind's eye she pictured herself as that strong woman in the collage encircled by mountains—an image that always feels safe to her. She stated her intention to feel the presence of the goddess, and then spontaneously decided to also call forth the "dark mother." Instantly, she was startled by an unexpected image of a "cosmically huge" black figure that towered over her. She said the figure represented "pure evil" and it really terrified her. She gasped and quickly put her mind on something more positive. The goddess (good mother) never appeared. I ask Jackie to draw a picture of that powerful experience. When she completes the drawing (*not shown*), she puts her hand over the tiny stick figure representing herself. I ask what her hand is doing in that gesture, and she responds that as she looks at the drawing, she feels a need to protect herself from that enormous threatening presence. *Two weeks ago, Jackie had said that she needed to own both the goddess and the dark mother within herself. What she has brought in today, the collage and the Active Imagination experience, indicate she is now willing to be conscious of the potential for both extremes of good and evil that coexist within her (as they do within everyone), yet the emotional impact of the spontaneous development scared her.*

*   *   *

August 8ᵗʰ

In a dream this week, Jackie saw herself in a forest wearing an orange sweater with jewels in it; this sweater reminded her of her mother. There were men in the trees (dark-skinned like her father), and she had something they wanted. I reverse the situation, asking what she had that her mother wanted; she says tearfully, "My dad." *Jackie's unconscious mind has formed a dream-symbol showing how she was a stand-in for her mother, and that her father wanted her. Appropriately enough, in some Eastern philosophies orange is the color associated with the second chakra located in the belly, which is the center of sexual energy—and—her orange sweater had jewels in it!*

In another dream, Jackie finds there is a mutual attraction between herself and a man. She is surprised that he likes her despite her weight.

In recent weeks, Jackie has expressed much anger, self-loathing, and shame about her excessive weight. At this time, her feelings about her size are as painful to her as the feelings she had regarding the incest. She says the wound from her father was more impersonal, and so her anger got projected out onto the male species in general. However, with her mother, the wound was more personal, and so her rage has been internalized, as witnessed by her self-loathing and abusive over-eating.

This week, Jackie's son got married; he and his bride eloped on a cruise ship. Jackie says she's surprised at the amount of grief she feels because "he was never a mama's boy." A wedding dinner will be held in a few weeks.

*   *   *

August 15ᵗʰ

As we begin, Jackie says she didn't do any collages this week and could barely remember having any dreams. A notable exception was one in which, she says, good and evil were being explained to her. In the dream she thought, "Oh, yeah, that makes sense," but when she awoke she couldn't remember the explanation. *Her dream has brought forth an answer to one of the core questions she has been struggling with in this second phase of her therapy. However, as often happens, the conscious mind cannot grasp and hold onto the meaning of the dream. This experience is frustrating to the waking mind, but it does not negate the fact that the understanding is, nonetheless, held within the maturing psyche on some deeper level. That new insight can then begin to affect the dreamer's waking perceptions of the world in subtle, but powerful ways.*

In this session, we do breathwork to "go within," as Jackie says, more deeply and process the image of the "pure-evil, dark mother" who arose so powerfully in her Active Imagination process at home two weeks ago. Once again she creates an internal image of the dark side of the feminine nature: it is overwhelmingly large as before. Jackie immediately gets tense and feels she can't breathe. In her visualization, she begins to shrink to about half her size and tearfully realizes that in diminishing herself, she is able to breathe more easily. She tells me she recognizes a parallel in her life; that is, when she holds herself back and doesn't claim her real strength, she feels safer and is more comfortable. By allowing herself to slip into the Abyss of self-denigrating depression, she has continued to give authority over her life to those who had abused her in her youth. Now Jackie says, "It shouldn't be like that."

As our session continues, she feels a need to confront the dark mother. Gradually, Jackie visualizes herself growing tall again until she can see the huge face that was looming above her. The dark mother says only, "I am you, and you are me." Then this ominous figure begins to shrink until there is nothing left of her but a black cape on the floor *strikingly like the wicked witch of the West in the Wizard of Oz.* Jackie is completely surprised and shocked by this spontaneous turn of events and says she doesn't understand what it means.

I suggest that in growing tall and confronting the "dark mother" face to face, it is as if she has looked into a mirror and found the same potential in herself to hurt others. In doing this, the possible threat others present is no longer overwhelmingly frightening, and the "evil mother" outside of her has lost all her power and simply melted away. I note that, in the process of integrating her own capacity to do harm, Jackie's internal image of herself did not become dark or evil; she is relieved to recognize this is so.

I comment that accepting one's own Shadow does not mean an individual no longer gets angry, fearful, jealous, and so on. Rather, it means that in becoming more conscious of those feelings in oneself, they will not be unconsciously projected onto others, seeing only evil in them, and exclusively goodness and righteousness in oneself. This is an ongoing process in life, requiring a great deal of honesty, courage, and sincerity.

Just two weeks ago Jackie had said, "If I'm going to meet the goddess inside, I guess I'll also have to find the dark mother in me." The experience today was a real breakthrough for her, demonstrating she has now begun that process in earnest.

*   *   *

August 22nd

Two collages were created this week, (not shown) both suggest the rebirth of a healthy woman. First, a nude woman who isn't felt by Jackie to be vulnerable, is seen from behind, emerging out of tidal pools at the shore. In the second, a woman rises out of water into a field of wild flowers.

In the week since her breakthrough experience of the integration of the "dark mother," Jackie has had several dreams in which she was having a positive relationship with a man. In the most significant one, a man reaches around her from behind to hug her. She thinks he will be turned off by her weight, but he's not. He says they're married, and he had lost her, but now he's glad he's found her again. They lie down together, and she is amazed she's married.

This latter dream reminds me of what C.G. Jung spoke of as the "coniunctio"[59] or sacred marriage of the masculine and feminine aspects of one's own psyche, which represents an important step in the inner healing and integration process.

Jackie says she's amazed and can't understand what's happened this week. In addition to those positive dreams of men she's had, she also realizes she's starting to develop a tentative, but increasingly sensual, image of herself as a woman. She feels there's a connection between those feelings and her experience of integrating the "dark mother" last week, but doesn't understand the relationship between these two phenomena.

I suggest a possible explanation. That is, the integration of the "dark mother" is an act of claiming her own power. That power is both her positive strength as well as her rage; this latter she had previously felt to be overwhelming and so until recent years had denied and repressed it. Now that she has begun to accept her own strength and self-worth, she no longer feels overly vulnerable and victimized by men or their strength, and can now deal with them as an equal. She's also gotten her old job back and has begun to work again.

Jackie has never consulted with me about taking medication, but has been seeing her psychiatrist for it. Today she tells me that for some weeks she has been cutting down on her anti-depressant medication, and two weeks ago she stopped taking it altogether. Now, as a result, she finds she is much more keenly in touch with her emotions. This week, everything sentimental is touching her heart and making her cry. Jackie says it's been a bit disturbing, but, nonetheless, she feels it's a good sign. Jackie tells me she now realizes her depression was caused primarily by her emotional problems rather than by a hormonal imbalance, as she had previously believed. She knows this because she has found that in effectively dealing

---

[59]Jung, C.G. *The Collected Works of C.G. Jung.* Vol. 14, "Mysterium Coniunctionis"

[60] *I've often heard people on the psychiatric units of hospitals where I worked say their depression is caused by a chemical imbalance in their brain. This is true; however, it implies one is helpless to do anything about it except take medication. In my years of studying healing methods based on working with the energy fields of the body, I've learned that negative emotional states due to trauma, stress, or other situations are often the underlying cause of those imbalances in the brain chemistry.*

There is a growing body of information from the medical community that also demonstrates how positive thoughts, emotions, visualizations, and various types of bodywork and energy healing processes can contribute significantly to the healing process, often without the need for medication. Each person needs to do whatever they feel is effective for them.

with her emotional issues in therapy, she has now been able to get off the medication and yet, in doing so, she has not gotten more depressed again. *I'm interested to hear Jackie describe this experience. While I recognize individual differences and needs in regard to antidepressant medications, her experience corroborates my basic perspective on this issue, although we have never discussed it.*[60]

*   *   *

In the early 20th century, Carl Jung, MD, was the first to explore and use art and inner visualizations to aid the healing of psychological, emotional, and spiritual problems. Since his visionary beginnings, many other medical doctors have incorporated complementary healing processes in their medical or psychiatric practices. A small sampling of some of the earliest include: Elizabeth Kübler-Ross, Bernie Siegel, Stanislav Grof, Richard Gerber, Christiane Northrup, W. Brugh Joy, O. Carl Simonton, John Weir Perry, and Richard Moss.

Fig. 36   "SHIPWRECKED DREAMS"

A mature woman, no longer the naively optimistic bride who was filled with hope and romance, now looks back and wonders about the path her life has taken, what the meaning of it all may be, and considers the possibility of a relationship again.

Fig. 36 "SHIPWRECKED DREAMS" 8/29/91

A beautiful woman, stylish and well-groomed, has a pensive expression. She appears to be thinking about something, or remembering. Behind her, separated by a wire fence, is a couple in close embrace, kissing. In the foreground is a sailboat model, grounded. The woman is in color, while the couple, as if in the woman's memory, are in black and white.

August 29ᵗʰ

In recent weeks, Jackie has been arriving about 10 minutes late for each session, whereas previously she had always been prompt. She tells me it's also been happening at work, and in that case it feels like being a rebellious adolescent. However, she says it's different here, and she can't imagine why she wouldn't be on time for her art therapy appointments. Yesterday she told a friend she had so much to tell me she'd probably never want to leave; yet she arrived late again. She says her feeling about not being on time for therapy is more like being a naughty child and that the feeling is internal—not a message from me. I ask if I am reminding her of her mother somehow. Tearfully, she says, "I don't want to think so, but probably, yes." Jackie hates this and feels she should be finished with "all this painful mother-daughter stuff." I respond that although she has owned *her* dark feminine side, she still has a raging anger against her mother, which she acknowledges is true. I suggest it might be beneficial for us to pursue this in a later session, when we have enough time for in-depth breathwork. Jackie agrees, and so for now we just talk about that relationship.

Once again, Jackie has been feeling much anger, self-loathing, and shame about her size; and says she will be very uncomfortable at her son's wedding reception in two months. She's experiencing sciatic pain in her leg and remembers she had that same pain when he was born. She tells me that she was extremely afraid to take her new-born baby home because she didn't know how to be a mother. She got headaches and soon chose not to nurse him—she says "it wasn't the thing to do at that time." In the first week, her mother came to help, but Jackie would not let her touch the baby. *Jackie felt protective of her baby around her mother, although she had not yet remembered the abuse.* Lately, she has seen herself as moving about in the same way her mother does, and she hates this similarity. I suggest she not judge it but hold it till her next session when she plans to address her feelings about her mother.

In addition to several collages, Jackie has brought in a painting. She had very energetically painted red mountains on a blue background with a white moon. She is surprised at my description of the image as "turbulent, angry, and passionate" because she had not been feeling that way while painting. Then she remembers that, in fact, her emotions had been very tumultuous this week, and recognized she had not let herself *feel* those emotions as much as she usually does when collaging, despite the fact that painting is a much more direct and sensuous process. Jackie laughs, saying my reading of her images is "often too perceptive."

*   *   *

Fig. 37 "NURSING CHILD"

The physical nurturance Child needs is never fully satisfied without an emotional and spiritual bond, and this will be true of both food and sexuality throughout her life.

Fig. 37 "NURSING CHILD" 9/4/91

A dark-skinned mother and child whose faces appear to be unwashed, as if the mother cannot properly care for them, are nursing amid a cascade of flowers. The mother's gaze is vague and distant; she does not appear at all emotionally connected with the daughter she feeds from her breast. The child is also distracted and seems outwardly vigilant.

September 5th

This week was a difficult one for Jackie: she tells me she felt depressed and withdrawn, yet she deliberately chose not to resume taking the antidepressant. She says with conviction, "I don't want to do that anymore."

However, she had run out of the paper she uses for collaging. Being unable to engage in this creative and therapeutic process, she began to feel depressed again. Finally, yesterday she was able to resume her artwork and in a burst of creativity, made four collages; she says that, after the artwork, she finally felt better. Jackie comments that she found herself *"craving"* the collage process—"like needing to eat food or go to the bathroom." I tell her this is a perfect metaphor because the artwork is both nourishment and a release for her. *Jackie has always been involved in art-making, but this realization that the creative process can replace her use of antidepressant medications is a major breakthrough. I'm delighted to hear her say it has been effective for her. This would not necessarily be the case for everyone.*

This collage is a good illustration of a dream Jackie had this week. In it she is watching a baby trying to suckle at its mother's breast which is flat and has no milk. The mother's skin is very dark (just as Jackie's father's complexion is, especially during the summer).
It is interesting that this dream came up at this time because Jackie said last week she wanted to work on her relationship with her mother this week.

The cascade of flowers in this image reminds Jackie of a funeral, and also that her mother gardened profusely. She says the child nurses "matter of factly, aware she is only getting physical food and nothing else; the food is empty because there is no emotional bonding; therefore, the child learns to be alone and survive" *reflecting her own childhood experience.* At first, Jackie says the child would feel safe if she were alone; she would not feel vulnerable to attack. Then she realizes she attacks herself by eating excessive amounts of food because, "if food is the only connection with the mother and she didn't get what she needed from the mother, she might keep eating as an effort to get what she still does need emotionally." She also remembers being overfed, as an infant, until she threw up. We speak of alternative ways to get emotional needs met more appropriately. I mention that Freud spoke about infant sexuality and how nursing is our first sensual/sexual experience. Jackie says she's never thought about a food/sex connection, but then she smiles and her face softens as she remembers her son's obvious bliss as she nursed him for a brief time.

*   *   *

Fig. 38   "EMPOWERED WOMAN"

Woman holds high the sword previously brandished only by men; yet she is not aggressive. She has returned from her descent into the depths and stands empowered on the shore. Her strength comes from within and brings with it a sense of humor.

Fig. 38 "EMPOWERED WOMAN"   9/4/91

A mature Aboriginal woman stands on the shore of the Sea. She is smiling, with one hand on her hip and the other raising a machete to the sky. She is bracketed by ancient petroglyphs of women.

September 5ᵗʰ *(continued)*

Empowerment as a woman was one of three specific goals Jackie defined when she resumed her art therapy a little over a year ago. Now, after so much painful processing, comes this strong and independent crone. Jackie tells me she loves this dark-skinned elder and feels she has a good sense of humor. *Her comments suggest that Jackie is beginning to value herself now. The stone carvings of women surrounding her symbolize Jackie's new alignment with her ancient feminine lineage, which she had disparaged for so many years. The stance of the crone at the edge of the Sea suggests Jackie has now emerged from the depths of the unconscious, empowered. The image is an interesting correlate to several of her earliest images in which there were statues of male equestrian figures brandishing swords on high (not shown).* Through this and other images she has made recently, Jackie says she realizes how much stronger and more positive her image of women is becoming, and she is now beginning to take this stance of strength and confidence in her life.

Another collage this week shows a white wolf cub baying at some houses on a distant cliff *(not shown)*. Jackie also loves this image and describes it first as "isolated," then as "safe and comforting." I ask if the cub feels safe because it is isolated. She says "Oh." She hadn't made that connection. She comments that the wolf cub is not wailing painfully, as in previous collages. *I see this as a projection of her new and more positive feelings, even though isolation still feels safer to her at times.*

*   *   *

Fig. 39 "SHE'S CONFINED"

Woman followed her dream to go to England, but upon returning finds she has more unresolved issues haunting her that she needs to address.

Fig. 39 "SHE'S CONFINED" 9/9/91

This collage is a view from the inside of an English country cottage. It is the traditional stuccoed, half-timbered type—small, but cozy and inviting. On the table is a white globe with blue stars on it, a blue-white china bowl, a glass, a vase of pink flowers and several flowering thistles. Hanging on the wall is a copper mold that has grapes embossed on it (hint of Bacchus). A ladder-back chair is pulled up to the table; and finally, a woman is framed in the open top half of an old-fashioned Dutch door.

Sept. 12th

This has been an incredibly creative week for Jackie—she has arrived with seven new collages (!) *Due to space limitations only the first will be shown here, and the second discussed.*

Of this first one Jackie says this image represents where she imagines Charles lives, yet she describes the woman, who is framed by the half-open door as "confined." *The woman does not look happy and that, in fact, was the reality of how Jackie felt while in Europe last year. The globe of stars suggests the cosmos or a crystal ball in which one might get a glimpse of the larger picture of one's destiny—a feeling of truly coming home to the meaning of one's life.*

In another collage *(not shown)* **Jackie places a picture of a family above a Civil War cemetery.** *A Civil War image is particularly relevant, since that was a time when families were divided and fighting against each other.* **This image brings up a lot in our discussion about the dynamics in Jackie's childhood home—especially between her parents. She says her father's behavior was very macho, domineering, and abusive; but her mother, who appeared weak, was really very controlling—like a puppeteer. She says this seems to be a picture representing her father and his unconscious behavior;** *it's my unspoken impression, too.*

A third collage features a very feminine woman standing with head down in a jacket with broadly padded shoulders. The ruins of an ancient church are behind her. The image reminds her of the feeling of shame, and she feels that perhaps she doesn't need to hide under a masculine persona any more. Again I sense Jackie's relationship to her feminine nature is becoming more positive. At first she's surprised by this change, but then quickly realizes that's exactly what a lot of her recent pictures have shown.

*   *   *

Fig. 40   "SKELETONS IN THE CLOSET OF THE ABYSS"

Much work has already been done, but now comes the recognition that there are yet more skeletons in the closet of Woman's psyche. They have been identified and will not go back into hiding. Notice is given: they will receive all the attention they require.

Fig. 40 "SKELETONS IN THE CLOSET OF THE ABYSS" 9/17/91

Here we see the vast barren canyons with a great black shadow/hole in the foreground. Above it is an old black door that has a large window, and through the glass is seen a skeleton cloaked in black. The sky is mostly clear, but there are some clouds moving in.

September 19ᵗʰ

Even as she is beginning to feel more positive, Jackie says this image reminds her of just how harsh her attitude toward herself has always been. She says the negative internal male voice (Alfred as father) always tells her she isn't *doing* something right. Whereas, the negative internal female voice (mother) always tells her it is *she herself* who isn't good enough. *Masculine energies are typically seen to represent the active "doing" aspect of the human psyche, and the feminine symbolizes one's essential "being." Jackie's feelings are an example of this.*

We spend much of today's session processing a dream. In it several men take her away to molest her. Jackie calls to a friend for help and yells "fire!" Somehow she manages to get away and asks her friend why she hadn't helped her. She says she was more puzzled than angry by that lack of response. The friend gets angry and says she will not talk about it now.

We examine this dream from three different perspectives. 1) Jackie's first thoughts were that the friend in the dream symbolized her mother who had not protected her from her father. 2) Also, through her associations to the actions in the dream, she realizes she has generalized her mistrust of what people say, based on her experience of sexual abuse. 3) In order to help her enter more personally into the image, I suggest a Jungian exploration in which all characters in the dream are seen as aspects of herself (as we have done with previous dreams). Jackie agrees to this process, although with some trepidation noted. Within this framework I ask, "What part of you is in danger?" "What aspect is abusive?" "What part is not acting in your own best interest?" and so on.

I ask Jackie if there is any way in which she is abusive of herself. "Yes." "How?" "With food." I ask if she knows how much she weighs now (that is, just how abusive has she been?) She says "More or less." I ask if she can tell me her weight, noting that she doesn't have to. *I don't need to know; I just want her to be aware of her own internal reactions.* She responds "No." "Can she get herself weighed?" "No." "Would it help to know my weight?" "No." Through this process it becomes clear that the aspect of her that doesn't protect her is the part that chooses to stay unconscious about the situation of her weight, and refuses to deal with it directly. Finally, her physical being is the part in danger because of the burden it carries. *Despite her initial hesitation to enter into this exploration, Jackie has shown courage in going through it, which has brought into consciousness her resistance to dealing with the issue.*

*　　　　　*　　　　　*

Fig. 41 "GRIEVING THE LOST CHILD"

A solitary wolf howls its grief for the infant abused by her sick mother, as well as by her father.

Fig. 41 "GRIEVING THE LOST CHILD" 9/21/91

The view is from the inside of what was once a beautiful home in ancient Pompeii—indicated by the richness of the mosaic-tiled floor. In the open doorway the skull of death leers over the charred remains of an infant's cradle. In the foreground, a lone wolf howls.

September 26th

I am deeply moved by the power and poignancy of this simple collage that utilizes only three images. I recall in the earlier segment of our work together, Jackie made a collage entitled "The Lament of the Unknown Knower" (Fig. 13). In it, the wolf was seen to represent the unconscious part of her that always held the memory of the incest, even when her conscious mind had banished it from awareness. Now, as the part of her represented by the wolf continues to grieve her lost childhood, Jackie is consciously working to reverse the negative self-image she had developed as a result of the years of abuse, and is actively taking steps to increase her sense of self-worth and confidence to be engaged in her life as a whole person.

Unfortunately, the notes for this session have been lost. However, I've chosen to include this collage because it is so poignant and important.

*   *   *

Fig. 42 "WOMAN BRINGING LIGHT TO THE DEAD FAMILY"

With a hooded figure in the background representing the abusing male, a holy woman with one hand compassionately over her heart, reverently brings light to bear witness to the sudden death of an entire family: entombed together in the "volcanic ash" created by the eruption of abuse flashbacks.

Fig. 42   "WOMAN BRINGING LIGHT TO THE DEAD FAMILY"   9/27/91

A holy woman, with one hand compassionately over her heart, brings a light to the skeletons in the foreground that have been entombed in volcanic ash. The skeleton of one adult embraces that of a small child in death. A third head is visible below. A hooded figure in the background represents to Jackie the "evil male."

October 2nd

This and other skeletal images Jackie has begun to use are from excavations of ancient Pompeii and Herculanium that were destroyed within minutes by a massive eruption of Mt. Vesuvius in 79 AD. The image is a visual metaphor for how the onset of abuse flashbacks abruptly destroyed her earlier positive memory of her childhood. The message is clear and we do not linger in discussion of this very moving collage.

Recently Jackie asked me to photograph her latest collages, as I had done with the early ones before she went to Europe. Today I have brought in the first two dozen pictures that have been developed. Because of their reduced size we are able to see all of them at once, which would not otherwise be possible given her prolific creativity. *As previously noted, Jackie created far more collages than I have been able to include in this book.*

We review and put them in chronological order just as we did a year ago. Jackie and I both note significant differences between the early works and these later ones. Seeing these images conjures up in Jackie memories of all the issues, emotions, dreams, and insights she has become conscious of in the last seven months of her art therapy. This review has been of great benefit to her—pictures often stimulate memory more clearly than words alone can.

*   *   *

Fig. 43 "THE TRAUMATIZED CHILD"

Beautiful flowers create an illusion of a loving, nurturing home.
But the truth that lies behind them is one of terror, rage, and devastation.

Fig. 43 "THE TRAUMATIZED CHILD" 10/6/91

A small doll, in a red dress, with a bizarre facial expression and hair standing on end, is outside a frame house. In the attic is a snarling wolf. Through the open doors are seen the skeletal remains of the inhabitants. In the foreground: a large bank of nasturtiums.

October 10ᵗʰ

When Jackie was a child her family lived in a frame house, such as the one in this collage. Having a special fondness for nasturtiums, I note them. She looks shocked to discover that is what they are. She remembers that her mother always had plastic nasturtiums in their house; she says she was not conscious of that while making this collage. *The flowers are a good example of relevant but unconscious elements often found in Jackie's collages. The attic can be seen to represent her mind, and the snarling wolf, the rage that has felt like a protector within her. This image is truly about her childhood home and how it felt to live there.*

Today Jackie talks about an important and surprising shift she is experiencing in her way of relating to men. She says the change seemed to happen abruptly, virtually from one day to the next, within the last two weeks. There are several men at her job who used to bother her a lot, but now she finds she is able to relate to them in a way that is more playful and meaningful. One man in particular has engaged her in conversations about all sorts of personal things, including sex. Also, her brother called on her birthday and they had a long and very personal conversation.

Jackie is left wondering what has happened to cause such a dramatic change in her feelings toward men and her ability to connect with them. I suggest the difference is due to all the work she has been doing on this issue, and it was foreshadowed by some recent images, most notably, the one of the couple kissing. *(Fig.36 "Shipwrecked Dreams"). This is an example of something I had previously said, namely, that spontaneous images which arise from the deep unconscious often precede insights and changes that are experienced later in waking life.*

In another collage Jackie places an image of a very slim woman moving away from an obese woman who is headless. She has put what she thought was a protective wolf in place of the woman's head. Jackie is disappointed when I point that out that it is actually a bear. Although Jackie thought this animal was a wolf, the image of a bear has its own relevance to her process.[61] Another component of this collage is the image of a male who has fallen on his own dagger.

Here, the phallic dagger has been turned back on the abuser; he has fallen, fatally wounded, and the woman's spirit is now free of the weight of her past relationship to him.

Our human parallel to the bear's going into the cave of Mother Earth, is that we need to go into the womb of the Eternal Mother, that is to say, the intuitive place of wisdom, which is the feminine aspect of the psyche. In that state, each person can quiet the chattering of the ego-mind and in that inner silence shift to other levels of consciousness and imagination where we can find the answers to our own questions. Native Americans refer to this as "the dream lodge." Australian Aboriginal people call it "the dream time." Both know it as the place of inner guidance.

I feel that through her involvement in this art therapy process, Jackie has truly been in the bear's dream-time.

---

[61] Sams, Jamie & Carson, David. *Medicine Cards - The Discovery of Power Through the Ways of Animals.* Illus. by Angela Werneke. (St. Martin's Press, New York, 1988)
According to the Native American "Medicine Cards," the bear is a very strong animal that seeks honey, which represents the sweetness of life. Also, the bear's pattern of going into hibernation, during which time it digests what it has taken in during the year, symbolizes the need for times of introspection.

Fig. 44   "DEATH OF THE EVIL MOTHER"

A lone wolf keeps vigil over the shrunken mummified figure.

Fig. 44 "DEATH OF THE EVIL MOTHER"   10/9/91

This collage is made up of only two pictures. In the foreground is the black, leatherized body of a person, naturally mummified by bog acids. Above and behind the figure is a lone white wolf.

October 17th

Although this is actually a bog-man, Jackie has chosen this image to represent her feelings that the dark influence of her abusive mother is now dead, and the wolf as her inner protector is standing guard to see it remains so.

Jackie again says because of her weight she is feeling intense anxiety about attending her son's wedding banquet that will be held this coming week. She says none of her clothes fit and that she's feeling "stressed to the max." She has a very nice light blue dress that she has worn here at times, which I suggest she could dress up a little more with a nice scarf and some jewelry.

Based on what Jackie has brought up about her weight, I ask, "Why does the image of a mountain always feel safe to you?" She confirms my unspoken conjecture, saying the mountain is a strong, feminine Earth image, and is related in her feelings to her own weight being a protection from any sexual advances by men. However, at this time, her weight feels more like a burden than a protection. She says she feels truly "imprisoned" in her body; and she's angry and dismayed that she has done this to herself, just as her parents had imprisoned her as a child.

I also ask: "Why was your rage in the early collages always expressed in religious images?" Jackie responds that she was angry at God for not protecting her as a child.

*   *   *

Fig. 45   "THE WELLSPRING OF LIFE"

Having reached the deep life-giving waters, Child proudly displays that which symbolizes her successful inner excavation. Now even this ancient male god, also present at the wellspring, appears to be celebrating her achievements.

Fig. 45   "THE WELLSPRING OF LIFE"   10/16/91

A stream flows through the bottom of a deep canyon. There in the depths stands a young girl who has been fishing. She smiles as she displays her catch in a basket. Together with a few fish are seven human skulls. Present also is an ancient figure of a male god holding a bird in one hand.

October 17th (continued)

In exploring this image of the young girl standing in a stream,[62] we talk about the fact that the child's basket originally had only fish in it, before Jackie added the skulls. A few of the fish can still be seen and she associates them with Jesus and the story of the loaves and fishes. Jackie recognizes that such a connotation represents spiritual nourishment from a male figure, and she feels this may be another positive shift in her feelings about men.

Neither Jackie nor I have any idea who the figure of the ancient male god represents. However, she tells me she feels that in this image, even the masculine aspect of consciousness is celebrating the healing and growth she has achieved in her therapy to this point.

An image that is frequently used to represent the work of uncovering painful memories in therapy is that of excavating— digging down very deep until we get to the core or to life-giving water. In this collage, the smiling girl who now stands in the flow of the life-spring at the very bottom of this deep canyon proudly displaying her catch, symbolizes Jackie's growing sense of satisfaction with the inner work she has done and her increasing feeling of self-esteem. Fostering this new positive sense of self will be an on-going process. Jackie has placed human skulls in the young girl's basket along with the fish. This image signifies that her inner child feels the past is dead and she is in control of the situation.

*   *   *

---

[62] *In mythology and dreams, the symbolism of water is varied. Among other things, it is seen to represent many elemental things such as: prime matter (from which all else comes), the source and preserver of earthly life, the feminine, the unconscious, emotions, cleansing, and healing. The ocean, specifically, signifies the deepest levels of emotion and the unconscious dimension that is hidden below the surface of our awareness. Considering what a deep dive Jackie has made for so long into her unconscious emotions and memories, this image seems particularly relevant, and it's surprising to me that the element of water has been so rarely seen in her artwork.*

Fig. 46   "PRIMAL ENERGIES"

Out of the primal rage has come a new marriage of male and female aspects of the psyche.

Fig. 46   "PRIMAL ENERGIES"   10/16/91

With a fiery red nuclear explosion in the background, a figure looks down at the skeletal remains of a body lying amid tombstones and the foundation stones of an ancient building. The superstructure has long-since been destroyed. However, the foundation is strong and forms a clearly defined circle with access through a stone threshold. The eyes of a living person look out through the white mask of a figure that appears androgynous—it wears a tuxedo jacket with boutonniere and top hat, yet a white wedding veil flows from under the hat down over the shoulders. (An interesting synchronicity is that the bolt of lightning runs parallel to the figure of the masked person.)

October 24th

Despite Jackie's dread about attending her son's wedding reception because of her weight, the experience turned out to be a major breakthrough for her. She says with the help of a lot of work in therapy and a couple of drinks(!), she relaxed and decided she would enjoy this celebration for her son. Standing in the receiving line, she greeted her ex-husband, introduced herself to everyone including her ex-husband's new wife, and was greeted by a number of her relatives like their prodigal daughter. She had not been in contact with them during the five years since the flashbacks began, so this was a wonderful reunion.

I am in awe as I witness the continuing flow of amazing synchronicities in Jackie's artwork—here she has found a unique composite bride/groom image and created this enigmatic collage in the week of her son's wedding. This picture speaks to several key issues: her feelings about her son's marriage and the integration of both the masculine and feminine aspects of her own psyche.

Jackie tells me she and her sister spoke at the wedding reception. Her sister apologized for hurting her so deeply, and they began a reconciliation process. In addition, she was greeted with great affection by her brother. She says the only thing unchanged was that her parents hardly greeted or made eye contact with her. The following day Jackie called her sister to make a date for breakfast together.

Most importantly, Jackie says much to her surprise, recently there have been times when she has begun to feel some compassion for her father, as she realizes his abuse came out of his weakness. *Clearly, another deep shift.* I ask Jackie what was the very best part of this extraordinary reconciliation and healing experience. Her immediate answer is "Me! I loved the way I felt! I even danced!"

I feel such joy hearing Jackie relate this wonderful experience that is the measure of all the healing work she has been doing for so long! Although Jackie's trepidation was mitigated by a couple of drinks to relax her tension, nonetheless, it's an example of how the process of releasing old rage and shame allows a person to move into joy and playfulness, centered within their own good nature.

*   *   *

Fig. 47   "INNER CHILD RETURNS FROM THE ABYSS"

Child is dressed in a pure white flowing dress and her spirit is light as she confidently returns to her little friends. They are all dressed up in long dresses and hats—like grown-up ladies.

Fig. 47 "INNER CHILD RETURNS FROM THE ABYSS"   10/29/91

A young girl, balanced like a tightrope walker, gingerly strides across a narrow bridge. We can see the last of the skeletal remains strewn about the desert, which she is now leaving behind. A low, white brick wall now separates her from that arid terrain. Two young friends witness her return.

October 31st

I find it interesting this collage was done in the week following Jackie's son's wedding reception. That experience was a benchmark, particularly in regard to her sense of self-worth and also the beginning of a reconciliation with her estranged sister. In this image, the child is leaving the devastation of the past behind and returning to those she loves.

After the reception, Jackie and her sister made a breakfast date. She tells me her sister seemed to be speaking on two parallel tracks. She had long denied there was any problem with their mother because she didn't want to acknowledge it. At first her sister said their mother was long suffering, always doing things for others. Jackie's response was "Huh?!" But then her sister also expressed her rage at their mother for how they were treated, and acknowledged she always tried to protect her children by keeping them from going to their grandparents' home. In an ironic twist of fate, Jackie's adolescent niece has recently moved in with her grandmother, and her sister is enraged because she says their mother "got one." Jackie tells me both she and her sister feel their mother "stole their children" to some degree.

Jackie tells me their conversation was meaningful because they both explored how much each had hurt the other without realizing the depth of it. Now they recognize that, although they have different styles and ways of dealing with their pain, each of them was doing essentially the same thing. They were trying to ignore their emotions and the inner knowing about how abusive their childhood home had been.

This week Jackie received a phone call from her brother who questioned her in an insistent way. She became agitated and said it made her feel like a mouse being played with by a cat before being eaten. I tell her that image is a good metaphor for childhood sexual abuse, that is, a small person being "played with" thoughtlessly before being "eaten." It's not surprising this kind of questioning would trigger feelings of anxiety about abuse, reminiscent of her father's way of always questioning her housework when she was young.

*   *   *

Fig. 48   "WOLVES INSPECTING THE BONES"

Pure white wolves, guardians of Child, return to make sure there is no further danger.

Fig. 48 "WOLVES INSPECTING THE BONES"   10/31/91

Three white wolves approach the skeletons of four people laid side by side in death. Above them is a rock outcropping.

October 31ˢᵗ (continued)

Jackie says the three wolves represent herself and her sister and brother; the four skeletons symbolize everyone in her family except herself; and the outcropping above signifies a safe cave where the wolves live. Jackie cries as she tells me when they were growing up her brother and sister were more like her children because, as oldest child, she had so much responsibility in their home. I comment that perhaps she is just now developing more of a sibling relationship with them. I ask what the wolves are doing there among the skeletons. Jackie responds that they are checking to make sure they are all dead, that is, all the pain associated with various family members.

When Jackie cut the paper for the "stone cave" she did not see anything else in that shape. However, as we look at it together, we both feel it suggests some kind of ominous animal—perhaps a cobra head or a vulture.

The picture is like an optical illusion, in that it sometimes looks like the profile of a dog (facing left), which is more in keeping with Jackie's initial feeling of this being a "safe cave where the wolves live." Here again I see how images in her artwork invite projections that can be quite disparate, which she did not consciously intend at the time she was creating them. In this case, the cave shape suggests both the earlier ominous feelings and her calmer/safer ones at present.

This week Jackie read a magazine article about incest in which the author discussed how abused children will frequently "leave their body." She reminds me of how she had spoken last year of having had that experience often between the ages of about two to eight years old, and how she loved the feeling of being free of her body.

Jackie tells me a dream in which she was adamantly saying: "I'll never, never, ever get married again—EVER!!!" Now she says if she ever does marry, it would have to be to a man who could match her depth—or she'd rather be alone. She will not enter into any intimate relationship out of a feeling of inadequacy or a sense of not being whole without a man.

Her comment is a hard-won and honest acknowledgment of her unique value as a woman, and I feel this attitude will serve her well whether she chooses to enter into a relationship or remain solitary.

Jackie says she just wants to be valued for herself. As I had done once before, I ask if *she* values herself. Several times, in a joking tone of voice, she says to me "Oh, shut up"—she doesn't want to talk about it, except to say, at this time, she values her inner being, but not her outer form.

Our conversation shifts to water images. Jackie tells me that images of whales and icebergs have always terrified her, even causing her to tremble. We explore their symbolism as representing the contents of the unconscious.

I remind her that Freud said the conscious mind is like the tip of an iceberg, and that, by far, the greater aspect of the mind is the unconscious realm, corresponding to the enormous mass of ice that is hidden beneath the water's surface and is very dangerous if not recognized.

In addition, whales are seen as phallic symbols. It is interesting to contrast Jackie's terror of water images, such as icebergs and whales (the unconscious and sexual domain), with her feeling of greatest safety with the land images of mountains (representing the feminine and a grounding). It is a measure of her courage that, despite these feelings, she has made such a deep dive in her healing work.

Fig. 49   "SELKET - GODDESS OF HEALING"

Safe in the presence of the great mountain temple, the goddess of healing is at peace amid the glowing symbols of the past. Her gesture suggests a strong, quiet feminine presence that can now embrace it all.

Fig. 49 "SELKET - GODDESS OF HEALING"   11/4/91

The beautifully feminine ancient Egyptian goddess, "Selket," stands with arms outstretched in a calming gesture of peace. On her head is a scorpion signifying this goddess is able to heal deadly bites from scorpions and snakes. The goddess stands on a spiral in a field of glowing petroglyphs. Behind her is the facade of a building in the ancient city of Petra in Jordan.

November 5th

Looking at this collage, Jackie says she feels the goddess is "cozy and safe" in this environment where she is backed by a great temple that has been carved out of the cliff. She deliberately placed the goddess off-center in the spiral because it is very important, she says, that the entrance to the temple be visible; she again says, "It feels safe."

In several of her early collages (some not included in this book) there were facades with small, round, open portals which seemed to be unconscious symbols of the vagina. These were seen in collages that expressed the original feelings of danger and of being personally and sexually unsafe. The first example was Fig.9, "The Father Wound: Altar of Sacrifice." It is therefore particularly significant that, after so much inner processing, this beautiful woman now stands with great presence and inner peace, and the open portal to the temple is immediately adjacent to her genital area. On a deep level, Jackie has begun to feel safe sexually. It is also interesting to me that she chose Selket for this collage, without knowing she is the goddess of healing.

Jackie tells me that twice in the past two weeks she was surprised to find herself defending a man's position in an argument, rather than agreeing with the woman's point of view. I offer the possibility that in coming to peace within herself, she may be moving beyond a militant feminism, where she previously could not accept anything about men as right, and is now moving into an attitude of greater openness to any human being. Jackie says this goddess is "ready to fly." I note her arms are in the same outstretched position as the child in last week's collage (*Fig. 47 "Inner Child Returns from The Abyss"*).

Two other collages this week both have a train motif. In the first, a distant train is winding its way around a hillside, and in the foreground, a swan with open wings is about to take flight. The second collage Jackie entitles "Night train to the Netherworld." In both cases the trains are moving away from the viewer. Jackie quotes the Jewish theologian, Martin Buber, who said, "Every journey has a destination the traveler does not know." This certainly is relevant to a therapeutic journey. Jackie says she loves the second train going "over" that hill. *It looks to me more like it's about to tunnel through the mountain; however, she does not see this sexual implication, and so I don't mention it.*

Her reaction to these train and snake images represents an enormous change from her earlier associations, for example, the father/cobra overshadowing her marriage (*Fig.17 "My American Gothic"*) or the serpentine monster representing her earlier sexual trauma (*Fig.35 "Pink and Blue Polka-Dot Monster"*) or the stone cave that suggests a cobra's head (*Fig.48 "Wolves Inspecting the Bones"*).

The last several collages are all giving hints that Jackie is feeling more and more at peace within herself.

Jackie cries as she says that for the first time ever she has begun to feel a deep grief for the loss of a truly loving father she never had. Prior to this time, she had grieved and longed for a loving mom who would nurture and protect her, but the lack of a caring dad was simply a dead issue—she never had one. Now she is letting herself feel that loss, too.

Fig. 50 "MONK BRINGING THE LIGHT"

Because Woman is now at peace within herself, Monk is allowed to carry the sacred light.

Fig. 50   "MONK BRINGING THE LIGHT"   11/10/91

A Buddhist monk approaches, carrying a glowing candle. He walks a lighted path with a feeling of deep inner peace, leaving behind an ancient temple that appears to be an embattled fortress.

November 14th

Today Jackie tells me she has just heard an interview with a well-known actor in which he talked about his Buddhist beliefs. He described his experience of sending out love and compassion from his heart to others and said this action has been an influence for positive change in himself and in those to whom he sent that energy. As she heard this, she cried and says she wants, once again, to feel love for others as she used to. Jackie says she meditated twice this week, for the first time since the memories came up. Prior to that, she had meditated daily for eleven years. *A personal sense of, and connection to, a Divine Presence in her life was one of her goals in resuming therapy and it has begun to return. Perhaps it will be different now–deeper and more authentically her own for having gone through the "dark night."* **Jackie sobs with relief as I affirm she is now coming out on the other side of her dark journey.**

Considering the grief Jackie has recently begun to feel in regard to her father, it seems particularly relevant that it is now a male–this monk–who is the light-bearer for her. In a previous image (Fig. 42), the light had been held by a compassionate woman, while the male was threatening.

Jackie brings in a dream, the significance of which is self-evident. In it she is walking down an exceptionally wide boulevard in what used to be a city. It is daylight and she is alone in the midst of a tremendous maelstrom. A tornado has struck and there is nothing left of the city. Bits of siding (*like the house she grew up in*), as well an enormous inflated red teddy bear (*her childhood anger*), were blowing by. She puts her hands up to protect her eyes, but then puts them down as she realizes she is not getting hurt by anything. She comes to an intersection and walks straight through; there is no question in her mind about which direction to go. She sees a house and some men ahead, but she does not feel threatened by their presence. They do not offer to help her; but then she realizes she doesn't need any help.

This past week, Jackie called her sister and was invited to her house for tea. Jackie went and surprised herself by staying four hours. She took the photographs of her collages in order to share this sensitive healing process with her sister. However, she was surprised I had not masked her parents' faces in the prints, as I had in the slides. She was afraid of what her sister's reaction would be, but no comment was made. Her sister seemed to see the collages only as works of art, not recognizing that the pain and rage represented in them were Jackie's reaction to their early family trauma. Jackie decided this limited level of communication was okay at this time. Her sister talked a lot about their parents. Jackie says she didn't comment on how much she wanted to change the subject because, without a deeper level of empathy between them at this time, she felt that to express her need would make her even more vulnerable than showing the collage images.

*　　　　　*　　　　　*

Fig. 51   "THE CHILDREN AT THE GRAVESITE"

The skeletons have now been interred, and a female-shaped tombstone marks the site. Child, who earlier held a machete against her own throat, has now matured and holds it as a weapon to protect the younger children. Together they have gathered to say goodbye.

Fig. 51 "THE CHILDREN AT THE GRAVESITE" 11/12/91

Two girls and a young woman with a machete are gathered together. Below them, in the graveyard beside a stone church, is an old tombstone carved in the shape of a woman. A Celtic cross is inscribed on it.

November 14th (continued)

This is one of five collages Jackie brought in today and it includes four figures: a young woman, two girls, and the female-shaped tombstone. *The latter representing the trauma of her past that is now dead and buried.* Above the tombstone figure, the young woman holds a machete; her eyes meet the viewers' gaze with what Jackie describes as "a determined look." In an earlier collage a young girl was holding a machete to her own throat (*Fig. 14*) and in another image, a child had been pierced from behind by a saber through her heart (*Fig. 18*). That child has grown up and now it is she who owns the sword, and she is prepared to use it if necessary to defend these children, that is, Jackie's inner children.

Leaning on her shoulder is a young girl whom Jackie describes as "sad, like I was as a child." This youngster can lean, i.e., depend, on the young woman *the part of herself that is now more emotionally mature* for protection. Above them both is another child Jackie says is "happy and normal," signifying to me, that the child who was injured in her now feels safe and has found her center of gravity. She has a beatific expression and I see her hand gesture as one of giving a blessing. Jackie, however, describes her gesture as either a message to "stop," or, she says, "the girl may be giving a slight wave."

Jackie surprises me at the end of this session by announcing she wants to start having just two sessions per month because she cannot afford weekly sessions at this time. When asked if she would like to negotiate with the counseling center for an adjustment in her fee, she declines and simply chooses to come less often. In fact, she says, it will be three weeks before she can come again.

I have been aware, particularly in the last month, that the images in Jackie's collages have been increasingly indicating a feeling of being at peace. Now I suspect she may have just heralded the end of our work together. In the session, when Jackie described the uppermost child's gesture as "stop," I initially thought that meant Jackie feels secure now about being able to protect herself from unwanted sexual advances. Now I'm thinking this may have been Jackie's first indication to me that she can soon stop her therapy, and that she is tentatively beginning to say goodbye.

A slight wave, indeed.

*   *   *

December 5th

In today's collage entitled "Crone with Posy Leaving the Iceberg" (not shown) an elderly woman, with a cane in one hand and a small bouquet of flowers in the other, walks briskly out of an iceberg. (In the text of Fig. 21–"Leaving the Past Behind"–Jackie said she dreamed that she had taken a love letter out of the freezer.)

I'm remembering that in the shamanic tradition of many native cultures, spirits are said to be able to "shape-shift." That is, at one time an entity may be seen in an animal form and at another time in a human form. Now, in Jackie's unconscious, that wise, knowing part of her psyche which has been represented by the wolf, has transformed into its more appropriate human form–the wise woman. The archetypal image of Wise Woman has been released from her unconscious, where it had been entombed in the frozen iceberg of her unexpressed rage.

Jackie and I talk about how beneficial it has been to be able to bypass her rational mind through this art process, to gain access to her deeper self. *She has done that so well as she allowed the collage images to form, often without a conscious understanding of their symbolism and without explanatory words. This non-rational way of working is precisely why the collages have been so deeply satisfying for her. It was only later, as she described those images in words, that conscious insights came, carrying her gradually forward.*

It has been three weeks since our last session, and Jackie says she hated having it be such a long time before she could come and process what has been going on in her feelings. For a while she stopped collaging and began feeling depressed, but just as before, her mood lifted when she resumed the artwork. We begin to explore this collage (one of five she has brought in today), and Jackie says that she has just realized the image of the wise old woman that has come up in several recent collages is related to the wolf, representing the unconscious part of her that held the memories.

Trust is the issue of the week. We talk about expectations and perceptions. Jackie and her parents have had no communication for five years since the flashbacks began, and now the recent reconciliation with her sister is on tenuous ground. She says both her sister and her parents have an "enthusiastic" relationship with her ex-husband, which they did not have before her divorce, and for that reason she feels she can't fully trust her sister's behavior. She feels that in aligning with him, they have deliberately rejected her. I wonder if their relationship with him may have been an unconscious way to maintain some contact with her, and ask Jackie if she could accept her sister's choices and, at the same time, honestly express her own feelings. I suggest that a deep level of acceptance of all aspects of one's self usually leads to a compassionate acceptance of others, even if they have another point of view.

In addition, Jackie has just discovered that everyone in her family has known about her incest memories, even though she had only told her sister and sister-in-law. Word had spread throughout the family; everyone knew and silently continued to keep the secret. *I feel this is a magnification of the original betrayal of her trust. Jackie told only two people in confidence and now finds her agonizing Secret was not a secret at all.*

Fig. 52   "JANUS AND THE MARRIAGE OF OPPOSITES"

In this pivotal point between the past and the future, male and female aspects of Woman are lovingly joined within her psyche, and there is now the potential for this marriage of opposites to manifest in her outer life.

Fig. 52 "JANUS AND THE MARRIAGE OF OPPOSITES"   11/27/91

In the foreground, as a foundation, is a contemporary sculpture of the ancient Roman god, Janus, who faces in opposite directions. The head of an axe forms a cleavage out of which is arising a mature couple who appear to be farmers.

December 5th (continued)

We now shift into a discussion of the symbolism of today's second collage.

Janus is the god of doorways and thresholds, of new beginnings, and of the rising and setting of the sun. This mythological figure is always pictured with two faces back to back, symbolizing the moment between looking back at the past and forward into the future. It is from Janus we derive the word "January," the pivotal point in the cycle of the year. An axe has come down between the two aspects of this figure signifying the necessary break between them. I suspect this symbol may be particularly relevant at this moment because I sense Jackie is approaching the end of her work with me, although, since she hasn't spoken of it directly, she does not yet seem to be consciously aware of it.

Out of the Janus figure now arise a couple—husband and wife whose expressions convey a sense of harmony and unity. The two heads of Janus are stony cold, split by the axe head. By contrast, this elder couple is warm and alive—brought together and transformed by the struggles and joys they've shared over many years. Just below the woman's right eye is a birthmark, perfectly shaped as a teardrop, suggesting life's sorrows. Here are the loving parents Jackie would like to have had, as well as the kind of loving, supportive relationship she is beginning to visualize as a part of her life in the future.

*   *   *

Fig. 53 "SPIRITUALITY, PSYCHOLOGY, AND WOMAN"

Both spirituality and psychology are here acknowledged as aspects of the healing process. Still, Woman maintains her vigilance.

Fig. 53 "SPIRITUALITY, PSYCHOLOGY, AND WOMAN" 11/27/91

In the lower right foreground is a medieval Byzantine image of Christ holding a bejeweled sacred text. Beside him is a box with many images of men and women and a scarab. In this double exposure a photo of Freud was superimposed on the box. His face has been cut out and replaced with a close up view of a woman's eyes.

December 5ᵗʰ (continued)

We examine a third collage Jackie created in the past week. The box on the left has many small compartments filled with pictures of men and women, both sacred and profane: some are dressed, some nude. They include: Adam and Eve, kings and queens, as well as saints and peasants from various time periods. From a Jungian perspective, an essential aspect of in-depth psychotherapy is finding a balance of feminine and masculine energies within a person and how that affects their relationships with others. All these figures together with Freud, whose emphasis was on sexuality, are particularly apt.

Two sections of the box are filled with the image of a beetle or scarab. Scarabs lay their eggs in a ball of dung, out of which the young hatch. To the ancient Egyptians this became a sacred symbol of the renewal of life out of what was thought to have no value. Both the scarab and Jesus symbolize rebirth or resurrection from the dead. As such they are relevant symbols of Jackie's psychological renewal as she is now making her Return.

My reading of the image is that it embodies the two essential components of a healing journey: the psychological and the spiritual. On the one hand, a solid psychological framework provides a crucial structure within which one can safely confront their inner demons: fear, rage, guilt, shame, grief. On the other hand, in order to solve a problem one must get a larger perspective on it. In a healing context, as I experience it, that involves coming to know one's wholeness which includes the spiritual dimension of the authentic Self, as well as the worldly level of the ego.

Freud, considered the father of psychoanalysis, believed dysfunction in the area of sexuality was the root of all psychological problems. In fact, he originally wrote about the prevalence of early sexual abuse, as it was reported to him by a number of his women patients.[63] However, after nine years of being ostracized by his peers and the public, Freud recanted, explaining that he hadn't understood how powerful women's fantasies can be, stating he now realized the reports of incest by his female patients were due to an intense fantasy life.[64] He then developed his new theory of the Oedipus Complex[65] to explain the source of the women's problems. This effectively placed the blame for women's incest trauma on women. Jackie has cut out the sections containing Freud's head and replaced it with the face of a woman whose eyes look out at the viewer with great caution and suspicion. She is fully alert and vigilant. After all Jackie's rageful decapitations in her earlier collages, it seems ironic that what may be her final act of decapitation, is of Freud—a little like putting her parents behind bars.

[63] *Freud, S. "The Aetiology of Hysteria." in The Standard Edition of the Complete Psychological Works of Sigmund Freud, Vol. III (1893-1899): Early Psycho-Analytic Publications, pp. 187-221., 1924 C.P., 1, 183-219. (TR. C.M. Baines.)*
[64] *Freud, S. "My Views on the Part Played by Sexuality in the Aetiology of the Neurosis." from The Complete Works, Vol. 7 pp. 271-279.*
[65] *Freud, S. "A Special Type of Choice of Object Made by Men" 1910. The Complete Works, Vol.11. Five Lectures on Psychoanalysis, Leonardo Da Vinci & Other Works. pp. 171.*

In contrast to Freud's view, Jung observed in his clients, both male and female, the cause of psychological problems, from their middle years on, was due to a one-sidedness, evidenced by a lack of connection with the spiritual dimension of their being. This became the focus of his later work.[66]

As I see it, each of these men brought out basic truths: sexuality being at the core of our outer, physical life, and spirituality, the core of our inner life. These two aspects are necessary in order to have a balanced and healthy system, and both are symbolized in this composite image.

*   *   *

---

[66] *Jung, C.G. The Collected Works of C.G. Jung. Bollingen Series XX, (Pantheon Books, a division of Random House. 1964) Ed. Note Vol. 4: "In the Editorial Note to Volume 1, it was pointed out that Jung's interest had gradually transferred itself, over the years, from psychiatry through psychoanalysis and typology to the theory of archetypes, and finally to the psychology of religious motifs." Ed. Note Vol. 11: "The title, Psychology & Religion: East & West, calls for comment, since no single volume can cover Jung's publications on a subject that takes so prominent a place in all his later works." Religious motifs are notably explored also in Vol. 9: Aion, Vol. 12: Psychology & Alchemy, and Vol. 14: Mysterium Coniunctionis.*

Fig. 54 "THE HANGED MEN"

The violating males are now under control and this is celebrated with a burst of vibrantly colored flowers.

Fig. 54 "THE HANGED MEN"   12/11/91

Four men are hanging in a sea of blue, suspended from their ankles by ropes. We see by their positions they are not dead, just immobilized. Above them is a virtual explosion of vibrantly colored flowers.

December 12th

Today Jackie mentions, somewhat sheepishly, that it wasn't until about two weeks ago she consciously realized she has been attracted to a man at work since before she went to England. A friend of hers is in an abusive relationship with a man, and that horrifies Jackie. Because of her attraction to the man at work, she fears she might get drawn into a relationship with someone like her father, and her inner children are anxious about that. She says the thought of it makes her depressed. As Jackie considers the possibility of a relationship, she wonders how she can avoid making the same kind of mistake she feels her friend has made. I tell her I believe when people develop a genuine love and respect for themselves, they are not likely to be attracted to an abusive partner.

We move into an exploration of today's collage. Jackie is aware of the Tarot cards that are a medieval system of divination. On one, "The Hanged Man," a man is suspended upside down by a rope tied around one ankle. This represents surrender or seeing one's situation from an entirely new perspective, and so symbolically, it is not as negative as one might think. This corresponds to Jackie's evolving feelings; the masculine element is now under control—not dead, but unable to be hurtful anymore.

Jackie seems to have completed the necessary work on her negative associations with men and for now they are simply being held in a kind of "suspended animation." She no longer feels threatened by them.

In this image, the background color is deep blue which can be seen to represent the waters of the unconscious, and the explosive vitality of the colored flowers above feels celebratory.

*   *   *

December 19th

Jackie says I'd better be sitting down for this one. Her brother called last night to say their father asked him to call Jackie and invite her to come for Christmas dinner with the family. I hope this may be an opportunity for further healing, but after five years of basically no contact between them, Jackie assumes it's just for good appearances. She cries, because it feels to her that if she goes, it will "trivialize" her incest trauma because they will ignore it and act as if it never happened.

I suggest she relax and breathe into the situation to find her own inner guidance by checking with her inner children. As Jackie drops into her feelings more deeply, she is surprised to find the children do not feel threatened by this invitation. I suggest she ask them what she should do. Jackie tells me the younger one says her father needs to be confronted directly about his motivation in extending this invitation. The older child wants her to simply walk away and ignore it. Jackie says she may call or write her father. *Jackie is surely adept at this process of Active Imagination that Jung used with his clients.*

Jackie has done no collages at all this week, and so she says maybe there's a shift happening in her. . . *I couldn't agree more.*

*   *   *

Fig. 55   "THE GRIEVING WOMEN"

The women weep, expressing a deep, universal, feminine grief over their losses.
Woman under veil suggests a deep leavening process is underway.

Fig. 55 "THE GRIEVING WOMEN"   1/1/92

Three women of different ages and races are weeping together. Above them, under a veil, is the head of a fourth woman who is seen in profile, facing right. Her hand is in front of her face and only her pinkie can be seen peeking out from under the dark veil.

IT IS NOW 1992

January 2ⁿᵈ

I was away last week over the Christmas holiday, and so it has been two weeks since we last met. Jackie did this collage and two others on New Year's Day. She tells me she had not done any artwork for over two weeks, and once again she felt great relief when she did these yesterday. She also realizes she's much more aware of her dreams when she's not collaging. *As mentioned before, they both arise from a deep place in her psyche and serve her needs in essentially the same way.*

In her book, Women Who Run with the Wolves,[67] *Jungian analyst Clarissa Pinkola Estes says the veil is an ancient motif. It signifies that after a woman has been in the Underworld and has endured a psychic death and rebirth, it takes time for her to re-emerge into the upper world of everyday life. Estes says the veil signifies "the preserving of the eros and mysterium of the wild nature. It is like a cloth covering bread dough as it rises; there is a potent leavening happening in the souls of women in descent. There is a powerful fermenting going on. To be behind the veil increases one's mystical insight."*

When she made this collage, Jackie had no idea of the significance of the veil over a woman's head, as described by Estes, but once again, I see how perfectly relevant are the images that "just feel right." Such a powerful expression of grief is appropriate now in this season of family gatherings and celebrations, as Jackie experiences her long estrangement from her family of origin.

Along with paisley patterns, the design on the woman's veil includes hearts, symbolizing loving feelings. The fact that one finger has come out from under the veil is a delicate, although tentative, indication that Jackie is now in the stage of Return.

In this session, Jackie tells me she called her father and asked him if his invitation to Christmas dinner was an acknowledgment of the incest. When he denied it again, she declined to attend. Outwardly she had remained calm during this conversation, however, she was aware of an inner hook: she feels a deep need for her father to someday own what he did, and as long as he does not take responsibility for his behavior, she is disturbed and feels there can be no relationship between them. Jackie says, even so, she's glad he invited her to the holiday dinner because at least it's an acknowledgment of her absence from the family, and that gives her some sense of satisfaction.

She was able to confront this situation directly and not feel overwhelmed by the interchange. At the beginning of her healing work, Jackie felt very intimidated as she prepared to confront her father in a legal situation. (See Fig. 26 "Bacchus Transformed.")

---

[67] Estes, Clarissa Pinkola. *Women Who Run with the Wolves, Myths and Stories of the Wild Woman Archetype.* Ballantine Books, New York, 1992

Jackie tells me that on Christmas morning her sister called. They had a long talk, and her sister asked many sincere and thoughtful questions about Jackie's memories. Her sister seemed to be struggling with her own feelings about how oppressive their parents had been, and yet still could not believe it had gone so far as to include prolonged incest for her older sister. She has really been thinking about this, though, and has come up with an alternative explanation. She wonders if perhaps Jackie had invented this story of incest because she was so angry at how oppressive their father was in so many other ways.

Jackie's response was that she has always been *consciously aware* of their father's other abusive treatment of them. She said, "I would not have had to make up such an awful explanation for my rage and put myself through such hell in the process of working through my memories and intensely painful emotions." Nonetheless, despite her sister's disbelief, Jackie felt a real caring from her and it made Jackie feel "safe." She tells me she felt non-defensive in their conversation and was no longer requiring her sister to believe her memories.

Fig. 56   "THE JOYFUL CRONE"

Sunlight streams down through the cathedral of verdant growth like a blessing from heaven. Now as a wise Crone seasoned by life experiences, Woman has retained her sense of humor and holds a staff for support on her continuing journey.

Fig. 56 "THE JOYFUL CRONE"   1/1/92

A white-haired woman with rosy cheeks smiles broadly as she stands in a tattered coat, holding a walking staff. Behind her, abundant vines and towering trees fade into the mists of the deep forest.

January 2ⁿᵈ (continued)

On New Year's Day, Jackie created both this and the previous collage expressing both grief and contentment. Like anyone who has grown to her age, this elder has surely experienced suffering, yet here she is smiling. In mythology, the crone signifies a wise and aged woman.

Jackie says that, as she made this collage, she felt very disturbed because the lower half of the woman's body was not in the picture. Jackie says it's very important for the old woman's "dignity" that she be whole. I comment, "Inwardly she *is* whole. You can see it in her eyes and in her smile. It is only in the picture of her that her lower torso (sexual area) and legs (to stand on) are not visible." *To me, Jackie's comment reflects her own deep need to feel whole again and to be able to take a strong stance in the world.*

I feel this figure is Jackie. To me she represents her wise, strong, and courageous inner being—her authentic Self, which she has reclaimed at a great price through all the intense healing work she has been doing. She has owned her Shadow, both its negative side—her rage, terror, guilt, shame, and grief; as well as its light side—her sense of humor, compassion, and creativity.

In this collage, Jackie has elegantly combined two images: the wise older woman, and the light illuminating her, as it filters down through the deep forest. Tucked into her pocket is a red handkerchief that may be seen to symbolize either that her anger is available if needed, but is no longer explosive, or the red vitality of life is emerging. Her staff may be seen to symbolize the supports she has for the next phase of her life. Jackie's struggles on this journey have yielded a positive view of life as she prepares to move forward. She has come to recognize her personal story as a microcosm of the larger universal cycles of life, death, and rebirth, as first recorded in the Myth of Inanna. After floating in amnesia for so many years due to the incest, Jackie is now fully grounded on the Earth. Being centered in a vision of hope that is also realistic, has given her the sense of inner peace this crone embodies.

*   *   *

"TOTEM POLE"   1/5/92 (see Frontispiece)

In this collage three photographs combine to create the illusion of a three-dimensional sculpture. They include a carving of an animal's head, half of which is a dark human face. Above that is a doll, and on top is a Samurai warrior. Protected by the enforced Silence of his victim, the warrior guards The Secret, rather than The Child. A totem pole is the symbolic record of a family's history and ancestry.

January 9th

Jackie begins this session saying she almost didn't come this week but then changed her mind at the last minute. She has brought in two collages. We look at this one first, but Jackie has no words of explanation for it, nor has she named it.

As Jackie and I translate this composite image into words, the story of her childhood abuse is told. On the bottom, a half-animal, half-human head smiles ominously and is surrounded by the red of passion and rage. In the middle, a doll-child without hands appears old and powerless. Dominating the image, a well-armored male warrior, with hands around the child's throat, protects himself by keeping her silent.[68] It is a representation of how the masculine animal-sexual instincts, when expressed inappropriately in an incestuous relationship, render an innocent child helpless, shamed, and old beyond her or his years.

In creating their totem poles, the Native Americans of the Pacific Northwest have a repertoire of symbols they understand—it is their common visual language through which they honor their ancestors and celebrate the accomplishments of their clans. Jackie's image differs from those traditional totem poles because these are her uniquely personal symbols. Her combination of pictures symbolize not only her experience, but also communicate the emotional tones of animal-passion, domination, and a victim's sense of helplessness, as well as the enforced silence around the Secret.

Initially Jackie was lost—submerged in her personal pain and shame. Gradually, as a result of the work in art therapy, I can see how her perception of her personal experience expanded. In this composite image, she has spontaneously elevated her individual experience to the mythic realm where she has found meaning and common ground with all who have endured the profound insult of sexual abuse. Because she is able to symbolize her experience in this way, Jackie shares with the world, as a storyteller might, that she is no longer lost in depression and in the unconscious denial that is amnesia.

Elegant in its simplicity, this image is a contemporary expression of the primal nature of sexual abuse and is emblematic of Jackie's rise into consciousness to transform the destructive effects of her experience of incest.

---

[68] *Joseph Campbell says that prominent in the folklore and mythologies of the peoples of the Arctic and north temperate zones is the idea of dual presences which may be animals in human guise or human beings seen as animals. The animal/human sculpture at the base of this collage is symbolic of that concept. The significance of their dual nature is that they are deceptive, which seems relevant to an abusive father who should, instead, be a protector. The deceptive quality would also relate to Jackie's use of the honorable Samurai warrior who in her collage represents patriarchal domination.*

Campbell, Joseph. Historical Atlas of World Mythology. Vol I: "The Way of the Animal Powers," Part 2: Mythologies of the Great Hunt. Harper & Row, Publishers, New York, 1988. p. 199.

Of all the collages she has created, I feel this is the single most comprehensive and specific symbolic statement of the issue that brought her into therapy. I am amazed Jackie has no words to describe the collage, yet they're not needed—her choice of images speaks eloquently.

The second collage *(not shown)* features a toy locomotive, stranded in snow and ice. Jackie describes it as having been "stopped dead in its tracks." Leaving the scene is a person dressed in a snow suit, trailing a rope that leads to the locomotive, but is not attached to it—rather like a severed umbilical cord. The engine seems to represent a source of movement no longer needed. Jackie says this person is going to "a nice warm place beyond our view." *This collage represents another preconscious message, namely, that her work here is coming to a halt; the "umbilical cord" of our connection is being severed, and she will soon be beyond my view.*

In leaving, Jackie says she will not be able to come for a session next week because she is short of money.

*   *   *

January 16ᵗʰ

Today I receive a message through the counseling center that Jackie has canceled this and next week's sessions, saying that she can't afford to come at this time. I remember her saying about a month ago that she felt a shift happening in her as her involvement in creating these collages began to taper down. I feel she is beginning to wean herself from this process and from her therapeutic relationship with me, though she still hasn't expressed this directly.

*   *   *

Fig. 57 "THE SNAKE GODDESS"

Proudly proclaiming her essential feminine nature, Woman is empowered and has taken control of her life. She is open to a relationship, but will never again be seduced into being a victim of a patriarchal mentality of abuse and domination.

Fig. 57 "THE SNAKE GODDESS" 2/9/92

The Minoan Snake Goddess stands alone in a triumphant position of feminine strength and power. She is bare-breasted and fearlessly holds up a snake in each hand. The Snake Goddess is standing on the ancient Israelite mountain of Masada. From this high vantage point she can survey great distances all around.

March 12ᵗʰ

It is now mid-March and there has been a full two-month hiatus since my last meeting with Jackie.

Today we resume the art therapy process. Jackie tells me she has done almost no collaging during that time (just this powerful image and some smaller cards), and yet this time she has not become depressed. *An important change.*

In Masada the ancient Israelites died rather than surrender and submit to the patriarchal domination of the Roman legions. I see this as a clear depiction of Jackie's contemporary triumph over the violence and domination that invaded the life of her childhood.

I ask Jackie if she feels she has begun a termination process she hasn't mentioned to me yet. She replies she hasn't really thought of it consciously in that way; but, yes, she does feel she is finished for now. However, she does not move into a discussion of that important issue in this session but, rather, speaks first about this collage and how it visually expresses a feeling of feminine empowerment. *This was the third of her goals when she returned to therapy and, increasingly, she is experiencing that feeling in herself.*

Jackie also brings up some important new insights about more ways in which she has taken on characteristics or behavior patterns of her parents. For example, she has had a realization about how food has represented the "good mother" for her because her mother was a "great cook" and, surprisingly, was taught this skill by Jackie's father. This was the nurturing mother, albeit the nurturing-mother-run-amok. Jackie reminds me again that at times when she was an infant, her mother overfed her with the bottle until she would vomit. She has continued the overeating pattern as an adult. She can now see that her own self-abuse through over-eating is a way in which she has perpetuated her parents' abuse of her.

Jackie tells me that in recent weeks she has also been *craving* alcohol. This has never been a problem for her, but it was a serious problem for her mother and her mother's family. I suggest she may once again, on a psychic level, be tapping into some of their dysfunctional behaviors. If she doesn't yield to those energies and get caught in acting them out, she will not perpetuate it in herself.

She tells me she's committed to being her own person and not a puppet of her sick parents. Another sign of growing self-esteem is that she has been doing aerobic exercises in order to lose weight.

March 26ᵗʰ

In this session, I focus our work on the question of termination and how we will structure that crucial aspect of the therapeutic process. Jackie and I agree to meet every other week for the next two months. She says after our last session she again realized how much she likes coming to see me to do the inner processing; yet, basically she is feeling she can stop soon without any trauma attached to the separation.

Jackie's inner processing continues to be intense even as her work is drawing to a close. She reports several dreams in which she was vehemently expressing rage at her mother. In the first, Jackie has a new baby, and she is shouting at her mother that she can't have the baby because she had really f——d up her own kids. She says she's surprised she still holds so much anger against her mother, even after all this therapy. *This dream is another image from her deep unconscious, showing once again Jackie's determination to no longer remain in the place of the victimized child. I see having a new baby in a dream as a wonderful indication from the unconsciousness that the dreamer has opened to new possibilities in his or her life. In this case, Jackie's dream indicates she is ready to protect that new aspect of herself, which she has so painfully birthed.*

In a second dream, Jackie is shouting at her father that her mother wanted to kill her and that she also wanted to kill her mother. Jackie's deep-seated rage continues to be safely vented through her dreams. She says that, in both these and other dreams recently, her father has appeared "wimpy"—no longer the strong, domineering figure he had been in her childhood.

These dreams indicate Jackie has claimed her rage on a deep level and is able to express it strongly and directly now. Typically, when such a change is clearly illustrated in our dreams, we are then ready to integrate and manifest those changes in our waking lives. This does not mean that now Jackie is going to start screaming at her parents, but rather that she will be able to stand her own ground in confrontations with them and other authority figures.

*   *   *

April 23ʳᵈ

Jackie is tearful as we discuss termination. We agree on her suggestion to meet three more times and bring to a close, in the first week of June, the work we have done together.
I ask Jackie what she has received here. "Above all," she says, "Myself! Also caring, validation, a sense of being valued, and a space in which to heal old wounds." I ask what she hasn't received. Immediately, and with surprise, she says, "A father - but I did get a 'good mother.'"

She wonders if we could go back to meeting weekly until the end, but we agree that would be counter-productive to the separation process. Jackie says if she were going to England now, she doesn't think she would be panicked, in the way she was after our first termination, because she feels her inner healing work is more complete at this time.

Jackie tells me that recently at work she has felt "stupid" because she is forgetting things a lot. She says that all through her early years, her father's demands that she be hyper-meticulous in all the housework (*the white glove gesture*), drummed into her that this was the only correct way to be. Now, as she is leaving Alfred, the critical voice, behind, she finds herself reverting to her natural personality type which is much more casual. I tell Jackie that as a result of the work she has done in art therapy, she is now able to immediately recognize the source of that critical voice in her head and not allow it to rule her life. Also if she's ever in a position of authority at work, she won't be projecting that negative image onto others. Jackie realizes that, of course, she is not stupid, just more relaxed and less vigilant.

In this past week, Jackie had a dream in which she was somehow both female and male, and she had lost her child. *The first part of this dream suggests she has integrated both the masculine and feminine aspects of herself on a deep psychological level, a process I have observed developing throughout the past year. Once again, this signifies the sacred inner marriage or integration of opposites that Jung referred to as the "coniunctio." As to the second part of the dream, in Jackie's present state of mind, losing her child would seem to signify that she is no longer in the victimized-child place in her feelings or possibly that she will need to take great care to nurture this newly developing aspect of herself. In another instance, the same image might have a more ominous meaning, for example, that she was out of touch with her playful, creative side, or is in denial about early wounds. Numerous interpretations are possible, depending on the state of the dreamer.*

Jackie describes another important change that has happened in her feelings as a result of this dream. This shift has to do with regaining a sense of her own personal spirituality, and she says now she is able to view God as the needed "good father," always absent in her family. *Regaining a sense of connection to Spirit was another of her goals for this second segment of her work in therapy, and she has now achieved it.*

*   *   *

May 7th

Jackie's dreams continue to express a wide range of emotions, both fearful and strong. In one of them, her old anxieties resurfaced. Men came with swords, and she was afraid of being overwhelmed by them. In a second dream, she had a new baby that "fails to thrive" *(a condition which often happens when there is a lack of physical touch and emotional connection with an infant)*. In that dream, Jackie felt horrified because she forgot to feed and care for her baby. In a third dream, she saw a very large, fat snake facing her, which had a man's head, *similar to her early collage, Fig.17 "My American Gothic."* She felt frightened, but not panicked, and decided that she'll just have to "meet it head on." *This aspect of the dream is reminiscent of Fig. 23 in the first segment of our work. In that collage the fearless, happy child is confronting the cobras eye-to-eye.* On the other hand, Jackie reports also having dreams of standing her ground and not yielding to domineering men.

Since the Snake Goddess collage done on Feb. 9th, Jackie's art process has been supplanted by her dreams. Again, collages and dreams have served the same function for her. If the collage of an empowered woman standing atop Masada, turns out to be her final one, it will be a fitting image with which Jackie can end the process of releasing her sense of being a victim and reclaiming her self-worth as a woman.

*   *   *

May 21st

I have completed photographing Jackie's collages from this second phase of her art therapy. Each collage and drawing was dated, and so, once again, we are able to spread them out in chronological order and view all the work Jackie has done during the last three years. In this way we have been able to see more clearly how the motifs in her collage images have evolved and changed.

In our initial work together the predominant themes included castles, sacrifice, blood, decapitation, religious images, Bacchus, and the goddess. In this second segment of her work the motifs included: returning from The Abyss, open windows and doors, new life emerging and being nourished, wolves, skeletons, and the crone. Jackie says in moving from the wounded child to the wise crone, she feels she has skipped her good middle years, but "somehow that's how it had to be." *This indicates to me a level of acceptance of her life's process. My feeling is that Jackie has now gotten in touch with all those ages and dimensions of herself.*

She brings in another collage, after all, saying she was beginning to fear she'd never do any more. In this collage (*not shown*) there's a picture of a bird caught in a wire fence. She says, "Maybe there's a wide opening we can't see on the other side so it can work itself out." *I hear this as her projection of feeling trapped and alone without help as our work together nears its end, but I also hear a voice of hope for change as she approaches her life on "the other side" of therapy. Once again, I think how the work of therapy is never a straight path from despair to joy; rather it is more like a roller coaster!*

And then, this dream:

> She's driving down a road in a huge truck, and a man is driving toward her in another one. They approach each other "head on," and she is determined not to yield to him. At the last minute, he swerves and she is pleased she stood her ground.

Recently Jackie drove by her parents' house and remembered a book title: *Living Well Is the Best Revenge.*[69]

In this context of healing from sexual abuse, far different than the memoir by Tomkins of that title, this means to me that the best way to reverse early victimization is to do the healing work of recognizing one's intrinsic worth, honoring oneself, and using one's energy for creative and meaningful pursuits—living well. Whereas, trying to get revenge by holding onto rage does nothing but keep one a victim, tied forever to the pain and grief and anger that drain away life's vitality.

Jackie is choosing to live well.

---

[69] *Tomkins, Calvin. Living Well is the Best Revenge. (Modern Library Publishers, Inc., 1971)*

Fig. 58   "GOLDEN GODDESS DANCING IN THE MOONLIGHT"

And finally to Woman's strength is added grace and beauty. She rejoices in the strength of her home and especially the light that shines out through the windows and door.

Fig. 58 "GOLDEN GODDESS DANCING IN THE MOONLIGHT" 6/3/92

A golden woman dances gracefully under a full moon, on a bed of russet Autumn leaves, with a tree stump to the left. Behind her is a strong old house with light shining out through the door and windows. The front door has a decorative iron gate for both beauty and protection.

June 4ᵗʰ, 1992   Termination (continuation of our final session)

And so we have arrived at our final session, and to it Jackie brings this last collage, a lovely counterpart to the Snake Goddess: this goddess who dances gracefully under a full moon is pure gold. *In philosophical/spiritual Alchemy, the goal was to find the pure "gold" of the whole Self.* Jackie says this is *her* house, representing her new sense of strength and stability.

I note that there is an iron gate over the front door (*clearly seen in the original*). Jackie is not at all pleased with this new information because she hadn't noticed it herself. She loved the fact that the light from within was radiating out through the door and all the windows, seeing this as a positive metaphor for herself at this time. She feels better when I say I don't see it now as defensiveness but rather as being able to keep her own personal and sexual boundaries safe even as her inner light shines through that protective gate. *I see the tree stump in the foreground as a phallic symbol, which I believe was also her intention.*

I ask Jackie how she is feeling now about ending this work we have done together. She responds, "Not great, but okay." Her tone of voice is wistful as she again wonders who will notice all the details in her collages that I pick up? And with whom will she share her later creations and inner process?

In regard to this final collage, I feel a sense of delight. Yes, there is a new-found strength, represented by the Snake Goddess, but the final touch is that now there is also a sense of grace and beauty within this woman.

*   *   *

After discussing the "Golden Goddess" collage, we move into a joint collage experience that Jackie had suggested in our last session.

JOINT COLLAGE   6/4/92 (*not shown*)

When we last met, Jackie said she would like us to create a collage together in our final meeting. I agreed and suggested because time would be limited, we each find some images ahead of time that could illustrate important aspects of the work and bring them into the session. We also have both brought bread and salad in order to share a meal; we decided to "break bread together" to reverently celebrate this time of healing.

The collage includes images we each feel symbolize aspects of her inner journey. They include a woman under a waterfall with a lizard beside her; a man looking out through a hole cut in a piece of sheet metal by a welding torch; a woman lighting a candle in three concentric rings of votive lights; a person climbing a sheer, vertical cliff; a statue of an angel holding a light, just above the climber's journey. There are also two smiling children sitting beneath a red and black Yin/Yang symbol, which represents the union of all duality; a road leading into the distance; a smiling child above a nest with birds hatching out of their eggs; a female weaver; a skier flying off the edge of a mountain in a totally free, spread-eagle position; a very happy little girl with arms open wide; and finally, top-center, an oval ring. The ring has four heads on the top, a howling wolf in the center, and above it is written: "The Power of Ancestors."

In the short time available, Jackie and I manage to create a reasonably coherent collage. Working together in this medium has brought up a variety of feelings in me. I first thought I would/should allow her to take charge of the choices and arrangement of pictures. Then, because as an artist I also wanted to make some choices, I began to feel it would be better for us to work as peers in this moment. In the end, I find myself hoping she has not felt I've been too much in charge (like a domineering parent). However, as this is our last session and time is limited, our conversation turns to summarizing her overall experience in art therapy. I am deeply touched that Jackie has chosen to share her creative process of collaging with me and am sorry we don't have time to discuss what today's experience has meant to each of us. As I look at the completed artwork I see it in a kind of "U" shape, and as I examine the images we put together, it strikes me that the content of them and the overall shape, are a microcosm of the Descent and Return theme, with wolf and ancestors in the center.

In that central image we have come full circle, as this work has been about family (ancestors) and of course, wolf represents the unconscious part of her that always held the memory of the incest, even while her waking mind could not bear to be conscious of it. Combining the two images here feels to me like a final acknowledgment of, and perhaps tribute to, wolf—her inner wisdom.

As we talk, we acknowledge several important measures of change in Jackie:

    1. She has submitted twelve collages to a fine art exhibit in New York City; all are from this second stage of her journey. By not including her early anguished pictures, Jackie is putting out to the world a whole new image of herself: no longer a suffering, raging victim, but rather a fine artist who has something significant to share with the world in the service of healing.

    2. Jackie also says that, in the future whenever she may exhibit her collages, she will now identify the problem as incest and claim this artistic body of healing work under her own name. She says she does not want to be seen as an incest survivor who happened to do some artwork, but rather primarily as an artist, who happens to also be an incest survivor. She is leaving behind her identity as a victim.

    3. Also, she can now stand up for herself firmly, for example, with her father or with her boss at work when there is a controversy.

    4. And finally, she finds herself thinking about Charles a lot lately, which signifies her growing openness to the possibility of a relationship with a man.

Jackie says from this art therapy process she has found her "whole Self." I ask what work has yet to be done. She responds it still has to do with her weight. She says she is clear now that her weight is connected with her shame about the incest. She feels it does not have to do with her anger at her mother. Lately she's thinking she should begin to visualize giving all her excess weight to her father "one pound at a time."

I can see Jackie is in a much better emotional and mental state now than she was at the completion of the first phase of her therapy. Although the inner work is never done—there is always more growth and healing that can be experienced on ever deeper levels—truly she has been on an amazing journey and has done her work thoroughly, with courage and integrity. Like Inanna, queen of the ancient Sumerian myth, Jackie has made a heroic Descent into the Underworld. She was stripped bare of all her happy childhood memories, her sense of competence and self-worth, and her spirituality. And as in the myth, when the flashbacks erupted her ego hung for a while on the "meat hook" and experienced a psychic death. Now she has returned to life. I feel deeply honored to have escorted her on that Descent and Return.

And so, again, our work has come to a close. Jackie and I give each other a warm hug upon leaving.

The inner work, of course, goes on. In the everyday process of life Jackie, like all of us, will continue to deal with feelings of fear, hope, rage, love, pain, grief, and self-acceptance on spiraling levels that go ever wider and deeper. Through it all, if we are sincere and attentive, we continue to grow, and to learn ever more about our Shadow as well as our Light—the miracle of our Wholeness.

          *   *   *

DESCENT AND RETURN:

AN INCEST SURVIVOR'S HEALING JOURNEY THROUGH ART THERAPY

AFTERWORD

"It is the Wise Fool who has the courage to set sail in search of the sacred Center of the Self."

Fig. 59   "SPIRIT OF THE SHAMAN: THE WOUNDED HEALER"

Woman has become shaman and her spirit is free; she is levitating. She has made her Descent into the Underworld and has returned from her long entombment in The Abyss. Now she rises above the field of death transformed and able to serve as healer for those who will never make the descent this fully, and as a guide for others who are now at The Edge.

Fig. 59 "SPIRIT OF THE SHAMAN: THE WOUNDED HEALER" 8/1/91

At the top of this configuration is an Australian Aboriginal petroglyph of a female who appears to be levitating. In that culture the stick that pierces her finger and the "dilly bag" that hangs from her shoulder (a pouch carrying sacred talismans) are the symbols of a shaman. Below her is an old burial ground and a stone wall that is smeared with something red—perhaps her blood.

The Shaman, the Wounded Healer, and the Fool in the Tarot are kindred spirits. All have made the journey into the Underworld of psyche.

The first 22 cards of the Tarot deck, the Major Arcana, symbolize the psychological process of individuation through the journey of the Fool. Filled with youthful naïveté and enthusiasm, Fool emerges from the womb of home, and sets out to explore the world, unaware of all the challenges that lie ahead. Along the way, the individual experiences universal life patterns or archetypes such as puberty, relationships, material and psychological challenges, successes and losses, maturity and mortality.

On this path of individuation, the Fool learns there is more to life than material gain and embarks on a spiritual quest. As this sojourner becomes increasingly attentive to the inner world, the demons of fear, rage, and shame are transformed through conscious attention and compassion. Ultimately, the wise Fool comes to experience the Self as an inextricable part of the Whole of creation. The Wounded Healer, like the Shaman and the Fool, then sets out to share what has been learned, healed, and integrated with those who are at the threshold of their own personal Abyss, and who may never make such a deep dive.

Jackie's experience embodies and illustrates one such journey.

Fig. 60   "BE TRUE IN HEART"

With quiet presence, She-Wolf looks out from the frozen darkness.

She has survived the trials of the night sea journey and is "True in Heart."

CRIE De COEUR – Cry of the Heart

The Children.
It's about the Children:
       innocent, beautiful, open, vulnerable,
       and oh, so wounded.
We are all wounded children
       who cry to heaven
       for protection
       for deliverance
       for love.......
and are answered, it seems, with Silence.

What monstrous thing is it that steals the Soul?
There is a universal myth of
       The Fire Theft.
Fire symbolizes the Sacred Life Force.
       Sexual abuse of children
       is the most profound theft.

I "rage against the dying of the light"
       in the Children
       who then grow tall
       and so often are crippled for life by
       insecurity, unworthiness,
       repressed rage, guilt, and shame;
or who, in their unhealed pain,
       inflict *their* wound on the next generation
       of Children.

Who speaks for the Children?
Who will protect, nurture, and deliver the Children
       from abuse?
Who will love the Children
       back into Life...?

Louise Lumen

APPENDIX I
BACKGROUND INFORMATION ON THE CLIENT

FAMILY OF ORIGIN

Jackie was the oldest of several children in a middle-class family. She completed approximately one year of college, with her major interests being in art and psychology; at one time she had thought of studying Art Therapy. She was married when she was nineteen years old and had two children before the marriage ended in divorce twenty-one years later. Since the divorce, she has worked to support herself (and her children, until they were out on their own).

Within her severely dysfunctional family of origin relationships were always strained. Jackie had been subjected to the incestuous acts and controlling tactics of her father since she was a toddler. The family dynamics deteriorated and Jackie reported that when she was eleven years old her mother began to "get sick;" that is, she became very depressed and would sleep much of the time or sit for hours gazing out the window. Her mother began to see a psychiatrist twice a week and this continued for the next ten years. She would frequently commit herself to the psychiatric unit of a local hospital, often staying as long as two weeks. (In the absence of parental acknowledgment of the incest, it remains a matter of conjecture as to whether or not Jackie's mother knew about it. If she did, it could have been a major factor contributing to her mother's depression.) Jackie says that her mother also received "lots" of ECT (electroshock therapy), which caused her to become very forgetful, and before her mother's 39th birthday her mother had become suicidal for a while.

As the oldest child, Jackie was cast in the role of filling her mother's empty shoes. She had to keep house and take care of her younger brother and sister. In addition to the on-going sexual abuse, when she was about eleven years old her father's fanatical "inspection tours" of her housework began. He was constantly observing and meticulously scrutinizing the cleaning she did - forever running his hand over even the most obscure surfaces, as if with a white glove, *always* making her redo what she had already done thoroughly, and telling her how stupid she was.

Jackie would sometimes use this "white glove" gesture as a symbol to express her father's omnipotence and extended domination of her. But the real trauma was having to be available to her father sexually, in the absence of her mother. The total effect was to make her feel helpless. In a letter to me, Jackie said: "Living in that house was like constantly walking on egg shells, never knowing what would happen next, what you would do wrong, when the other shoe would drop. And I NEVER, EVER, EVER felt comfortable or like I could be myself, EVER."

RELIGION/SPIRITUALITY

In light of Jackie's frequent use of religious symbols in the collages she created to express her deep pain, it is important to note her religious background and subsequent spiritual development. She was brought up in a Protestant denomination, and although neither of her parents ever went to church, she and her siblings were always required to attend Sunday school and then church when they were older.

When she was twenty-seven, Jackie got involved in Transcendental Meditation, which was very important to her and the beginning of many changes. She found that the various meditations and visualizations were very helpful in developing a satisfying and closer relationship with God than she had gotten in her early church-going years. Several years later, involvement in the 12-Step program, Overeaters Anonymous, opened her further to the spiritual realm.

In subsequent years, she was also involved in several spiritually oriented study groups: "Pathways to the Immortal," "Search for God" based on the work of the renowned clairvoyant Edgar Cayce, and "A Course in Miracles." However, all of these sincerely nurtured aspects of her spiritual development, as well as every other grounding, orienting belief she ever had, were wrenched away from her by the surfacing of the incest memories.

MARRIAGE/WEIGHT

Other relevant background information has to do with the interrelated issues of her marriage and a problem with obesity. Jackie says she always had a perception of having a weight problem. Throughout at least the first half of her marriage she had a serious struggle with eating binges that she said had a strong PMS (Pre-Menstrual Syndrome) component. She reported that at those times she would become completely non-functional, just as an alcoholic would be on a drinking binge. Her husband *was* an alcoholic, and thus isolation and a mutual lack of communication became a way of life. As their emotional connection continued to deteriorate, Jackie felt that her excessive weight served to "protect" her from the possibility of any sexual advances from her husband. She commented that their marriage of nineteen years was already in ruins when the incest memories finally surfaced.

And so it became clear to Jackie that the long years of sexual abuse had done their destructive work on the deepest unconscious levels of her psyche, causing a profound self-loathing in which, she said, food and her body became the battleground. The incest had destroyed her sense of self-worth and her capacity for trust and genuine relatedness in a marriage, long before it ever surfaced in consciousness.

THE SURFACING OF MEMORIES

Several years before beginning Art Therapy, Jackie used her art materials to make a small, coffin-like box. She put some things in it that represented the negative experiences she had with men in her life. Jackie then designed a ritual in which she symbolically buried this internal negative male voice, renounced all of the controlling male influences in her life, and vowed to take care of herself. Burying this psychologically laden "coffin" apparently had the effect of making it safe for her to allow the unspeakable memories to surface, because the flashbacks began shortly after that.

Jackie began to work with a therapist because of the discomfort she had long felt in her relationships. She said that when the first memory burst into her conscious awareness she "felt crazy in that instant because it was so weird" and she didn't want to think about what the implications would be. When she told her therapist about this spontaneous and very disturbing experience, the therapist did some "inner child" work with Jackie in a way that helped her feel safe; she was then able to explore the erupting memories that felt so bizarre and frightening to her. Jackie continued with her therapy for about six months, but then felt that particular therapist could not help her with the level of psychic trauma she was experiencing. That may be true, or it is also possible that Jackie was simply not able to cope with her flashbacks at that time because she stopped her therapy and fell into a deep depression.

She was referred to me for art therapy and the rest is chronicled in the text.

APPENDIX II
THE COLLAGES

All of the artwork in this book was created by Jackie and is less than half of all she made during the three years we worked together. Some of the others are described, but not shown. As with any creative process, this body of artwork was not done in a rational, linear sequence. Rather than always being a mirror of how this client-artist was feeling at any given moment, the process was a more dreamlike, intuitive one. The collages sometimes reflected changes Jackie had experienced weeks before, sometimes they expressed her immediate feelings, or at other times the images were the heralds of changes going on deep in her unconscious, that had not yet manifested in her outer life. As a result, the collages shown here are not always specific illustrations of the text that accompanies them.

In the first segment of her therapy, Jackie made these collages on very heavy brown paper. She tore it into irregular shapes and left the rough edges. This "not pretty" look to the ground she worked on was very important to her and was integral to the form through which she was trying to communicate her pain.

It is notable that in the second segment of the work, Jackie created her collages on a fine-quality drawing paper, which immediately indicated that she was now valuing her artwork in a new way. As an aspect of our termination processes for both Part I and Part II, Jackie asked me to photograph her work. This provided us with a manageable way to review all the changes in the form and content of her images.

PART I: THE FIRST 15 MONTHS

BEFORE "THE TURNING"
ISSUES in therapy:
Rage at father: incest
Rage at mother: lack of protection and active abuse
Pain, guilt, shame
Death of the ego's self-image

FORM of the artwork:
Done on torn brown paper
Images from "National Geographic": religious, nature, primitive cultures, etc.
Intricate, complex, irrational combinations: dream-like
THEMES in the artwork:
Blood, Sacrifice, Decapitation, Religious images,
Castles, Snakes, Goddess

AFTER "THE TURNING"
ISSUES in therapy:
Grieving the past
Growth of self-esteem
Positive, energetic movement
FORM of the artwork:
Torn brown paper
Contemporary images of active, happy women
Simple, block forms
Visually less interesting
THEMES in the artwork:
Leaving the past behind
Moving into the future
Dreams and plans of going to England
Possibility of a positive relationship with a man
Termination of the therapy process

INTERIM - NINE MONTHS
Letters from Europe on small collage cards containing words as well as images

PART II: THE SECOND 15 MONTHS

ISSUES in therapy:
Mother: rage, guilt
Spirituality
Personal empowerment
FORM of the artwork:
Done on good-quality drawing paper
Return to images from "National Geographic"
Simple, elegant, more integrated
THEMES in the artwork:
Return from The Abyss; empowerment
Repairing broken dreams; Possibility of Relationship
Balance of Masculine and Feminine
Skeletons, Wolves, Crone, Goddess

THE PROCESS OF CREATING THE COLLAGES

The word "collage" is a noun. The dictionary defines it as "the technique of creating a work of art by pasting on a single surface various materials not normally associated with one another, as newspaper clippings, theater tickets, fragments of an envelope, etc."[70] It is interesting that this was the medium Jackie chose to use because, by its very nature, creating a collage is a process of putting together separate and disparate elements to create an integrated whole, and so was an apt metaphor for what was happening internally throughout the therapy process. Jackie is the first person I have ever heard use the word as a verb: she was "collaging." This is significant because it indicates clearly that this was an active process for her, as well as an end product.

As previously mentioned, Jackie began to make the collages spontaneously at home after we had been working together several months; this was not my suggestion. She would page through magazines and tear out any pictures that appealed to her. She would have a table filled with pictures and then begin to choose images and cut and glue them down in whatever way she felt. Often the pictures would dictate, as it were, where they wanted to be. They seemed to take on a life of their own - a process with which any artist is familiar. That is, she might *think* she would put an image in one place, but then intuitively *feel* it belonged someplace else, or that a different image altogether was required. Like any true artist, Jackie would always follow the intuitive promptings and leave her initial, conscious plan behind. In so doing she found the collages always "spoke to her" from a much deeper level of her being and brought unexpected insights into her situation.

It was clear that, at times, when the collages were being created, Jackie had been in a somewhat altered or dissociated state of consciousness. The measure of this is that quite often, as we reviewed them together, I would comment on some element and she would be genuinely startled because she had not seen that aspect of the picture and yet it was perfectly relevant to what she was experiencing. Or at other times she had no memory of having altered a picture in some significant way, for example, several of the "decapitations."

Most of the time, of course, she was making conscious choices in the pictures she used and how they were placed. However, the number of times that the relevant, but unconscious, elements arose in her "collaging" was striking. She often had no explanation for why she had chosen a particular image. She would simply say, "It just felt right."

The collages, in fact, are very dream-like in the sense that non-rational combinations of disparate images are juxtaposed and, at first glance, do not appear to make sense. For example, a cobra with a human face, a living child with a saber through her heart, or a window entirely filled with one large eye. However, when described in words, the symbolism begins to emerge revealing its direct relevance to her experience and feelings.

It is notable that at one point near the end of the therapy process Jackie's "collaging" involvement began to taper off and she commented at that time that she was remembering her dreams more. Clearly, the two processes were serving the same purpose on her inner journey.

---

[70] *Webster's New International Dictionary of the English Language, 2nd Edition, unabridged, (G & C Merriam Co., pub., Springfield, MA. 1951)*

Once, in the latter part of the work, as we talked about a collage she brought in, I reached out and felt the artwork with my fingers. Sometime later, this came up and Jackie said how upset she had felt in that moment because she assumed that I was cleaning off some bit of glue that she thought had showed; that is, she took my action as an unspoken correction or criticism, yet, she didn't say anything at that time. Her reaction indicated how fragile her self-confidence still was at that time. Several weeks later, when she brought it up, she was surprised and touched when she heard that, on the contrary, rather than my gesture being a criticism, it could be taken as a compliment. At that point, her assemblage of pictures created such an integrated whole that I could not tell where one picture ended and the next began. I had to "see" with my fingers - I was feeling for the edges my eyes could not perceive.

THE MEANING OF THE IMAGES

A word now about the "interpretations" or understandings that Jackie and I came to about the meaning inherent in these complex images. Their individual significance was often recognized as we worked together in the sessions, or later in reviewing them in both of the termination sessions. But the larger understanding of the organic unity of her internal process as recorded externally in these collages - and how well her art was illuminating the archetypal pattern of a deep Descent and Return - came later. This happened as I looked at them ever more closely in order to photograph them and to research certain elements and write about them. It was at this time I discovered the beheading of the wolf in Fig.13, the beheadings in the "Judith" and "Medusa" stories, and the unexpectedly relevant changes and progressions in the goddess, Bacchus, and castle images. In doing this research, the depth of relevance of these images and myths to her personal healing process became ever more apparent.

I also began to see the correspondence between the symbolism of the collages and what Jung referred to as the "collective unconscious," that is, the deeper strata of the psyche that is made up of the instincts and archetypes that are universal rather than unique to the individual. This realm is the source of dreams, myths, and legends.

Jackie's journey is, I believe, an excellent illustration of precisely *why* myths are so meaningful to us. They portray in symbolic terms various aspects of the wider human condition in a way that helps us to understand our own personal experiences - including this particularly difficult cycle of an inner death and rebirth.

Thus, myths function both as a container that provides some supportive boundaries to our journeys and as a mirror that reflects back to us some specific patterns of the life process. In this way they add a dimension of universality that grounds the individual's journey in a larger context.

Choosing to share this therapeutic process is an important measure of the inner strength and self-assurance Jackie gained. The creative art therapy process and its visible, tangible result in the artwork has become an important means through which Jackie can claim her worth as a woman and also as an artist who has something of value to contribute to the world. She said she did not want to be seen as a victim of sexual abuse who happened to do some art work, but rather as an artist who happened to be a survivor.

After the first presentation of this work in 1993 at a nearby art museum, Jackie was given a two-week, one-woman exhibit of 15 of these pieces at the museum. Clearly, the curators there saw the value of these collages as "works of art," as well as the products of the art therapy process. Since then, Jackie has participated in several exhibits of artwork by sexual abuse survivors, and with her permission I have presented the work in slide lectures many times.

Jackie worked from a place of deep feeling in herself and followed her intuitive promptings; and while her drawing skills are not refined, she has an exquisite sense of design. This combination of uncensored, primal emotion and images, together with her elegant sense of design made these works deeply satisfying to her as well as poignant and moving to others who have viewed them. Often, as a result of seeing the collages and hearing the story of the process, people comment about how deeply they have been touched by the work, how it has helped them, and also what courage this woman has in, first of all, doing the healing work and then also in being willing to share it in order to help and encourage others. Once, when I told Jackie of this consistent response that her work was engendering, she said that perhaps being able to help others in this way is one reason for having gone through all the pain. One woman commented that Jackie "must be a giant." I fully concur. It takes a great deal of courage to do what Jackie has done here.

APPENDIX III
ON DEPRESSION AND SUICIDAL IDEATION

Jackie and I spoke of the concept of having choice when in a depression. I would like to clarify my understanding of that idea. It is not so much that one can choose how one feels. Choice becomes possible in regard to the actions one can take to move out of that state. The human brain is astonishingly complex and many factors may come into play to cause depression. Emotional stresses, genetics, seasonal changes, family coping patterns, nutrition, and other factors need to be considered. At times, psychotropic medications are essential and bring blessed relief from dark despair by altering the chemistry of the brain - releasing endorphins that stimulate positive feelings.

In addition, it is well known in medical and psychiatric circles that our emotions directly affect our physical condition, causing a wide variety of symptoms: the headaches Jackie had are an immediate example. In such a case, therapy can help a person examine the issues that are causing depression. When doing the work of healing, the individual learns to more quickly identify what emotions they are feeling, and also what wounds in their past are being stirred up again. With that awareness, a freedom is experienced in regard to how they may react or respond. If those feelings are not conscious, one will either contract into fear or react with blind anger. Fueled by the unhealed wounds, anger quickly becomes rage, often disproportionate to the immediate situation.

There is no criticism, blame, nor judgment of an individual for being ensnared in a painful depression. Rather, it is empowering when a person begins to realize they don't need to be at the mercy of their emotions. In some situations, even when there is a physiological component, it can be helpful to see if there is some emotional stress that could also be contributing to or altogether causing the miasma. In doing energy healing, it is seen that there is always an emotional component to any physical symptom. Depression is a serious and debilitating condition that all too often can even result in suicide, and it requires both skill and compassion from the therapist, and equally - willingness on the part of the one who is suffering - to take whatever steps are needed to return to a meaningful life.

In the ancient myth, it was Inanna's conscious choice to go into the Underworld to console her (sister's) grief, which then resulted in a death of who she thought she was. But she also made provision to get help if she got ensnared in the dark, and so it was also the compassion of the little emissaries from the gods for the suffering of her grieving sister that made Inanna's return to life possible.

A word here about how I work with people who express a desire to commit suicide. When a person's experience of life becomes so desperately unhappy, confused, and apparently without meaning that the only solution they can see is suicide, the safe container of a hospital's psychiatric unit or psychotropic medication may be absolutely necessary to get them through that critical stage. On the other hand, I know from my experience (both as therapist and as client) that this is not always necessary, and for some may not even be preferable. I believe that the question of whether or not one should be committed to an in-patient psychiatric unit at such a time of crisis, and whether or not to take medication, depends on the person's basic ego strength and willingness to resolve the issues, as well as the external supports and guides that are available to them. (See reference to Dr. Perry in the Prologue.)

I have worked for years with individuals in out- as well as in-patient settings, helping them examine and resolve their suicidal feelings. Especially in the hospitals, many persons in the most extreme pain of depression told me they felt alone, unloved, or abandoned, due to abuse or other traumatic experiences; and that they could find no inner or outer meaning in their lives. In some cases, they confided to me that they believed their depression was hurting those they loved and that everyone would be better off if they were dead. In this state of mental anguish, they went on to say it seemed to them the only way to end their intolerable emotional pain, and ironically, be kind to those who loved them, was to kill themselves. This is certainly a rationalization because I have also seen persons on a psychiatric unit whose deep pain was at least partially due to the fact that they had never been able to get over the suicide of a loved one: spouse, relative or friend. Some expressed rage at being abandoned by the one who chose to die. At times they also felt guilt as they anguished over the thought they might have done something to prevent their loved one from taking that irrevocable step.

There are reports that come back from The Edge, so to speak - from mystics of all religions and those who have had "near death experiences" telling us that the soul continues to live after the body dies. Truth is, until that time comes, none of us can know with certainty what will happen to us after we die. Consequently, death is the ultimate change we can imagine. The process I have found most effective in working with those who are experiencing suicidal feelings is to help them see their death-wish as a metaphor for a drastic change that needs to happen in order that the loving and meaningful life they long for may be achieved.

Of course, care must be taken to assess each client's capacity and willingness to do such a deep level of healing work. Some may choose not to do the work of therapy out of fear of what may come up, feeling they could be overwhelmed and so unable to function in their life. Also, for a variety of reasons, some people do not have the basic ego-strength to do in-depth psychotherapy, and that must be carefully ascertained.

Over the years I have learned that just as the body is always working to maintain an internal balance or homeostasis, our entire being - body, emotions, mind, and spirit - is also trying to achieve and maintain equilibrium. When a person's life has become so extremely out of balance that the body lacks vitality, the emotions are constricted or numb, the mind is confused, and contact has been lost with one's deep spiritual essence, that person may desperately want to end what seems to them to be random, meaningless pain. Therein lies the confusion: trying to resolve emotional, mental, or spiritual anguish by eliminating the physical body.

In my experience, the way to heal that suffering when possible, is to support the suicidal person in finding the inner courage and outer supports needed to enter fully into their pain and explore all its dimensions and significance, in order to find some resolution that will bring balance, meaning and joy back into their life. Once again, the key, as I see it, is to view the suicidal feelings as a metaphor for the client's profound wish for a total change in how they are experiencing life; and then through their work in therapy, enable that person to make the needed changes. Such in-depth psychotherapy is likely to be an intensely painful process, requiring psychological courage, such as Jackie exhibited during her three years of work in art therapy to heal her incest wound.

Finally, I remember something I observed in the first few months of working as an art therapist on an in-patient psychiatric unit. The core problem can be manifested in a wide range of diverse symptoms of neuroses or psychoses. But my conviction grew as I heard from the souls who were suffering in that intense way, that the problem ultimately always had to do with love: feeling unloved, unable to love, or believing they were essentially unlovable. It is a tragedy I feel is at the root of all intrapsychic conflict, which then creates interpersonal crises in the family, at work, and on ever larger stages of society.

In a way that is related to my work of helping clients explore the meaning of what their suicidal feelings signify, Jungian analyst, Arnold Mindell, in his work with what he terms the "Dreambody" describes how helping clients enter into and amplify their physical symptoms brings psychological insights that often facilitate healing of the physical body.

Also, in Dr. Perry's book, *The Far Side of Madness*, (see the Prologue) he describes a similar way of working with persons having an acute schizophrenic breakdown. By not numbing the symptoms with medication, he and his staff very carefully allow a patient, under close and loving supervision, to fully experience their mental pain and confusion until it has revealed the underlying cause and is resolved.

[44] *Mindell, Arnold. Working with the Dreaming Body. (Routledge & Kegan Paul, London and New York, 1985)*

APPENDIX # 4
FORGIVENESS/COMPASSION AS AN ESSENTIAL ASPECT OF HEALING

We can think of "forgiving" as "fore-giving." That is, the one who has been violated "gives" up their demand for an apology or for vengeance "before" any such apology is ever offered by the abuser, even as they realize that the apology they so desperately need, may never be forthcoming.

If our happiness and peace of mind are dependent on an apology that probably will never come, or on punishment that may never be meted out, then the victimized person remains a victim - a captive of their own rage. And often, that unresolved rage will be acted out either against others, or it may be turned in upon one's self in self-hurtful or even self-destructive behavior. In this way, the unresolved/unforgiven rage at having been violated by another often turns the victim into a perpetrator of violence against one's self. It is that unresolved rage that continues to be hurtful and even dangerous.

It must be completely clear that I am not implying that everyone who has been abused becomes an abuser of others. But when one is an abuser, it's likely they were abused and that wound was never healed. On the other hand, it is reasonable to assume that, in most cases, if a person who has been victimized goes on to become a truly healthy, happy person, able to live a productive and meaningful life, then in some way they have achieved resolution of their pain whether in therapy, in their spiritual practice, or in some other way. In my experience, it is this process of "forgiving," that is, giving up that demand for retribution, that provides the most complete resolution of rage, which is freeing for the wounded one.

In my work with sexually abused persons, I often find that if the experience remains unhealed, like a raw open wound, the victims continue to feel shamed and unlovable; they are rageful because the abuse has made them feel such self-loathing. Typically, people who have been victimized feel that they are "bad" or "unworthy" and they often have very low self-esteem as a result of those experiences. Consequently, some seem to consider themselves to be an exception to the rule that says we should not hurt someone, and they turn their rage against themselves. They either feel that they deserve to be punished or that this is the only permissible way to express their rage at the one who hurt them. Since there are laws against hurting others or because the victims of abuse are too afraid to express their anger directly to the person(s) to whom it belongs, they often take out their anger in self-abusive ways, which may include sexual promiscuity, eating disorders, drug and alcohol abuse, or inflicting pain on oneself by cutting or burning one's own body.

It is also important to note that often an abused person is reluctant to "forgive" their abuser because they believe that to do so would have the effect of minimizing their pain and trauma - implying that all the suffering they endured would mean nothing. So they hold onto their rage rather than let it go; but it is in the letting-go that they themselves are freed. Forgiving will not in any way minimize the suffering of the past, and it certainly does not mean that the abuse was acceptable, it will simply prevent it from continuing into the future, endlessly.

When engaging in this process, it is also essential to remember that we cannot leap from victimization and rage to forgiveness and peace in one easy step. This is sometimes referred to as a "spiritual by-pass." That never works. It is necessary to move through, rather than around, our pain and shame in order to fully acknowledge our feelings, and then release them when we are ready.

Forgiveness is a process that heals the old rage that has continued to fester and poison the life of the one who was abused. It is a letting go that frees one's energies to be redirected into the more enjoyable and creative aspects of life. When people have been sexually violated, they are always made to feel that it is their fault, and therefore they are "bad," etc. However, this "letting go" process is one in which the "victim" moves out of the captivity of keeping the shameful Secret, and into the empowered stance of "survivor," fully at peace within one's self, knowing that having had very bad experiences does not make one a bad person. In recognizing this, they come, at last, to honor their own intrinsic goodness and integrity.

Because "forgiveness" is such a charged word for many people, perhaps "compassion" would be a better choice. "Compassion" means to "feel with" another, and is the basis for the higher awareness that recognizes we all have the potential for both greatness and cruelty within us. In addition, we begin to see that when one person abuses another in any way, that behavior does not come from a place of nobility of character in the abuser; rather it comes out of that person's own unresolved pain. Being able to recognize the wounded child in the abusing adult is a helpful way to diminish the sense of power in the abuser. Recognizing this, we lay down the arms that we have ragefully turned against ourselves when we feel guilty, or against others when they have hurt or violated us. When we can "feel with" another, we recognize that on a deep inner level we are all one, and that we all have the potential to experience and express the entire spectrum of emotions and behaviors - the dark, as well as the light.

As I see it, forgiveness is primarily for the benefit of the one who was the victim of abuse; only secondarily is it for the abuser. After owning and expressing all our rage, terror, grief, shame, and guilt, we come to the place of letting go; the place of stopping our demands for retribution; the place of forgiveness; the place of peace within ourselves. Yet it is also important to be aware that a deep healing journey is never a straight uphill progression from agony to ecstasy. Rather, it has its ups and downs, breakthroughs and regressions, before a client can move to the higher ground of genuine self-esteem and compassion. This was certainly true of Jacqueline's healing process.

APPENDIX V
THE "RECOVERED MEMORY SYNDROME" CONTROVERSY
A WORD ABOUT REPRESSED MEMORIES AND FORGIVENESS

What is related in *Descent and Return* is the story of a person who, having been sexually abused by her father and otherwise abused and not protected by her mother throughout her childhood, lost all conscious awareness of that early trauma when it stopped in her early adolescence. She was in a state of amnesia about it for twenty-four years until the memory of it suddenly and spontaneously erupted into conscious awareness. These experiences had a profoundly negative effect on all areas of her life, and when the memory of them surfaced, she was cast into the depths of the Abyss of depression. This is, therefore, a classic example of what has come to be known as "repressed memories." I wish to acknowledge the fact that there is an intense controversy about such memories and much has been written on both sides of this issue. However, it is neither my intent nor purpose to engage in that discussion here.

As a therapist, it is not my job to determine the objective reality of what a client brings into the therapeutic setting. As I see it, my work is to assist my clients to deal with all their emotions: the rage, fear, and grief they feel in regard to others in their life, and whatever guilt or shame they may be carrying that robs them of true self-esteem. Moving out of the place of wounded victim in which one feels helpless and hopeless, and into the empowered stance of knowing one's true self-worth, requires that a person take responsibility - not for what was done to harm them - but for their own emotions in the present. It takes true courage to allow oneself to consciously feel underlying rage, terror, guilt, and shame, but the process is freeing. Instead of continuing to carry the blame for an abuser's actions and often, therefore, punishing oneself by self-injurious behavior, the responsibility is given back to the abuser, and those who were victimized are able to redirect their energies into more creative, meaningful, and enjoyable activities.

I am not a judge of what has caused those feelings; rather, I am an escort and guide for another person who is on the path of healing. So, regardless of their perspectives on this issue, readers will, at the very least, be witness to the process that one woman went through in returning from the Abyss of depression to reclaim her life.

It is helpful to remember that when we feel good about ourselves, we wouldn't think of hurting another person - particularly a child. When someone abuses another, it is always because that person has been wounded in some way and the resulting anger about the experience has never been resolved. Abuse arises out of weakness and insecurity in the perpetrator, masked by brute strength and machismo. For those who have difficulty with the notion of "forgiveness," a more acceptable idea might be to consider having *compassion* on the wounded child whose feelings are still held within the psyche of the adult who is directing his or her unresolved rage onto someone weaker. In my experience forgiveness/compassion is a crucial aspect of healing and there are increasing numbers of examples in the world that bear witness to the effectiveness of this process. A particularly good example is to be found in the difficult and poignant process of the "Council for Truth and Reconciliation," which was instituted by Archbishop Desmond Tutu, to work toward the healing of years of extreme racial conflict in South Africa. Forgiveness is never a simple wave of the hand to dismiss the deep pain that has been sustained by victims. Rather, it is a soul-searching experience for all who have the courage to engage in the process. Jacqueline is such a person and her struggles with this issue are an important aspect of this journal.

About the Author

Louise Lumen was born and raised in St. Louis, Missouri. For as long as she can remember art has always been a central means of expression for her. She is youngest of three girls born to deaf parents whose profound hearing impairments were due to early childhood illnesses (scarlet fever and spinal meningitis), and so their hearing loss was not congenital. Because of this, she and her sisters grew up bridging two worlds—the one hearing and the other deaf—the latter of which represented a unique culture in which communication was the primary difficulty. She found that speech through sign language was either painful and embarrassing, or at other times, a source of humor for the family.

Seeing first-hand the difficulties of that disability fostered in her an acute sensitivity to other people with various physical or mental challenges. This experience also helped her to choose a career path that eventually led to her becoming an art therapist, working mainly with those who suffered from early sexual abuse or life-threatening illnesses.

She received her B.A. in Liberal Arts with an Art major from Webster College in St. Louis, MO; an M.F.A. in painting from Mills College in Oakland, CA; and later an M.A. in Art Therapy from The George Washington University in Washington, DC.

As a Registered Art Therapist (ATR), she has worked for thirty years in counseling centers, private practice, and psychiatric hospitals mostly with women who were sexually abused as children, and also with persons with life-threatening illnesses or those who are bereaved. As a Hospice volunteer, she has utilized Art Therapy with cancer patients and has also run support groups for medical staff and other volunteers to help them to process their ongoing work-related losses.

Her previous publication was a case study entitled "Michael: An Illustrated Story of a Young Man with Cancer," published in the *American Journal of Art Therapy*, precursor to *The Journal of the American Art Therapy Association*. Three pieces of her artwork were published as cover designs for *Tiferet: A Journal of Spiritual Literature. Descent and Return: An Incest Survivor's Healing Journey through Art Therapy* represents for her the fruition of a life's work, and for which she is grateful to have received the wise, patient, and skillful help of many friends.

CPSIA information can be obtained
at www.ICGtesting.com
Printed in the USA
FSOW04n1851090117
29434FS

9 781630 513818